||| ||| ||| ||| ||| ||| ||| ||| ||| |||

✓ **S0-BIL-793**

IMPORTAN

HERE IS YOUR REGISTRATION CODE TO A~~CCESS MCGRAW-HILL~~
PREMIUM CONTENT AND MCGRAW-HILL ONLINE RESOURCES

For key premium online resources you need THIS CODE to gain access.
Once the code is entered, you will be able to use the web resources for
the length of your course.

Access is provided only if you have purchased a new book.

If the registration code is missing from this book, the registration screen
on our website, and within your WebCT or Blackboard course will tell you
how to obtain your new code. Your registration code can be used only
once to establish access. It is not transferable.

To gain access to these online resources

1. USE your web browser to go to: **www.mhhe.com/wi**

2. CLICK on "First Time User"

3. ENTER the Registration Code printed on the tear-off bookmark on the right

4. After you have entered your registration code, click on "Register"

5. FOLLOW the instructions to setup your personal UserID and Password

6. WRITE your UserID and Password down for future reference. Keep it in a safe place.

If your course is using WebCT or Blackboard, you'll be able to use this code to access the
McGraw-Hill content within your instructor's online course.

To gain access to the McGraw-Hill content in your instructor's WebCT or Blackboard course
simply log into the course with the user ID and Password provided by your instructor. Enter
the registration code exactly as it appears to the right when prompted by the system. You will
only need to use this code the first time you click on McGraw-Hill content.

These instructions are specifically for student access. Instructors are not required to register
via the above instructions.

The McGraw-Hill Companies

**Mc
Graw
Hill Higher Education**

Thank you, and welcome to your
McGraw-Hill Online Resources.

0-07-322856-7 T/A MAIMON, WRITING INTENSIVE, 1/E

3HK9-CAFT-YPWX-MBWG-B

REGISTRATION CODE

Catalyst 2.0

Use this registration card to access *Catalyst 2.0: the premier on* *resource for writing, research, and editing.* Available free with ev student and instructor copy of *Writing Intensive*, online access includes:

- The *Factiva* online database with thousands of full text articles and images from periodicals and journals
- Interactive tutorials on document design and visual rhetoric
- Guides for avoiding plagiarism and evaluating sources
- Electronic writing tutors for composing informative, interpretive, and argumentative papers
- *Bibliomaker* software for the MLA, APA, Chicago, and CSE styles of documentation
- More than 4,500 exercises with feedback in grammar, usage, and punctuation

In addition, *Catalyst 2.0* offers writing instructors a new, state-of the-art course management and peer review system that allows users to do the following:

- Embed comments and links contextually alongside reviewed papers
- Create and select from lists of 'favorite' comments
- Drag and drop editing abbreviations and symbols into papers that link to *Catalyst* grammar coverage online
- Create and comment on multiple drafts among groups of student reviewers
- Use instructor-created review questions to respond to drafts

Writing Intensive

Intensive

Essentials for College Writers

Elaine P. Maimon
University of Alaska Anchorage

Janice H. Peritz
Queens College,
City University of New York

Boston Burr Ridge, IL Dubuque, IA Madison, WI New York
San Francisco St. Louis Bangkok Bogotá Caracas Kuala Lumpur
Lisbon London Madrid Mexico City Milan Montreal New Delhi
Santiago Seoul Singapore Sydney Taipei Toronto

Higher Education

Published by McGraw-Hill, an imprint of The McGraw-Hill Companies, Inc.,
1221 Avenue of the Americas, New York, NY 10020. Copyright © 2009, 2007. All
rights reserved. No part of this publication may be reproduced or distributed in
any form or by any means, or stored in a database or retrieval system, without
the prior written consent of The McGraw-Hill Companies, Inc., including, but
not limited to, in any network or other electronic storage or transmission, or
broadcast for distance learning.

3 4 5 6 7 8 9 0 DOC/DOC 0 9

ISBN-13:   978-0-07-332768-6   ISBN-10:   0-07-332768-9

Editor in Chief: *Michael Ryan,* Publisher: *David S. Patterson,* Sponsoring
Editor: *Christopher Bennem,* Director of Development: *Dawn Groundwater,*
Marketing Manager: *Allison Jones,* Development Editor: *Anne Kemper,* Media
Producer: *Alex Rohrs,* Production Editor: *Chanda Feldman,* Manuscript Editor:
Amy Marks, Design Manager: *Cassandra Chu,* Text and Cover Designer:
Maureen McCutcheon, Art Editor: *Robin Mouat,* Production Supervisor: *Randy
Hurst,* Composition: *9/11 pt. New Century Schoolbook by Thompson Type,*
Printing: *PMS 355 and PMS 648, 45# New Era Plus, R. R. Donnelley & Sons*

Credits: The credits section for this book begins on page C-1 and is considered
an extension of the copyright page.

Library of Congress Control Number: 2005054421

The Internet addresses listed in the text were accurate at the time of
publication. The inclusion of a Web site does not indicate an endorsement
by the authors or McGraw-Hill, and McGraw-Hill does not guarantee the
accuracy of the information presented at these sites.

www.mhhe.com

How to Find the Help You Need in *Writing Intensive*

Writing Intensive is a reference for all writers and researchers. When writing in any context, you are bound to come across questions about writing and research. *Writing Intensive* provides you with answers to your questions.

Check the tables of contents.
If you know the topic you are looking for, try scanning the brief contents on the inside front cover or the complete contents on the inside back cover. The brief contents lists all part and chapter titles in the book. The complete contents also includes each section number and title in addition to the part and chapter numbers and titles. If you are looking for specific information within a general topic (how to correct an unclear pronoun reference, for example), scanning the detailed table of contents on the inside back cover will help you find the section you need.

Look up your topic in the index.
The comprehensive index at the end of *Writing Intensive* (pp. I-1–I-40) includes all of the topics covered in the book. For example, if you are not sure whether to use *I* or *me* in a sentence, you can look up "*I vs. me*" in the index.

In the List of Discipline-Specific Resources.
In Chapter 13 (pp. 86–92), you will find a comprehensive list of sources that have already been checked for relevance and credibility.

Check the documentation flowcharts.

By answering the questions posed in the charts on pages 94–96 (for the MLA documentation style) and 143–45 (for the APA documentation style), you can usually find the model that you are looking for.

Look up a word in the Glossary of Usage or a term in the Glossary of Grammatical Terms.

If you are not sure that you are using a particular word such as *farther* or *further* correctly, try looking it up in the Glossary of Usage on pages 257–70. If you need the definition for a grammatical term such as *linking verb,* consult the Glossary of Grammatical Terms on pages G-1–G-15.

Use the reference tools on each page.

The reference features shown on page vii, most of which appear throughout *Writing Intensive,* will help you find the advice you need:

- The **chapter number and title** give the topic of the chapter.
- The **running head** gives the topic covered on the page.
- The **marginal reference to *Catalyst 2.0*** provides the URL for *Catalyst 2.0* and a path to follow for more information and practice exercises on the topic.
- The **main heading** includes the chapter number and section letter (for example, 29a) as well as the title of the section.
- **Examples,** many of them with hand corrections, illustrate typical errors and how to correct them.
- **Thumb tabs,** each containing the number and letter of the last section on the page (for example, 29a on p. 229) and an abbreviation or symbol for that section, help you find the topic you are looking for.
- The **"Identify and Edit" boxes** help you recognize and correct errors.

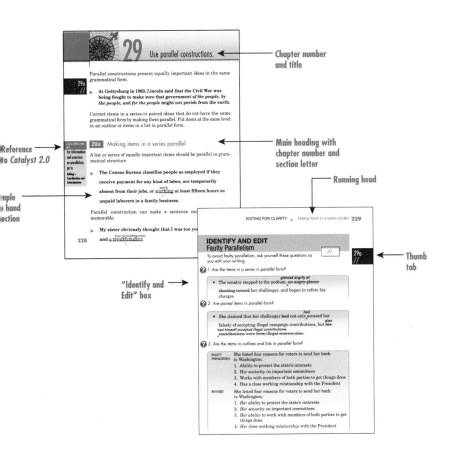

29 Use parallel constructions. ◄——— Chapter number and title

Parallel constructions present equally important ideas in the same grammatical form.

29a //

> At Gettysburg in 1863, Lincoln said that the Civil War was being fought to make sure that government *of the people,* by *the people,* and *for the people* might not perish from the earth.

Correct items in a series or paired ideas that do not have the same grammatical form by making them parallel. Put items at the same level in an outline or items in a list in parallel form.

www.mhhe.com will
For information and exercises on parallelism, go to
Editing >
Coordination and Subordination

29a Making items in a series parallel ◄——— Main heading with chapter number and section letter

A list or series of equally important items should be parallel in grammatical structure.

> The Census Bureau classifies people as employed if they receive payment for any kind of labor, are temporarily absent from their jobs, or ~~working~~ at least fifteen hours as unpaid laborers in a family business.

Reference to *Catalyst 2.0* ———►

~~mple~~ ~~n hand~~ ~~ection~~ ———►

Running head ———►

Parallel construction can make a sentence mo memorable.

> My sister obviously thought that I was too yo and ~~a troublemaker.~~ *too troublesome*

228

EDITING FOR CLARITY ■ Making items in a series parallel **229**

IDENTIFY AND EDIT
Faulty Parallelism

To avoid faulty parallelism, ask yourself these questions as you edit your writing:

? 1. Are the items in a series in parallel form?

◆ The senator stepped to the podium, ~~an angry glance~~ ~~shooting toward~~ her challenger, and began to refute his charges. *glanced angrily at*

? 2. Are paired items in parallel form?

◆ She claimed that her challenger ~~had~~ not only accused her falsely of accepting illegal campaign contributions, but ~~his~~ ~~contributions were from illegal sources also.~~ *had* *also had himself accepted illegal contributions.*

? 3. Are the items in outlines and lists in parallel form?

FAULTY PARALLELISM She listed four reasons for voters to send her back to Washington:
1. Ability to protect the state's interests
2. Her seniority on important committees
3. Works with members of both parties to get things done
4. Has a close working relationship with the President

REVISED She listed four reasons for voters to send her back to Washington:
1. *Her ability* to protect the state's interests
2. *Her seniority* on important committees
3. *Her ability* to work with members of both parties to get things done
4. *Her close working relationship* with the President

29a // ◄——— Thumb tab

"Identify and Edit" box ———►

Refer to Chapter 43 if you are a multilingual student.
Chapter 43 provides help with the use of articles, helping verbs, and other problem areas for multilingual students.

Go to *Catalyst 2.0* for online help with learning, writing, research, and editing.
Catalyst 2.0 includes diagnostic tests; practice exercises in grammar, punctuation, and mechanics; *Bibliomaker* software that formats source information in the MLA, APA, Chicago, and CSE documentation styles; access to the Factiva database with thousands of full-text articles; a tutorial on recognizing and avoiding plagiarism; and much more.

> Anybody who is involved in working across the disciplines is much more likely to have a lively mind and a lively life.
>
> —MARY FIELD BELENKY

PART 1

Common Assignments across the Curriculum

1

Most college courses require at least some writing, including one or more formal papers. Your writing projects might be case studies in the social sciences, lab reports in the hard sciences, texts for oral presentations in business studies, and analyses in the humanities, to name a few possibilities. Writing is a way to learn about the conventions of different disciplines and to make sense of your intellectual experiences.

1a Learning about common college assignments

No matter what your course of study, writing will be an important part of your college experience. Understanding what is being asked of you as a writer is a critical ingredient of your success.

www.mhhe.com/
wi

For help with
writing any
kind of
assignment,
go to

**Writing >
Paragraph/
Essay
Development**

Although writing assignments can differ, all writing has elements in common. There are also common writing assignments—types of writing required by courses in many different disciplines. The three most common types of papers are informative reports, interpretive analyses, and arguments.

- **Informative reports** occur in all disciplines. In an informative report, the writer passes on what he or she has learned about a topic or issue.

- **Interpretive analyses** explore the meaning of written documents, cultural artifacts, social situations, and natural events.

- **Arguments** are valued in all fields of study. These types of papers support a point or justify an opinion through logic and concrete evidence.

1b   Learning how to understand assignments

From a journal entry to an essay exam to a research report, college writing assignments aim to enhance your knowledge while stimulating your creativity. Even when an instructor provides explicit and specific directions, you still need to make the assignment your own in order to write an effective response to it.

The following questions and suggestions will help you begin figuring out your assignments:

- **What has the professor said in class about the purpose of the assignment?** Check your notes and consult with classmates.

- **What are some key terms in the assignment that might give you a clue about what is being asked of you?** Terms like *comment, consider,* and *discuss* do not point to a particular purpose. *Classify, illustrate, report,* and *survey* are frequently associated with the task of **informing.** *Analyze, compare, explain,* and *reflect* are often associated with **interpreting.** *Agree, assess, defend,* and *refute* go with the task of **arguing.**

- **What type of project are you being asked to write?** Is it one of the common assignments, or is it particular to a discipline?

- **How long is the paper supposed to be, and when is it due?** Many topics must be narrowed to be completed on time and within the specified number of pages. Some instructors may note due dates for progress reports or first drafts.

- **What format is required for the assignment?** Some assignments, like a laboratory report, must follow a conventional form. When research is assigned, instructors generally will prefer a particular style of documentation. Check with your instructor. (*See the documentation sections, Parts 3–5.*)

2 Informative reports

2a Understanding the assignment

www.mhhe.com/
wi
For online
guidance as
you write an
informative
paper, go to
Writing >
Writing Tutor:
Informative
Reports

An **informative report** passes on what someone has learned about a topic or issue; it teaches. When your instructor assigns an informative report, he or she expects you to find out about some topic and to present what you discover in a clear and unbiased way.

An informative report gives you a chance to do the following:

- Read more about an issue that interests you
- Make sense of what you have read, heard, and seen
- Teach others what you have learned

Note: Instructors sometimes assign a special kind of informative report called a *review of the literature.* Here the term *literature* refers to published research reports, and the term *review* means that you need to present an organized account of the current state of knowledge in a specific area, not refute the research or argue for your opinion.

2b Approaching writing an informative report as a process

- **Select a topic that interests you.** The major challenge of writing informative reports is engaging the reader's interest. Selecting a topic that interests you makes it more likely that your report will interest your readers.
- **Consider what your readers know about the topic.** Assume that your readers have some general familiarity with your topic area but that most do not have clear, specific knowledge of your particular topic.
- **Develop an objective stance.** A commitment to objectivity gives your report its authority. Present differing views fairly, and do not take sides in a debate. For instance, if there are three different viewpoints on proposed anti-logging legislation, you would want to give equal time to each one in an informative report on this topic.
- **Compose a thesis that summarizes your knowledge of the topic.** An informative thesis typically reports the results of the writer's study or states an accepted generalization. Before you decide on a thesis, review the information you have collected. Compose a thesis statement that summarizes what the information in your paper shows. In an informative report on the work of Alfred Stieglitz, you might have the following thesis:

www.mhhe.com/
wi
For more information on developing a thesis, go to
Writing >
Paragraph/
Essay
Development >
Thesis/Central
Idea

EXAMPLE

Alfred Stieglitz promoted photography as an art in three key ways: he started a journal, opened a gallery, and joined a group of avant-garde modernists.

2b
writing

- **Provide context in your introduction.** Informative reports usually begin with a simple introduction to the topic and a straightforward statement of the thesis. Provide some context or background, but get to your specific topic as quickly as possible and keep it in the foreground.

- **Organize your paper by classifying and dividing information.** Clarity matters. Develop ideas in an organized way by classifying and dividing information into categories, subtopics, or the stages of a process.

- **Illustrate key ideas with examples.** Use specific examples to help readers understand your most important ideas. Examples make reports interesting as well as educational.

- **Define specialized terms and spell out unfamiliar abbreviations.** Specialized terms will probably not be familiar to most readers. Explain these terms with a synonym (a word with the same meaning) or a brief definition—as we have just done. Spell out unfamiliar abbreviations the first time you use them, with the abbreviation in parentheses: *In September, the union will present its case to the National Labor Relations Board (NLRB).*

www.mhhe.com/ wi

For an example of an informative paper, go to

Writing > Writing Samples > Sample Informative Paper

- **Conclude by answering "So what?"** Conclude with an image that suggests the information's value or sums it all up. The conclusion reminds readers of the topic stated in the introduction and answers the question "So what?"

3 Interpretive analyses and writing about literature

3a Understanding the assignment

Interpretation involves figuring out a way of understanding a written document, literary work, cultural artifact, social situation, or natural event and presenting your understanding so that it is meaningful and convincing to readers. When an assignment asks you to compare, explain, analyze, discuss, or do a reading of something, you are expected to study that subject closely. An interpretive analysis moves beyond description, however, and examines or compares particular items for a reason: to answer a critical question in ways that enhance your reader's understanding of people's conditions, actions, beliefs, or desires.

www.mhhe.com/
wi
For online
guidance as
you write an
interpretive
paper, go to
Writing >
Writing Tutor:
Interpretive
Analysis

3b Approaching writing an interpretive analysis as a process

- **Discover an aspect of the subject that is meaningful to you.** Think about your own feelings and experiences while you read, listen, or observe. Connecting your feelings and experiences with what you are studying can help you develop new ideas and fresh interpretations.
- **Develop a thoughtful stance.** Think of yourself as an explorer. Be thoughtful, inquisitive, and open-minded. When you write your paper, invite your readers to join you on an intellectual journey, saying, in effect, "Come, think this through with me."

3b
writing

- **Use an intellectual framework.** To understand your subject, use a relevant perspective or an intellectual framework. For example, the basic elements of fiction, such as plot, character, and setting, are often used to analyze stories. Sigmund Freud's theory of conscious and unconscious forces in conflict has been applied to various things, including people, poems, and historical periods.

  No matter what framework you use, analysis entails figuring out how the parts make up a meaningful whole. Treat the whole as more than the sum of its parts and recognize that interpreting meaning is a complex problem with multiple solutions.

www.mhhe.com/
wi

For more
information on
developing a
thesis, go to
Writing >
Paragraph/
Essay
Development >
Thesis/Central
Idea

- **List, compare, classify, and question to discover your thesis.** To figure out a thesis, explore separate aspects of your subject. Try one or more of the following strategies:
  - Take notes about what you see or read, and if it helps, write a summary.
  - Look for and list points of likeness and difference.
  - Name the class of things to which the item you are analyzing belongs (for example, memoirs), and then identify important aspects of that class (for example, scene, point of view, helpers, turning points).
  - Ask yourself questions about the subject you are analyzing, and write down any interesting answers. Imagine what kinds of questions your professor or classmates might ask about the artifact, document, or performance.

- **Make your thesis focused and purposeful.** To make a point about your subject, focus on one or two questions that are key to understanding it. Resist the temptation to describe or comment on everything you see.

EXAMPLE

3b
writing

In the first section of Schubert's *Der Atlas,* both the tempo and the harmonic progression express the sorrow of the hero's eternal plight.

Although you want your point to be clear, you also want to make sure that your thesis anticipates the "So what?" question and sets up an interesting context for your interpretation. Unless you relate your specific thesis to some more general issue, idea, or problem, your interpretive analysis may seem pointless to readers.

- **Include in your introduction the general issue, a clear thesis or question, and relevant context.** In interpretive analyses, an introduction needs to do the following:
  - Name the specific item or items you will focus on.
  - Identify the general issue, concept, or problem at stake. You can also present the intellectual framework being applied.
  - Provide relevant background information.
  - State the thesis you will support and develop or the main question(s) your analysis will answer.

Even though you may begin with a provocative statement or an example designed to capture your readers' attention, make sure that your introduction does the four things it needs to do.

- **Plan your paper so that each point supports your thesis.** After you pose a key question or state your thesis, work point by point, organizing the points to answer the question and support your interpretive thesis. Readers must be able to follow your train of thought and see how each point you make is related to your thesis.

**4a
writing**

www.mhhe.com/
wi

For an
example of
an interpretive
paper, go to

Writing >
Writing Samples
> Sample
Interpretive
Paper

▪ **Conclude by answering "So what?"** The conclusion of an
interpretive analysis needs to answer the "So what?" question
by saying why your thesis—as well as the analysis that supports and develops it—is relevant to the larger issue identified in the introduction or to our understanding of people's
conditions, actions, beliefs, or desires.

4 Arguments

4a Understanding the assignment

www.mhhe.com/
wi

For online
guidance as
you write an
argument,
go to

Writing >
Writing Tutor:
Arguments

Writing arguments is a way to form reasoned positions on debatable
issues. When you write an argument paper, your purpose is to take
part in the debate by stating and supporting your position on an issue.
In addition to position papers, written arguments appear in other
forms, including critiques, reviews, and proposals.

▪ **Critiques** focus on a position someone has taken on an issue.
The critique fairly summarizes that position and either
refutes or defends it. Refutations use one of two basic strategies: either the presentation of contradictory evidence or the
exposure of inadequate reasoning. Defenses make use of three
strategies: clarifying the author's reasoning, presenting new
arguments to support the position, and showing that criti-

cisms of the position are unconvincing. Critiques address the question "What is true?"

■ **Reviews** evaluate an event, artifact, practice, or institution. Judgments in reviews should be principled; that is, they should be determined by reasonable criteria. Reviews address the question "What is good?"

■ **Proposals,** sometimes called **policy papers,** are designed to cause change in the world. Proposals ask readers to see a situation and to act on that situation in a certain way. Proposals address the question "What should be done?"

4b Approaching writing an argument as a process

■ **Figure out what is at issue.** Before you can take a position on a topic like air pollution or football injuries, you must figure out what is at issue. Ask questions about your topic. Are there indications that all is not as it should be? Have things always been this way, or have they changed for the worse? From what different perspectives—economic, social, political, cultural, medical, geographic—can problems be understood? Do people interested in the topic disagree about what is true, what is good, or what should be done?

Based on your answers to such questions, identify the issues your topic raises and decide which of these issues you think is most important, interesting, and appropriate for you to write about.

■ **Develop a reasonable stance that negotiates differences.** You want your readers to respect your intelligence and trust your judgment. Conduct research to make yourself well

4b
writing

informed. To enhance your thoughtfulness, find out what others have to say. Pay attention to the places where you disagree with other people's views, but also note what you have in common—shared interests, key questions, or underlying values.

Avoid language that may promote prejudice or fear. Misrepresentations of other people's ideas are out of place, as are personal attacks on character. Write arguments to open minds, not slam doors shut.

Trying out different perspectives can also help you figure out where you stand on an issue. (*Also see the next item, on stating your position.*) Make a list of the arguments for and against a specific position; then compare the lists and decide where you stand. Does one set of arguments seem stronger than the other? Do you want to change or qualify your initial position?

www.mhhe.com/
wi

For more
information on
developing a
thesis, go to

Writing >
Paragraph/
Essay
Development >
Thesis/Central
Idea

▪ **Compose a thesis that states your position.** A strong, debatable thesis, or claim, on a topic of public interest is a key ingredient of an effective written argument. Without debate, there can be no argument and no reason to assert your position. Personal feelings and accepted facts are not debatable and therefore cannot serve as an argument's thesis.

PERSONAL FEELING, NOT A DEBATABLE THESIS

I feel that professional football players are treated poorly.

ACCEPTED FACT, NOT A DEBATABLE THESIS

Many players in the NFL get injured.

DEBATABLE THESIS

Current NFL regulations are not enough to protect players from suffering the hardships caused by game-related injuries.

In proposals and policy papers, the thesis presents a solution in terms of the writer's definition of the problem. Because this kind of thesis is both complex and qualified, you will often need more than one sentence to state it clearly. You will also need numerous well-supported arguments to make it credible.

4b writing

- **Use reasoning to support and develop your thesis.**
A thesis needs to be supported and developed with reasoning. As you conduct research for your paper, note evidence—facts, examples, and expert testimony—that can be used to support each argument for or against your position. Usually an argument includes more than one type of claim and more than one kind of evidence. Besides generalizations based on empirical data or statistics, it often includes authoritative claims based on the opinions of experts and ethical claims based on the application of principle.

  You can think of an argument as a dialogue between the writer and readers. Anticipate questions and answer them by presenting claims (reasons) that are substantiated with evidence and by refuting counterarguments, substantiated claims that do not support your position. Consider using one of the following strategies to take **counterarguments** into account:
  - Qualify your thesis in light of the counterargument by including a word such as *most, some, usually,* and *likely:* "Although many people—fans and nonfans alike—understand that football is a dangerous sport, few realize just how hard *some* NFL players have it."
  - Add to the thesis a statement of the conditions for or exceptions to your position: "The NFL pension plan is unfair to the players, except for those with more than five years in the league."

■ Choose one or two counterarguments and plan to refute
their truth or their importance in your paper. A writer arguing that the NFL pension plan is unfair to players could
refute the counterargument that the pension plan is good
for players by pointing out specific problems with it.

■ **Create an outline, including a linked set of reasons.**
Begin drafting by writing down your thesis and outlining
the way you will support and develop it. Your outline should
include the following parts:
  ■ An introduction to the topic and the debatable issue.
  ■ A thesis stating your position on the issue.
  ■ A point-by-point account of the reasons for your position,
  including the evidence (facts, examples, authorities) you
  will use to substantiate each point.
  ■ A fair presentation and refutation of one or two key counterarguments to your thesis.
  ■ A response to the "So what?" question. Why does your argument matter?

■ **Use responses from peers to help you understand your
audience.** Having peers review your work is especially important when you are writing arguments about debatable issues.
You cannot assume that readers will agree with your position,
so asking your peers to critique your draft will give you clues
about your readers' reactions. As you revise your argument,
incorporate what you have learned from your peers.

■ **Emphasize your commitment to dialogue in the introduction.** You want your readers to listen to what you have to
say. When you present the topic and issue in your introduction, you should establish some kind of common ground or

shared concern with them. If possible, return to that common ground at the end of your argument.

**4b
writing**

- **Conclude by restating your position and emphasizing its importance.** After presenting your reasoning in detail, remind readers of your thesis. The version of your thesis that you present in your conclusion should be more complex and qualified than the thesis statement you included in your introduction. Readers may not agree with you, but they should know why the issue and your argument matter. If your paper is a proposal, readers will finally want to know that the proposed solution will not cause worse problems than it solves; they realize that policy papers and proposals call for actions, and actions have consequences.

- **Reexamine your reasoning.** After you have completed the first draft of your paper, take time to reexamine your reasoning. Ask yourself the following questions:
  - Have I given a sufficient number of reasons to support my thesis, or should I add one or two more?
  - Have I made any mistakes in logic? (*See the list of Common Logical Fallacies on pp. 16–17.*)

- Have I clearly and adequately developed each claim presented in support of my thesis? Is my supporting evidence accurate, sufficient, and relevant? (*For more on quoting, paraphrasing, and documenting sources, see Part 2: Researching, pp. 76–77 and 82–84, and Parts 3–5.*)

www.mhhe.com/
wi

For examples
of argument
papers, go to
**Writing >
Writing Samples
> Sample
Argument Papers**

COMMON LOGICAL FALLACIES

Non sequitur: A conclusion that does not logically follow from the evidence presented or one that is based on irrelevant evidence: "Students who default on their student loans have no sense of responsibility." [*Students who default on loans could be faced with high medical bills or unemployment.*]

Red herring: An argument that diverts attention from the true issue by concentrating on an irrelevant one: "Hemingway's book *Death in the Afternoon* is not successful because it glorifies the brutal sport of bullfighting." [*Why can't a book about a brutal sport be successful? The statement is irrelevant.*]

Bandwagon: An argument that depends on going along with the crowd, on the false assumption that truth can be determined by a popularity contest: "Everybody knows that Hemingway is preoccupied with the theme of death in his novels." [*How do we know that "everybody" agrees with this statement?*]

Ad hominem: A personal attack on someone who disagrees with you rather than on the person's argument: "The district attorney is a lazy political hack, so naturally she opposes streamlining the court system." [*Even if the district attorney usually supports her party's position, does that make her wrong about this issue?*]

Circular reasoning: An argument that restates the point rather than supporting it with reasonable evidence: "The wealthy should pay more taxes because taxes should be higher for people with higher incomes." [*Why should wealthy people pay more taxes? The rest of the statement doesn't answer this question; it just restates the position.*]

Begging the question: A form of circular reasoning that assumes the truth of a questionable opinion: "The president's poor relationship with the military has weakened the armed forces." [*Does the president really have a poor relationship with the military?*]

Hasty generalization: A conclusion based on inadequate evidence: "Temperatures across the United States last year exceeded the fifty-year average by two degrees, thus proving that global warming is a reality." [*Is this evidence enough to prove this very broad conclusion?*]

Biased language: Words with strong positive or negative overtones that are designed to sway opinion: "The opposition of self-indulgent hippies added to the burdens of our government during the Vietnam War." [*Does "self-indulgent hippies" accurately describe the people who objected to the war, or is it meant to evoke negative reactions?*]

Either/or fallacy: The idea that a complicated issue can be resolved by resorting to one of only two options when in reality there are additional choices: "Either the state legislature will raise taxes or our state's economy will suffer." [*Are these really the only two possibilities?*]

False analogy: The assumption that some similarities between two things indicate total similarity between the two: "If the United States negotiates with aggressive nations, we will pay for our weakness the way England did when it negotiated with Hitler before World War II." [*Is there a danger of war every time the United States negotiates with an aggressive nation?*]

5a   Personal essays

The personal essay is literary, like a poem, a play, or a story. It feels meaningful to readers and relevant to their lives. It speaks in a distinctive voice. It is both compelling and memorable.

- **Make connections between your experiences and those of your readers.** When you write a personal essay, you are exploring your experiences, clarifying your values, and composing a public self. The focus, however, does not need to be on you. You might write a personal essay about a tree in autumn or an athletic event, but whatever focus you choose, remember that your readers expect to learn more than the details of your experience. They expect to see connections between your experience and their own.

- **Turn your essay into a conversation.** Personal essayists usually use the first person (*I* and *we*) to create a sense that the writer and reader are engaged in the open-ended give-and-take of conversation. How you appear in this conversation—shy, belligerent, or friendly, for example—will be determined by the details you include as well as the connotations of the words you use.

- **Structure your essay like a story.** There are three common ways to narrate events and reflections:
  - **Chronological sequence** uses an order determined by clock time; what happened first is presented first, followed by what happened second, then third, and so on.
  - **Emphatic sequence** uses an order determined by the point you want to make; for emphasis, events and

reflections are arranged either from least to most important or from most to least important.

- **Suspenseful sequence** uses an order determined by the emotional effect the writer wants the essay to have. To keep the reader hanging, the essay may begin with a puzzling event, then flash back or go forward to clear things up. Some essays may begin with the end and then flash back to recount how the writer came to that insight.

- **Make details tell your story.** Details shape a story. The details you emphasize, like the words you choose and the characters you create, communicate the point of your essay. Often it is not even necessary to state your thesis.

  Details also control the pace of your essay. To emphasize a particular moment or reflection, provide numerous details to slow the reader down. As an alternative, use details sparingly to surprise the reader, especially in a context otherwise filled with rich detail.

- **Connect your experience to a larger issue.** To demonstrate the significance of a personal essay to its readers, writers usually connect their individual experience to a larger issue. A personal essay about a misunderstanding in an Internet chat room might be connected to the issue of the contrast between face-to-face and online communication.

5b   Lab reports in the experimental sciences

Without writing, science would not be possible. Scientists form hypotheses and plan new experiments as they observe, read, and write. When they work in the laboratory, they keep well-organized and detailed notebooks. They also write and publish lab reports, using a format that reflects the logic of scientific argument. In this way, they share their discoveries and enable other scientists to use their work.

Lab reports usually include seven distinctive sections in the following order: Abstract, Introduction, Methods and Materials, Results, Discussion, Acknowledgments, and Literature Cited. Organize your writing as follows:

- Begin with the methods-and-materials and results sections.

- Next, draft your introduction and discussion sections, making sure your introduction includes a clearly stated hypothesis.

- Finally, prepare the literature cited section, the acknowledgments, and the abstract.

Follow the scientific conventions for abbreviations, symbols, and numbers and revise to make sure that each part of your lab report does what it is expected to do.

- **Abstract.** An abstract is a one-paragraph summary of what your lab report covers. Scientists often skim professional journals, reading nothing more than the titles and abstracts of articles. Abstracts generally use about 250 words to answer the following questions:

  - What methods were used in the experiment?

  - What variables were measured?

  - What were the findings?

  - What do the findings imply?

- **Introduction.** The introduction gives readers the information they need to understand the focus and point of your lab report. State your topic, summarize prior research, and present your hypothesis.

**5b
writing**

Use precise scientific terminology, spell out the key terms that you will later abbreviate, and whenever possible, use the active voice instead of the passive. (*For a discussion of active and passive voices, see Part 6: Editing for Clarity, pp. 244–46.*) The present tense is used to state established knowledge ("the rye seed *produces*"), whereas the past tense is used to summarize the work of prior researchers ("Haberlandt *reported*").

- **Methods and materials.** Experiments must be repeatable. The purpose of the methods-and-materials section is to answer the *how* and *what* questions in a way that enables other scientists to replicate your work. Select the details that they will need to know to do the experiment again. Using the past tense, recount in chronological order what was done with specific materials.

- **Results.** In this section, tell your readers about the results that are relevant to your hypothesis, especially those that are statistically significant. Results may be relevant to your hypothesis even if they are different from what you expected. An experiment does not need to confirm your hypothesis to be interesting.

  To report what you have learned, you might provide a summarizing table or graph. Every table and figure you include in a lab report must be referred to in the body of your report. Do not repeat all the information in the display, but do point out relevant patterns. If you run statistical tests on your findings, be careful not to make the tests themselves the focus of your writing. Refrain from interpreting why things happened the way they did. Interpretation belongs in the discussion section.

Note: Terms like *correlated, random,* and *significant* have specific meanings for scientists and should therefore be used in a lab report only in their scientific sense.

■ **Discussion.** In your discussion section, explain how and why your results do or do not confirm the hypothesis. In discussing your results, do the following:
  ■ Interpret your major findings by explaining how and why each finding does or does not confirm the original hypothesis.
  ■ Connect your research with prior scientific research. How and why do your findings and interpretations agree or disagree with the prior research summarized in your introduction?
  ■ Look ahead to future research: what do researchers need to investigate now?

■ **Acknowledgments.** In professional journals, most reports of experimental findings include a brief statement acknowledging those who assisted the author(s) during the research and writing process.

■ **Literature cited.** Include in this section a listing of all manuals, books, and journal articles you used during your research and writing process. Use one of the citation formats developed by the Council of Science Editors (CSE style), unless another citation format is favored by those working in the area of your research. (*See Part 5: Other Documentation Styles.*)

5c Case studies in the social sciences

Social scientists observe and record the behavior of individuals and groups, research that depends on writing. Accurate observations are essential starting points for a case study, and writing helps observers see more clearly and precisely.

- **Choose a topic that raises a question.** When doing a case study, you need to connect what you see and hear with issues and concepts in the social sciences. Choose a topic and turn it into a research question. Before engaging in your field research, write down your hypothesis—a tentative answer to your research question—as well as some categories of behavior or other things to look for.

- **Assume an unbiased stance.** As you collect and present empirical findings, your stance should be that of an unbiased observer. Make a detailed and accurate record of when and how as well as what you observe. Whenever you can, count and measure, and take down word-for-word what is said. Avoid value-laden terms and unsupported generalizations.

- **Discover meaning in your data.** As you review the notes you made during your observations, try to uncover connections, identify inconsistencies, and draw inferences. For example, ask yourself why a subject behaved in a specific way, and consider different explanations for the behavior.

- **Start your paper with a research review, a statement of your hypothesis, and a description of your methodology.** The introduction presents the framework, background, and rationale for your study. Begin with the topic, and review

5d
writing

related research. Follow that with a statement of your hypothesis, accompanied by a description of your **methodology**—in other words, when and where you made your observations and how you kept records.

■ **Present your findings in an organized way.** There are two basic ways to present your findings in a case study:
  ■ As stages of a process: If you organize your study this way, transform your observations into a pattern or story with distinctive stages.
  ■ In analytic categories: You might use categories from your course textbook to present your findings.

  Note: If possible, develop stages or categories while you are making your observations. In your paper, illustrate your stages or categories with material drawn from your observations.

■ **In the conclusion, discuss your findings.** Answer the following three questions: (1) Did you find what you expected? (2) What do your findings show, or what is the bigger picture? (3) Where should researchers working on your topic go now?

5d Essay exams

Essay exams can be stressful because you are writing under the pressure of the clock. Thinking strategically as you prepare for the test will reduce the stress and may even transform the exam into a learning experience.

- **Understand your assignment.** Your purpose in writing an essay exam is to demonstrate informed understanding. An essay question may require you to do the following:

  - **Explain** what you have learned in a clear, well-organized way. (*See question 1 in the box on p. 26.*)
  - **Connect** what you know about one topic with what you know about another topic. (*See question 2 in the box on p. 26.*)
  - **Apply** what you have learned to a new situation. (*See question 3 in the box on p. 26.*)
  - **Interpret** the causes, effects, meanings, value, or potential of something. (*See question 4 in the box on p. 26.*)
  - **Argue** for or against some controversial statement about what you have learned. (*See question 5 in the box on p. 26.*)

- **Prepare with the course and your instructor in mind.** Consider the specific course as your writing context and the course's instructor as your audience.
  - What questions or problems did your instructor explicitly or implicitly address?
  - What frameworks did your instructor use to analyze topics?
  - What key terms did your instructor repeatedly use during lectures and discussions?

- **Plan your time.** During the exam, quickly look through the whole exam, and determine how much time you will spend on each part or question. You will want to move as quickly as possible through the questions that have lower point values so that you can spend the bulk of your time responding to the questions that are worth the greatest number of points.

5d writing

CHARTING the TERRITORY

Essay Exam Questions across the Curriculum

During finals week, you may be asked to respond to essay questions like the following:

1. Discuss the power of the contemporary presidency as well as the limits of that power. (from a political science course)
2. Compare and contrast the treatment of labor supply decisions in the economic models proposed by Greg Lewis and Gary Becker. (from an economics course)
3. Describe the observations that would be made in an alpha-particle scattering experiment if (a) the nucleus of an atom were negatively charged and the protons occupied the empty space outside the nucleus and (b) the electrons were embedded in a positively charged sphere. (from a chemistry course)
4. Explain two ways in which Picasso's *Guernica* evokes war's terrifying destructiveness. (from an art history course)
5. In 1800, was Thomas Jefferson a dangerous radical? Be sure to define your key terms and to support your position with evidence from specific events, documents, and so on. (from an American history course)

▪ **Answer short identification questions by showing the significance of the information.** The most common type of short-answer question is the identification question: Who or what is X? In answering questions of this sort, present just

enough information to show that you understand X's significance within the context of the course.

▪ **Be tactical in responding to essay questions.** Keep in
mind that essay questions usually ask you to do something
specific with a topic. Begin by determining precisely what you
are being asked to do. Before you write anything, read the
question—all of it—and circle key words.

EXAMPLE   (Explain)(two) ways in which Picasso's *Guernica*
               evokes war's terrifying (destructiveness.)

To answer this question, you need to focus on two of the
painting's features, such as coloring and composition, not
on Picasso's life.

▪ **Use the essay question to structure your response.** Usually, you will be able to transform the question itself into the
thesis of your answer. If you are asked to agree/disagree with
the Federalists' characterization of Thomas Jefferson in the
election of 1800, you might begin with the following thesis:

> **In the election of 1800, the Federalists characterized
> Jefferson as a dangerous radical. Although Jefferson's
> ideas were radical for the times, they were not dan-
> gerous to the republic.**

Take a minute or two to list evidence for each of your main
points, and then write the essay.

▪ **Check your work.** Leave a few minutes to read through
your completed answer, looking for words you might have
omitted or key sentences that make no sense. Make corrections neatly.

5e Oral presentations

When we write, we imagine the presence of absent strangers. When we speak, the strangers are there in front of us, expecting us to connect with them. To do so, prepare a speech that is appropriate, clear, and memorable.

- **Imagine the occasion and your audience.** An oral presentation should suit the occasion. Who is likely to be there to listen? How and why have these people come together as an audience? What do they have in common, and what are they expecting to hear?

- **Decide on the purpose of your presentation.** Do you want to intensify your audience's commitment to what they already think, provide new and clarifying information, provoke more analysis and understanding of the issue, or change what the audience believes about something?

- **Make the focus of your presentation explicit and the organization clear-cut.** Select two or three ideas that you most want your audience to hear—and to remember. Make these ideas the focus of your presentation, and tell your audience what to expect by previewing the content of your presentation.

- **Make your opening interesting.** Get your listeners' attention. Surprising statements, quotations, images, and anecdotes are all effective ways to begin.

- **Be direct.** For clarity, speak in basic sentence structures, repeat key terms, and pay attention to the rhythm of your speech.

- **Use visual aids.** Consider using slides, posters, objects, video clips, and music. Visual aids make your focus explicit while you are speaking. The twelve PowerPoint slides in Figure 5.1 on pages 30–31 offer advice on how to design effective slides for a presentation.

www.mhhe.com/
wi
For a PowerPoint® tutorial, go to
Writing > PowerPoint Tutorial

- **Make eye contact and keep your audience interested.** A written script can be a barrier between you and your audience. If you speak from an outline, make eye contact with your listeners to monitor their responses and adjust what you have to say accordingly. Write out only those parts of your presentation where precise wording counts, such as quotations.

   For most occasions, it is inappropriate to write out everything you want to say and then read it word for word. In some formal settings, however, precise wording may be necessary, especially if your remarks are to be published or quoted in the media. If a script feels necessary, triple-space the typescript of your text; avoid carrying sentences over from one page to another; and mark your manuscript for pauses, emphasis, and the pronunciation of proper names. You should also practice your delivery. It should take about seventy-five seconds to deliver one triple-spaced page of text.

- **Conclude in a memorable way.** Your final comments will be the part of your speech that your audience remembers most.

- **Rehearse.** Whether you are using an outline or a script, practice with a clock, and leave yourself time to insert occasional remarks during the actual performance.

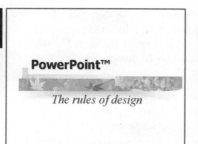

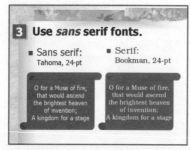

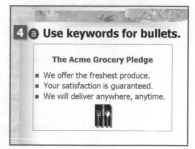

FIGURE 5.1 Advice on designing PowerPoint slides.

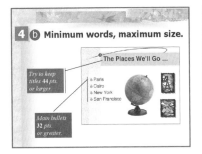

4 ⓑ Minimum words, maximum size.

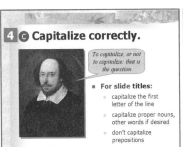

4 ⓒ Capitalize correctly.

■ **For slide titles:**
  - capitalize the first letter of the line
  - capitalize proper nouns, other words if desired
  - don't capitalize prepositions

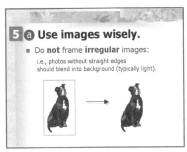

5 ⓐ Use images wisely.

■ Do **not** frame **irregular** images:
i.e., photos without straight edges should blend into background (typically light).

5 ⓑ The clip-art hall of shame

6 Strive for visual balance.

■ Avoid dead space.
■ Avoid lopsidedness.
■ Position items for legibility & clarity.

Some final observations

■ Break any rule if you have a good reason.
■ Observe copyright laws on photos & artwork.
■ You control every aspect of a slide's design. Have a purpose for everything that happens.

5f   Coauthored projects

A project is coauthored when more than one person is responsible for producing it. In many fields, working collaboratively is essential. Here are some suggestions:

- Decide on some ground rules with your partners, including meeting times, deadlines, and ways of reconciling differences.
- Divide the work fairly so that everyone contributes to the project. Keep in mind that each group member should do some researching, drafting, revising, and editing.
- If the group's dynamics begin to break down, seek the assistance of a third party.
- After each group member has completed his or her assigned part, the group should negotiate to create a focused piece of writing with a consistent voice. Tact is essential. Keep the excellence of the project in the forefront, and all should go well.

5g   Portfolios

A **portfolio** is an ordered selection of your work. The principles that guide selection and order depend on the occasion, purpose, and audience.

As soon as you select a major, you should consider keeping an organized folder of your work in that area. The folder can be organized chronologically, by field or subfield, or by issue. Each year, it is a good idea to create a portfolio that reflects what you have learned and how you learned it. Successful job candidates often prepare well-organized portfolios of carefully selected materials to take with them to job interviews.

6 Design documents for page and screen.

Like writing decisions, design decisions must be purposeful to be effective. Consider your purpose for writing, as well as the needs of your audience. Your goal is to enhance the content of your text, not just decorate it.

6a Getting the margins, spacing, type, and page numbers right

The way you format a document determines how your text appears on the page—and how it affects readers. Here are a few basic guidelines for formatting academic papers:

- **First page:** In a short paper, less than five pages, page 1 contains a header with your name, your professor's name, your course and section number, and the date. If your paper exceeds five pages, page 1 is usually a title page.
- **Type:** Select a common typeface, or **font,** such as Courier, Times, or Bookman, and choose an 11- or 12-point size. Avoid display fonts—Antique, Calligrapher, Old English, and others—in academic writing.
- **Margins:** Use one-inch margins on all four sides of your text. Line up, or **justify,** the lines of your document along the left margin but not along the right margin. This procedure enables you to avoid odd spacing between words.

33

6b
design

- **Line spacing:** Double-space your paper unless you are instructed to do otherwise.

- **Page numbers:** Page numbers typically appear in the upper right-hand corner of all pages after the first.

CHARTING the TERRITORY

Style Guides

The Modern Language Association (MLA) and the American Psychological Association (APA) have developed widely used guidelines for documentation and manuscript format. For more about the basic document styles recommended by MLA and by APA, see pages 93–141 and pages 142–75, respectively. For style guides in math, physics, chemistry, and other fields, see page 85.

6b Thinking intentionally about design

From straightforward academic papers to more elaborate documents such as reports, newsletters, or brochures, the same design principles apply.

1. Get to know your computer toolbar.

The toolbars on your computer give you a range of options for editing, designing, and sharing your documents. In Figure 6.1, three toolbars are open in Microsoft Word: the standard, drawing, and reviewing toolbars. The standard toolbar allows you to choose different typefaces; bold, italic, or underlined type; numbered or bulleted lists; and so on. The drawing toolbar allows you to insert boxes, drawings, and clip art into your text; and the reviewing toolbar enables you to mark changes, add comments, and even send your document to a reader.

6b design

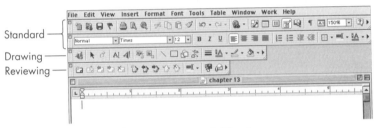

Standard
Drawing
Reviewing

FIGURE 6.1 Three toolbars in Microsoft Word.

If you are using a word-processing program other than Microsoft Word, take some time to learn the different toolbars and formatting options that are available to you.

2. Use design to organize information.

Group related items as closely together as your space allows. Use graphic accents such as boxes or indents, headings, spacing, and numbered or bulleted lists to indicate emphasis and importance. These variations in text appearance help readers scan, locate information, and dive in when they need to know more about a topic.

**6b
design**

Headings interrupt the text in short papers. In longer papers, though, they help you organize complex information. Effective headings are short, descriptive, and, like lists, consistent in emphasis and parallel in grammatical structure. All headings in a paper might be in the form of questions, declarative or imperative sentences, or phrases beginning with -*ing* verbs. (*For more on parallel structure, see Part 6, Editing for Clarity, pp. 228–29.*)

Place and highlight headings consistently. For example, you might center all first-level headings and put them in bold type. If you have second-level headings, you might align them at the left margin and underline them.

First-Level Heading

<u>Second-Level Heading</u>

3. Use design to emphasize information.

You can emphasize elements in your text by varying your type style and using lists. You can emphasize a word or phrase by making it **bold,** *italicizing it,* or <u>underlining it.</u> You can also use ALL CAPITAL LETTERS or SMALL CAPS for emphasis, although this option is seldom appropriate for academic papers.

4. Use design elements effectively.

In design, simplicity, contrast, and consistency matter. If you emphasize an item by putting it in italic or bold type or in color, or if you use a graphic accent such as a box to set it off, consider repeating this effect for similar items to give your document a unified look.

5. Use restraint.
Avoid using too many graphics, headings, bullets, boxes, or other elements in a document. Standard fonts have become standard because they are easy on the eye. Unusual typefaces get readers' attention, but they lose their force when overused. Bold or italic type, underlining, or any other graphic effect should not continue for more than one sentence at a time.

6c Using and integrating visuals

Effective visuals are used for a specific purpose, not for decoration, and each type of visual illustrates some kinds of material better than others. Make your visuals simple and clear. If a chart is overloaded with information, separate it into several charts instead. Because visual elements are more accepted in some fields than in others, ask your instructor for advice before including a visual in your paper.

1. Using tables
Tables are made up of rows and columns of cells; each cell presents an element of textual, numeric, or graphic information. Tables organize data for readers. Consider Table 1 on page 38, which was taken from the Web site of the Environmental Protection Agency.

2. Using bar graphs
These graphs show relationships and highlight comparisons between two or more variables. The example in Figure 6.2 compares the frequency of three kinds of activities during certain periods of the year.

TABLE 1. U.S. Emissions of Criteria Pollutants, 1989–1996 (million metric tons of gas)

SOURCE	1989	1990	1991	1992	1993	1994	1995	1996
Carbon monoxide	93.5	91.3	88.3	85.3	85.4	89.6	83.5	NA
Nitrogen oxides	21.1	20.9	20.6	20.7	21.1	21.5	19.7	NA
Nonmethane VOCs	21.7	21.4	20.8	20.3	20.5	21.1	20.7	NA

NA = not available.

Note: Data in this table are revised from the data contained in the previous EIA report, *Emissions of Greenhouse Gases in the United States 1995,* DOE/EIA-0573(95) (Washington, DC, October 1996).

Source: U.S. Environmental Protection Agency, Office of Air Quality Planning and Standards, *National Air Pollutant Emission Trends,* 1900–1995, EPA-454/R-96-007 (Research Triangle Park, NC, October 1996), pp. A-5, A-9, and A-16.

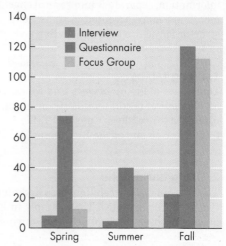

FIGURE 6.2 Market research activities.

3. Using pie charts

Pie charts are circles divided into segments, with each segment representing a piece of the whole. The segments must add up to 100 percent of something. See the pie chart in Figure 6.3.

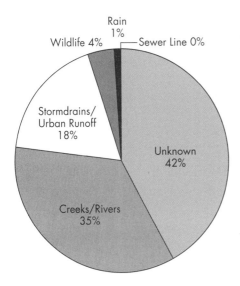

FIGURE 6.3 Sources of contamination resulting in warnings posted statewide in year 2000 (Based on Beach Mile Days).

4. Using line graphs

Line graphs or charts are used to show changes over time or to show the relationship, as shown in Figure 6.4.

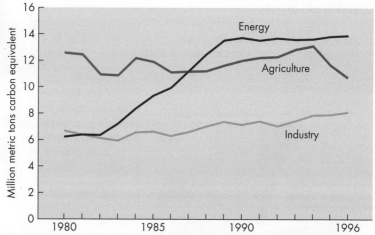

FIGURE 6.4 U.S. nitrous oxide emissions by source, 1980–1996.

5. Using diagrams

Used to show concepts or structures visually, diagrams are often included in scientific or technical writing. The diagram in Figure 6.5, for example, shows the factors involved in the decision to commit a burglary.

FIGURE 6.5 Event model for a burglary.

6. Using photographs and illustrations

Photographs and illustrations can reinforce a point you are making in your text, showing readers what your subject actually looks like or how it has been affected or changed. When you use photographs or illustrations, always credit your source, and be aware that most photographs and illustrations are protected by copyright. If you plan to use a photograph as part of a Web page, for example, you will usually need to obtain permission from the copyright holder.

6c
visuals

7. Integrating visuals into documents

If you decide to use a table, chart, or diagram, keep this general advice in mind:

1. **Number tables and other figures** consecutively throughout your paper, and label them appropriately: Table 1, Table 2, and so on. Do not abbreviate *Table. Figure* may be abbreviated as *Fig.*

2. **Refer to the visual element in your text** before it appears, placing the visual as close as possible to this reference. Always refer to a visual by its label: for example, "See Figure 1."

3. **Give each visual a title and, if necessary, a caption** that clearly explains what the visual shows.

4. **Include explanatory notes below the visuals,** and use the word *Note* followed by a colon to introduce explanations of the visual as a whole. To explain a specific element within the visual, use a superscript *letter* (not a number) both after the specific element and before the note. This footnote should appear directly beneath the graphic, not at the foot of the page or at the end of your paper.

5. **Credit sources for visuals.** Use the word *Source,* followed by a colon and complete documentation, including the author, title, publication information, and page number if applicable.

Note: The Modern Language Association (MLA) and the American Psychological Association (APA) provide other guidelines for figure captions and crediting sources of visuals. (*See Part 3: MLA Documentation Style, p. 93, and Part 4: APA Documentation Style, p. 142.*)

6d Designing pages for the Web

The best known part of the Internet, the World Wide Web is a gigantic intertwined network of information as well as a publishing network. Not too long ago, writers who wanted to publish their ideas on the Web had to learn to write in hypertext markup language (HTML) or extensible markup language (XML). Now programs such as FrontPage, PageMill, Dreamweaver, and Netscape Composer provide a WYSIWYG (what you see is what you get) interface for creating Web pages.

Visitors to a Web page decide in ten to twenty seconds whether to stay. Consequently, on good Web sites, you will find such easy-to-follow links as "what you'll find here" and "FAQs" (frequently asked questions).

As you surf the Internet, observe how the different Web sites you visit address various audiences and have different purposes. As you design your own Web page, ask yourself the following questions: Who is

For MULTILINGUAL STUDENTS

Designing a Web Site Collaboratively

If you are asked to create a Web site as part of a class assignment, try to make arrangements to work with a partner or a small group. The kind of interaction involved in writing the content and designing the site will provide you with beneficial language support. At the same time, you will be able to provide the project with the benefit of your unique multicultural viewpoint.

my audience? What is my purpose in publishing on the Web? Remember that if your visitors do not find your site engaging, they can easily hop to another one.

1. Design a Web site with a unified look.

Because the Web is a visual medium, readers appreciate a site with a unified look. Design your home page to complement your other pages, and do the following:

- Include a site map, a Web page that serves as a table of contents for your entire site.
- Select elements such as buttons, signs, animations, sounds, and backgrounds with a consistent design.
- Use colors that provide adequate contrast and fonts that make text easy to read. Pages that are too busy are not visually compelling.

For example, Figure 6.6 is the table of contents and site navigation page from the Web site of the *Literature, Arts, and Medicine Database*.

2. Identify the site on each page, and include a date.

People will not always enter your Web site through the front door. Therefore, include the title of the site on each page in your Web site. Every time you change the content of your Web page, change the date as well so that your visitors will know you have updated it.

3. Provide a navigation bar on each page.

A **navigation bar** can be a simple line of links that you copy and paste at the top or bottom of each page. Provide a navigation bar on each page to make it easy for visitors to move from the site's home

Advanced Educational Systems

About Us | Research Projects | Learning Tools | People | Gallery

Virtual Patient

Infrastructure for
Rich Media
Educational
Environments

Patient Education
Research and
Development
Initiative

Psychosocial
Aspects of
Bioterrorism

Medical
Humanities

Physical
Computing

Medical Humanities

The Medical Humanities project, a
collaboration with Felice Aull, Ph.D.,
M.A., Head, Literature, Arts, and
Medicine Project at the New York
University School of Medicine,
provides several resources for the
medical humanities field including an
international directory of people and
programs, syllabi of courses and
teaching materials from many
institutions, archives of a literature
and medicine list serve, and The
Literature, Arts, & Medicine Database.

**The Literature, Arts, & Medicine
Database** is an annotated
bibliography of prose, poetry, film,
video and art which was developed to
be a dynamic, accessible,
comprehensive resource for use in
health/pre-health and liberal arts
settings. It is a multi-institutional
project initiated by Drs. Felice Aull,
Martin Nachbar, Karen Brewer, Roy
Smith and Irene Chen '96 of the New
York University School of Medicine in
the summer of 1993. This Web site is
produced and maintained by the AES.

Editor-in-Chief:

Felice Aull, Ph.D., M.A.
Head, Literature, Arts, and Medicine
Project
New York University School of
Medicine

Co-editors:

Catherine Belling, M.A., Ph.D.
Associate Director, Institute for
Medicine in Contemporary Society
Stony Brook Health Sciences Center

Sandra L. Bertman, Ph.D.
Palliative Care/Boston College Graduate School of Social Work

Stephanie Brown Clark, M.D., Ph.D.
Medical Humanities/University of Rochester Medical Center

Jack Coulehan, M.D., M.P.H.
Director, Institute for Medicine in Contemporary Society/Stony Brook Health Sciences
Center

FIGURE 6.6 The home page for the *Literature, Arts, and Medicine
Database.*

page to other pages. Always include a link to the home page on the navigation bar.

4. Use links to make connections.

"Hot links" are anchored to specific text. When activated, the link opens another Web page. Web writers use these hypertextual links to connect their interests with those of others and to provide extra sources of information. Hypertext links also give readers and writers ways to create their own reading and writing paths. Avoid using the command "Click here" on your Web site. Instead, make links part of your text.

5. Use relevant, easy-to-load graphics.

Even though a picture may be worth a thousand words, your Web site should not depend on graphics alone to make its message clear and interesting. Graphics should be used to reinforce your message.

When adding graphics to your Web site, you should use photographs saved in JPEG (pronounced *"jay-peg"*) format. The file extension is .jpg or .jpeg. Be sure to minimize the size of your images so that they will load quickly on any computer.

6. Use peer feedback to revise your Web site.

Before publishing your site, proofread your text carefully, and ask a couple of friends to look at your site and share their responses. When you publish on the Web, you offer your work to be read by anyone in the world. Make sure your site reflects favorably on your abilities.

For all knowledge and
wonder (which is the seed
of knowledge) is an impression
of pleasure in itself.

—FRANCIS BACON

PART

2

Researching

7 Understand the purpose of research projects.

College faculty in all fields are researchers. Besides searching out existing information about a particular subject in their specialty, they do research to create new knowledge about that topic. Joining the academic community means becoming a researcher.

7a Understanding primary and secondary research

Primary research means working in a laboratory, in the field, or with an archive of raw data, original documents, and authentic artifacts to make firsthand discoveries.

Secondary research means looking to see what other people have discovered, learned, and written. Knowing how to identify facts, interpretations, and evaluations is key to good secondary research:

- **Facts** are objective. Like your body weight, facts can be measured, observed, and independently verified in some way.

- **Interpretations** spell out the implications of facts. Are you as thin as you are because of your genes—or because you exercise every day? The answer to this question is an interpretation.

- **Evaluations** are debatable judgments about a set of facts or a situation. Attributing a person's thinness to genes is an interpretation, but the assertion that "one can never be too rich or too thin" is an evaluation.

Once you are up to date on the facts, interpretations, and evaluations in a particular area, you will be able to design a research project that adds to this knowledge. Usually, what you will add is your *perspective* on the sources you found and read:

- Given all that you have learned about the topic, what strikes you as important or interesting?
- What patterns do you see, or what connections can you make between one person's work and another's?
- Where is the research going, and what problems still need to be explored?

7b Recognizing the connection between research and college writing

In one way or another, research informs all college writing. But some assignments require more rigorous and systematic research than others. These **research project** assignments offer you a chance to go beyond your course texts—to find and read both classic and current material on a specific issue.

Classic sources are respected older works that made such an important contribution to a particular area of research that contemporary researchers use them as touchstones for further research. In many fields, sources published within the past five years are considered current. A research paper constitutes your contribution to the ongoing conversation about a specific issue.

7c Choosing an interesting research question

If you choose an interesting question, your research is likely to be more meaningful.

7c
research

1. Choose a question with personal significance.

Get personally involved in your work. Begin with the wording of the assignment, analyzing the project's required scope, purpose, and audience (*see Part 1: Common Assignments across the Curriculum, pp. 3–4*). Then browse through the course texts and your class notes, looking for a match between your interests and topics, issues, or problems in the subject area.

2. Make your question specific.

The more specific your question, the more your research will have direction and focus. Make a question more specific by asking about the *who, what, why, when, where,* and *how* of a topic.

CHARTING the TERRITORY

Typical Lines of Inquiry in Different Disciplines

Research topics and questions differ from one discipline to another, as the following examples show:

- **History:** Explain the meaning of the events leading up to the fall of the Berlin Wall in 1989.
- **Education:** How do textbooks used in German schools deal with the Nazi period?
- **Political science:** What is the German concept of citizenship, and how does this concept apply to people born in Germany who are not of German ethnicity?
- **Sociology:** What factors determine social class in twenty-first-century Germany?

After you have compiled a list of possible research questions, choose one that is relatively specific or rewrite a broad one to make it more specific and answerable. For example, a student could rewrite the following broad question about Germany to make it answerable:

7c
research

TOO BROAD   **What are Germany's prospects in the twenty-first century?**

ANSWERABLE   **In terms of international trade and capital investment, what are Germany's current economic prospects?**

3. Find a challenging question.

To be interesting, a research question must be challenging. If a question can be answered with a simple yes or no, a dictionary-like definition, or a textbook presentation of information, you should choose another question or rework the simple one to make it more challenging.

NOT CHALLENGING   **Have Germany's capital investment inflows increased since reunification?**

CHALLENGING   **How likely is it that the current trends in Germany's capital investment inflows will continue in the same direction?**

4. Speculate about answers.

Sometimes it can be useful to develop a **hypothesis**—an answer to your research question—to work with during the research process. Keep an open mind as you work, and be aware of the assumptions embedded in your research question or hypothesis. Consider, for example, the following hypothesis:

**7d
research**

HYPOTHESIS **With the problems caused by reunification behind it, Germany should enjoy a strong economy during the coming decades.**

This hypothesis assumes that the worst is over for the German economy. But assumptions are always open to question. Researchers must be willing to adjust their ideas as they learn more about a topic.

7d Creating a research plan

Take some time at the beginning to outline a research plan. Even though you will probably modify your plan later, your work will go more smoothly if you have definite goals from the beginning. As a starting point, use the following outline.

Outline for Scheduling Research

Project Planning (three days for an assignment due in one month): Activities include the following:

- Analyzing the assignment
- Deciding on a topic and a question
- Outlining a research plan

Research Phase I (five days for an assignment due in one month): Get a general overview of your topic by doing the following:

- Reading **reference works**
- Making a list of relevant **keywords**
- Compiling a **working bibliography** of print and online sources
- Sampling some of the items in your bibliography

Research Phase II (twelve days for an assignment due in one month): Most likely you will spend twice as much time in the second phase as you did in the first phase. Activities include the following:

- Locating, reading, and evaluating selected sources
- Taking notes
- Conducting primary research

Research Phase III (ten days for an assignment due in one month): Count on spending one third to one half of the available time working on the paper that grows out of your research:

- Drafting your paper
- Revising and editing your paper

8 Find print and online sources.

The amount of information available in the library and on the Internet is vast. Usually, a search for sources entails three activities:

- Collecting keywords from reference works
- Using library databases
- Finding material in the library and on the World Wide Web

For MULTILINGUAL STUDENTS

Researching a Full Range of Sources

Relying on what is available in your first language will severely limit the range of materials you have to choose from and may cause you to miss important sources of information. Although you may find reading research in English challenging, it is important to broaden the scope of your search as soon as you can to include the full range of print and Internet resources written in English.

 8a Consulting sources

Consult more than one source and check out more than one kind of source. These are some of the kinds of sources available to you:

- **General Reference Works**
  Encyclopedias, annuals, almanacs
  Computer databases, bibliographies, abstracts

- **Specialized Reference Works**
  Discipline-specific encyclopedias, almanacs, and dictionaries

- **Books and Electronic Texts**

- **Periodical Articles**
  In newspapers
  In magazines
  In scholarly and technical journals
  On the World Wide Web

- **Web Sites**

- **News Groups, ListServs, E-mail, and Virtual Communities (MUDs and MOOs)**

- **Pamphlets, Government Documents, Census Data**

- **Primary Sources**
  Original documents like literary works, art objects, performances, manuscripts, letters, and personal journals
  Museum collections; maps; photo, film, sound, and music archives
  Field notes, surveys, interviews
  Results of observation and lab experiments

8b library

8b Using the library

Librarians know what is available in your library and how to get material from other libraries. They can also show you how to access the library's computerized book catalog, periodical databases, and electronic resources or how to use the Internet to find information relevant to your research project.

www.mhhe.com/
wi
For links to
online libraries,
go to
Research >
Using the Library

Discipline-specific **help sheets,** found at most college libraries, list the location of relevant periodicals and noncirculating reference books, along with information about special databases, indexes, and sources of information on the Internet.

8b
library

1. Reference works

Reference works provide an overview of a subject area and are less up to date than the specialized knowledge found in academic journals and scholarly books. There is nothing wrong with consulting a general encyclopedia for your own information, but for college research you will need to explore your topic in more scholarly resources. Sometimes, the list of references at the end of an encyclopedia article can lead to useful sources.

Reference books do not circulate, so plan to take notes or make photocopies of the pages you need to consult later. Many college libraries subscribe to services that provide access to online encyclopedias. Check your college library's home page for a link to reference materials like online encyclopedias. As you consult reference works, collect ten or more key terms associated with your topic and learn how those terms are related conceptually. The more keywords you have, the better your chances of retrieving a reasonable number of relevant sources.

Here is a list of some other kinds of reference materials available in print, on the Internet, or both:

ALMANACS	*Almanac of American Politics*
	Information Please Almanac
	World Almanac
BIBLIOGRAPHIES	*Bibliographic Index*
	Bibliography of Asian Studies
	MLA International Bibliography

BIOGRAPHIES	*African American Biographical Database* *American Men and Women of Science* *Who's Who*
DICTIONARIES	*Dictionary of American History* *Dictionary of the Social Sciences* *Oxford English Dictionary (OED)*

8b
research

2. Books

A search of the library's catalog will provide you with a list composed mostly of books. Online library catalogs can be searched by author, title, or keyword or by a subject term listed in the *Library of Congress Subject Headings (LCSH)*. The *LCSH* provides a set of key terms that can be used in your search for sources. Record the **call number** of each book that might prove useful so that you will know where to look for the book on the shelves. Your library's online catalog may list books available in affiliated libraries. A librarian can help you obtain books that are not in your college's library through an interlibrary loan process. This process can take time, however. Consult your librarian.

3. Periodicals

Newspapers, magazines, and scholarly journals that are published at regular intervals are classified as **periodicals.** Scholarly and technical journals, which publish articles written by experts and based on up-to-date research and information, are more reliable than articles written by journalists for newspapers and magazines. Ask your instructor or librarian which periodicals are considered important in the discipline you are studying.

8b
library

Articles published in periodicals are cataloged in general and specialized indexes, many of which are available in electronic formats, known as **databases,** as well as in print volumes shelved in the library's reference section. Many databases provide abstracts of the works they list. If you are searching for articles that are more than twenty years old, use printed indexes. Otherwise, see what your library has available through an online subscription service or on CD-ROM. (*For help with search terms, see pp. 57 and 63.*) The following list includes many of the most popular online indexes to periodical articles.

- *ABC-CLIO:* This Web-based service offers one interface for searching two indexes: *American History and Life* and *Historical Abstracts.*

- *Academic Universe (Lexis-Nexis):* Updated daily, this online service provides full-text access to around 6,000 newspapers, professional publications, legal references, and congressional sources.

- *EBSCOhost:* The Academic Search Premier service provides full-text coverage for more than 3,000 scholarly publications and indexes articles in all academic subject areas.

- *ERIC:* This database lists publications in the area of education.

- *Factiva:* This database offers access to content from Dow Jones and the Reuters news agency, including over 1,000 newspapers; over 3,000 magazines, journals, and newsletters; and over 10,000 news and business Web sites.

- *FirstSearch:* Offering a common interface for access to general databases such as NetFirst and WorldCat, this service

www.mhhe.com/
wi
To conduct a
search using
the Factiva™
database, go to
Research >
Factiva
PowerSearch

also permits searches of such subject-specific bibliographic databases as ERIC, *Medline,* and the *MLA Bibliography*.

- ***General Science Index:*** This index is general rather than specialized. It lists articles by biologists, chemists, and other scientists.

- ***GDCS:*** Updated monthly, the Government Documents Catalog Service (GDCS) contains records of all publications printed by the United States Government Printing Office since 1976.

- ***Humanities Index:*** This index lists articles from journals in language and literature, history, philosophy, and similar areas.

- ***InfoTrac SearchBank:*** This Web-based service searches bibliographic and other databases such as the General Reference Center Gold, General Business File ASAP, and Health Reference Center.

- ***JSTOR:*** This electronic archive provides full-text access to scholarly journals in the humanities and social sciences.

- ***MLA Bibliography:*** Covering from 1963 to the present, the *MLA Bibliography* indexes journals, essay collections, proceedings, and series published worldwide in the fields of modern languages, literature, literary criticism, linguistics, and folklore.

- ***New York Times Index:*** This index lists major articles published by the *Times* since 1913.

- ***Newspaper Abstracts:*** This database provides an index to twenty-five national and regional newspapers.

- ***PAIS International:*** Produced by the Public Affairs Information Service, this database indexes literature on public policy,

8c
research

social policy, and the general social sciences from 1972 to the present.

■ *ProQuest:* This database offers access to many newspapers and journals, as well as historical sources dating back to the nineteenth century.

■ *PsycInfo:* Sponsored by the American Psychological Association (APA), this database indexes and abstracts books, scholarly articles, technical reports, and dissertations in psychology and related disciplines such as psychiatry, medicine, nursing, and education.

■ *PubMed:* The National Library of Medicine publishes this database, which indexes and abstracts journal articles in biomedicine and provides links to related databases.

■ *Sociological Abstracts:* This database indexes and abstracts journal articles, books, conference papers, and dissertations in the area of sociology.

■ *Social Science Index:* This index lists articles from journals in such fields as economics, psychology, political science, and sociology.

www.mhhe.com/
wi

For advice on
locating and
using online
sources, go to
Research >
Using the Internet

8c Searching the Internet

The **Internet** is a global network of computers. The easiest and most familiar way to gain access to the Internet is through the **World Wide Web,** which uses hypertext links. Besides providing access to online databases, reference works, and periodicals, the Internet can bring you closer to primary materials that were once difficult to examine firsthand. It can also put you in touch with a research community through e-mail, chat rooms, online class discussions, MOOs (multiuser dimensions, object-oriented), MUDs (multiuser dimensions), discussion lists, news groups, and blogs.

Resources that you find on the Web must be critically evaluated for their reliability because unlike most books and articles, Web sites usually do not go through peer review and evaluation before publication. (*For help with evaluating Web sources critically, see pp. 66–67.*)

Learn how to use search engines and keywords to find useful Web sites, as well as how to gain access to and use other Internet resources such as discussion groups (ListServs), Usenet news groups, MOOs and MUDs, and blogs.

8c research

1. Search engines

To search for sources on the Web, type a keyword or phrase into a **search engine,** a software program that returns a list of Web sites that include your keyword. Most researchers find it necessary to use more than one search engine. To learn how a search engine can best serve your needs, look for a link labeled "search help," "about us," or something similar in any search engine you use.

Simple search engines, or *directories,* use hierarchical indexes to categorize information. These directories are easy to use and selective in the results they return.

- *Yahoo!* <http://www.yahoo.com>
- *Galaxy* <http://www.galaxy.com>

Standard search engines send "robots" or "spiders" to all points on the Web to return results, putting the most relevant items at the top of the list.

- *AltaVista* <http://www.altavista.com>
- *Go.com* <http://infoseek.go.com>
- *All the Web* <http://www.alltheweb.com>
- *HotBot* <http://www.hotbot.com>

8c
Internet

Other search engines allow users to ask for information in different ways.

- *Google* <http://www.google.com>: Responds to a query in a way that ranks relevant Web sites based on the link structure of the Internet itself.
- *Ask Jeeves* <http://www.ask.com>: Supports natural language searching. Type a question and click on "ask."

Meta search engines return results by searching other search engines. They provide more sites than a simple search engine, but they are not as selective.

- *Dogpile* <http://www.dogpile.com>
- *MetaCrawler* <http://www.metacrawler.com>

CHARTING the TERRITORY

The following sites list online academic resources by subject or field of research:

- *Academic Info* <http://www.academicinfo.net>
- *Infomine: Scholarly Internet Resource Collections* <http://infomine.ucr.edu>
- *Voice of the Shuttle General Humanities Page* <http://vos.ucsb.edu/index.asp>
- *World Wide Web Virtual Library* <http://www.vlib.org>

2. Keyword Internet searches

To fine-tune your search process, adjust your keyword or phrase. Altering the keyword to make it more specific narrows the results significantly.

Many search engines allow you to refine a keyword search by using these strategies:

8c
Internet

- **Group words together.** Put quotation marks or parentheses around the phrase you are looking for—for example, "Dixieland Jazz."

- **Use Boolean operators.**

  AND (+)   Use AND or + when words must appear together in a document: Germany + Economy.

  OR   Use OR if one of two or more terms must appear in your results: jazz OR "musical improvisation."

  NOT (–)   Use NOT or – in front of words that you do not want to appear together in your results: Germany NOT west.

- **Add a wildcard.** For more results, combine part of a keyword with an asterisk (*) used as a wildcard: German* AND econom* or +German* +econom*.

- **Search the fields.** Some search engines enable searching within fields, such as the title field of Web pages. You will find Web pages that are about your topic by doing a title search: TITLE: +Louis +Armstrong will give you pages about the great jazz musician Louis Armstrong.

3. Online communication

The Internet provides access to communities with common interests and varying levels of expertise on different subjects. Discussion lists (electronic mailing lists), Usenet news groups, MOOs, and MUDs are the most common communities. Online journals or blogs offer another way to connect with people interested in a given topic.

▪ **Discussion lists (electronic mailing lists)** are networked e-mail conversations on particular topics. Lists can be open (anyone can join) or closed (only certain people, such as members of a particular class or group, can join). If the list is open, you can subscribe by sending a message.

▪ **Usenet news groups** are one of the oldest features of the Internet. Like lists, news groups may exist on topics relevant to your research. You must subscribe to read postings since they are not automatically distributed by e-mail.

▪ **Multiuser dimensions,** known as **MUDs,** or **multiuser dimensions, object-oriented,** known as **MOOs,** exist in many disciplines, including biology (BioMOO) and French (MOOFrancais). Participants interested in a topic meet and interact with each other in a virtual space, where they use writing to create a world of objects and actions and feelings. To join a MUD or MOO, you need to apply to the managers for a password and character.

▪ **Web logs, or blogs,** are Web-based journals that offer information and commentary on a variety of topics. Blog authors may or may not be experts in their fields of study, so be cautious about using blog content as a source.

Who is speaking affects the credibility of what is said. When you are doing research, you must evaluate the reliability of your sources. Even a reliable source may have little to do with your research questions, however, so be sure to assess the relevance as well as the reliability of your sources.

9a
research

9a Print sources

Here are some questions to ask about any source you are considering:

Reliability

- **What information can you find about the writer's credentials?**
- **Who is the publisher?** University presses and academic publishers are considered more scholarly than the popular press.
- **Does the work include a bibliography of works consulted or cited?** Trustworthy writers cite a variety of sources and document their citations properly.
- **Is there any indication that the writer has a particular point of view on your topic or that the writer is biased?**

Relevance

- **Do the source's title and subtitle indicate that it addresses your specific research question?**

www.mhhe.com/
wi
For help with
evaluating print
and online
sources, go to
Research >
CARS Source
Evaluation Tutor

- **What is the publication date?** Is the material up to date, classic, or historically pertinent?
- **Does the table of contents indicate that the source covers useful information?**
- **If the source is an article, does it have an abstract at the beginning? Is there a summary at the end?**
- **Do subheadings in the work indicate that the source covers useful information?**
- **If the source is a book, does the index include keywords related to your topic?**

Relevance can be tricky. Be prepared to find that some promising sources turn out to be less relevant than you first thought.

9b Internet sources

The Internet is a free-for-all. You will find up-to-the-minute material there, but you must carefully question every source you find on the Internet. Here are some points to keep in mind.

- **Authority and credibility.** Look for information about the individual or organization sponsoring the site. The following extensions in the Web address, or uniform resource locator (URL), can help you determine the type of site (which often tells you something about its purpose):

.com commercial (business)	**.edu** educational	**.mil** military
.org nonprofit organization	**.gov** U.S. government	**.net** network

A tilde (~) followed by a name in a URL usually means the site is a personal home page not affiliated with any organization.

- **Purpose.** A site's purpose influences its presentation of information and its reliability. Is the site's main purpose to advocate a cause, advertise a product or service, provide factual information, present research results, provide news, share personal information, or offer entertainment?

- **Context.** Search engines retrieve individual Web pages *out of context.* Always return to the site's home page to determine the source and to complete your citation.

- **Timeliness.** Reliable sites usually post the date an item was published or loaded onto the Web or tell you when the information was last updated.

- **Objectivity and reasonableness (bias).** Look carefully at the purpose and tone of the text. Clues that indicate a lack of reasonableness include an intemperate tone, broad claims, exaggerated statements of significance, conflicts of interest, no recognition of opposing views, and strident attacks on opposing views.

- **Relevance.** Is the information appropriate for your research? Consider the intended audience of the site, based on its purpose, content, depth of coverage, tone, and style.

9c research

9c   Evaluating a source's arguments

As you read the sources you have selected, you should continue to assess their reliability. Look for arguments that are qualified, supported with evidence, and well documented. Avoid sources that appeal to emotions unfairly or promote one-sided agendas. A fair-minded researcher needs to read and evaluate sources on both sides of issues, including the relevant primary sources that are available.

10a
research

10 Conduct research in the archive, field, and lab.

Often research involves more than finding answers to questions in books and other printed or online material (secondary research). When you conduct primary research—examining authentic documents and original records in an archive, observing behavior and other phenomena in the field, and experimenting in the laboratory—you participate in the discovery of knowledge.

10a Adhering to ethical principles

In the archive, field, or lab, you are working directly with something precious and immediate: an original record, a group of people, or special materials. An ethical researcher shows respect for materials, experimental subjects, fellow researchers, and readers. Here are some guidelines to follow:

■ Handle original documents and materials with great care, always leaving sources and data available for other researchers.

- Accurately report your sources and results.
- Follow proper procedures when working with human participants.

Research with human participants should also adhere to the following basic principles:

- **Confidentiality:** People who fill out surveys, participate in focus groups, or respond to interviews should be assured that their names will not be used without their permission.

- **Informed consent:** Before participating in an experiment, participants must sign a statement affirming that they understand the general purpose of the research.

- **Minimal risk:** Participants in experiments should not incur any risks greater than they do in everyday life.

- **Protection of vulnerable groups:** Researchers must be held strictly accountable for research done with the physically disabled, prisoners, those who are mentally incompetent, minors, the elderly, and pregnant women.

When you refute the primary research of others, state their viewpoints in words that they themselves would recognize as accurate.

10b Preparing for archival research

Archives of specialized or rare books, manuscripts, and documents are accessible in libraries, in other institutions, in private collections, and on video- and audiotape. The more you know about your area of study, the more likely you will be to see the significance of an item in an archival collection.

Some archival collections are accessible through audio- and video-tape as well as sites on the Internet such as *American Memory* <http://memory.loc.gov> and the *U.S. National Archives and Record Administration (NARA)* <http://www.nara.gov>. Others you must visit in person. If you intend to do research in a rare-books library, you will need a letter of introduction, usually from your professor or your college librarian.

10c Planning your field research

Field research involves recording observations, conducting interviews, or administering surveys.

1. Observing and writing field notes
When you use direct observation, keep careful records in order to retain the information you gather. (*For advice on conducting and recording direct observation, see Part 1: Common Assignments, pp. 23–24.*)

2. Conducting interviews
To be useful as research tools, interviews require systematic preparation and implementation.

- Identify appropriate people for your interviews.
- Do background research, and plan your questions.
- Take careful notes, and if possible, tape-record the interview. (Be sure to obtain your subject's permission if you use audiotape.)
- Follow up on vague responses with questions that get at specific information.

- Probe inconsistencies and contradictions politely.
- Write thank-you notes to interviewees, and later send them copies of your report.

3. Taking surveys

Conducted either orally or in writing, **surveys** are made up of structured questions. Written surveys are called **questionnaires.** The following suggestions will help you prepare informal surveys:

- Define your purpose.
- Write clear directions and questions. For example, if you are asking multiple-choice questions, make sure that you cover all possible options and that none of your options overlap.
- Make sure that your questions do not suggest a preference for one answer over another.
- Make the survey brief and easy to complete.

10d Keeping a notebook when doing lab research

To provide a complete and accurate account of your laboratory work, keep careful records in a notebook. The following guidelines will help you take accurate notes on your research.

1. Record immediate, on-the-spot, accurate notes on what happens in the lab.

Write down as much detail as possible. Measure precisely; do not estimate. Identify major pieces of apparatus, unusual chemicals, and laboratory animals in detail. Use drawings, when appropriate, to illustrate complicated equipment setups.

2. Follow a basic format.

Present your results in a format that allows you to communicate all the major features of an experiment. The five basic sections that must be included are title, purpose, materials and methods, results, and conclusions. Include tables, when useful, to present results. (*For more advice on preparing a lab report, see Part 1: Common Assignments, pp. 19–22.*)

3. Write in complete sentences, even if you are filling in answers to questions in a lab manual.

Resist the temptation to use shorthand to record your notes. Later, the complete sentences will provide a clear, unambiguous record of your procedures and results. Highlight cause-effect relationships in your sentences by using the following transitions: *then, next, consequently, because,* and *therefore.*

4. When necessary, revise and correct your laboratory notebook in visible ways.

If you make a mistake in recording laboratory results, correct them clearly by erasing or by crossing out and rewriting on the original sheet. If you make an uncorrectable mistake in your lab notebook, simply fold the sheet lengthwise and mark *omit* on the face side.

If you add sheets to your notebook, paste them permanently to the appropriate pages. Unanticipated results often occur in the lab, and you may find yourself jotting down notes on a convenient scrap of paper. Attach these notes to your laboratory notebook.

Work with sources and avoiding plagiarism.

Once you have a research question to answer, an idea about what the library and Internet have to offer, and a sense of the materials you need, you are ready to begin selecting and using sources.

11a Maintaining a working bibliography

As you research, compile a **working bibliography**—a list of those books, articles, pamphlets, Web sites, and other sources that seem most likely to help you answer your research question. Maintain an accurate, complete record of all sources you consult. For each source, record the following bibliographic information:

- Call number of book, reference work, or other print source; URL of each Web site
- All authors, editors, and translators
- Title of chapter, article, or Web page
- Title of book, periodical, or Web site in which the chapter, article, or page appears
- For books: date of publication, place, and publisher as well as edition or volume numbers, if applicable
- For periodical articles: the date and edition or volume number, issue, and page numbers if applicable
- For a Web source: the date you consulted it

Record bibliographic information on printouts, on photocopies of source material, or on 3" × 5" cards. (*See pp. 111, 119, and 129 for examples of bibliographic information in a book, an article, and an online source in MLA style and pp. 157, 161, and 167 for examples in APA style.)*

11b
research

1. Printouts
When you conduct online searches, the screen may offer you the option of printing out the results or saving them on a disk. On the printout or disk, be sure to note all relevant bibliographic information, including the database you used.

2. Photocopies
When you photocopy articles, essays, or pages from a print or micro-form source, note the bibliographic information on the photocopy.

3. 3" × 5" cards
Before computers became widely available, most researchers used 3" × 5" cards to compile the working bibliography, with each potential source getting a separate card. This method is still useful. You can use the same cards to record brief quotations from or comments on those sources.

www.mhhe.com/
wi
For more on
taking notes,
paraphrasing,
and
summarizing,
go to
Research >
Research
Techniques >
Learn to Take
Notes

11b Taking notes, paraphrasing, and summarizing

Take notes on your sources by annotating photocopies of your source material or by noting useful quotations and ideas on paper, on cards, or in a computer file.

1. Annotation

One way to take notes is to annotate photocopied articles and print-outs. Write the following notes directly on the page:

11b
research

- On the first page, write down complete bibliographic information for the source.

- As you read, record your questions, reactions, and ideas in the margins.

- Comment in the margin on ideas that agree with or differ from those you have already learned about.

- Put important and difficult passages into your own words by paraphrasing or summarizing them in the margin. (*For help with paraphrasing and summarizing, see pp. 76–77.*)

- Use a highlighter to mark statements that are key to understanding an issue or are especially well expressed.

After annotating the article or printout, use a research notebook to explore some of the comments, connections, and questions you recorded in the margins.

2. Separate notes

If you do not have photocopies to annotate, take notes on paper, index cards, or a computer. Use a separate page or card for each idea. Be sure to record the source's bibliographic information as well as the specific page number for each idea.

Enclose in quotation marks any exact words from a source. Label the passage a "quote." Unless you think you might use a particular quotation in your paper, express the author's ideas in your own words by using a paraphrase or a summary.

3. Paraphrases and summaries

When you **paraphrase,** you put someone else's statements into other words. A paraphrase is not a word-for-word translation. Even though you express the source's ideas *in your own way,* you must still give credit to the original writer by citing his or her work properly. If your paraphrase includes any exact phrasing from the source, put quotation marks around those phrases.

In the first, unacceptable paraphrase that follows, the writer has used synonyms for some terms but retained the phrasing of the original. The writer also failed to enclose all borrowed expressions—highlighted here—in quotation marks. The acceptable paraphrase, by contrast, is more concise than the original, and although it quotes a few words from the source, the writer has expressed the definition in a new and different way.

SOURCE

Scat singing. A technique of jazz singing in which onomatopoeic or nonsense syllables are sung to improvised melodies. Some writers have traced scat singing back to the practice, common in West African musics, of translating percussion patterns into vocal lines by assigning syllables to characteristic rhythms. However, since this allows little scope for melodic improvisation and the earliest recorded examples of jazz scat singing involved the free invention of rhythm, melody, and syllables, it is more likely that the technique began in the USA as singers imitated the sounds of jazz instrumentalists.

—J. BRADFORD ROBINSON,
The New Grove Dictionary of Jazz

UNACCEPTABLE PARAPHRASE: PLAGIARISM

Scat is a way of singing that uses nonsense syllables and extemporaneous melodies. Some people think that scat goes back to the custom in West African music of turning drum rhythms into vocal lines. But that doesn't explain the free invention of rhythm, melody, and syllables of the first recorded instances of scat singing. It is more likely that scat was started in the U.S. by singers imitating the way instrumental jazz sounded (Robinson 515).

11c
research

ACCEPTABLE PARAPHRASE

Scat, a highly inventive type of jazz singing, combines "nonsense syllables [with] improvised melodies." Although syllabic singing of drum rhythms occurs in West Africa, scat probably owes more to the early attempts of American singers to mimic both the sound and the inventive musical style of instrumental jazz (Robinson 515).

When you **summarize,** you state the main point of a piece, condensing a few paragraphs into one sentence or a few pages into one paragraph. Here is a summary of Robinson on scat singing:

Scat singing probably originated in the United States when singers tried to mimic the sound of instrumental jazz.

11c Avoiding plagiarism and copyright infringement

Knowledge develops in a give-and-take process akin to conversation. In this kind of situation, it is a matter of integrity and honesty to

11c
research

CHARTING the TERRITORY

Using Data

Statistics—numerical data and methods of interpreting those data—are part of research in many disciplines, particularly the social sciences. When providing statistics, always cite the source of the information, as the writer has done in this example:

> In 1993, 11.7% of Germany's exports went to France, while 11.3% of its imports came from France (CIA, 1996).

www.mhhe.com/
wi
To learn
more about
plagiarism and
how to avoid it,
go to
Research >
Avoiding
Plagiarism

acknowledge others, especially when you use their words or ideas. The failure to acknowledge sources correctly—either intentionally or inadvertently—is **plagiarism.** Writers who unfairly use copyrighted material found on the World Wide Web or in print are legally liable for their acts.

To avoid plagiarism, adhere to these guidelines:

- Do not rely too much on one source, or you may slip into using that person's thoughts as your own.

- Keep accurate records while doing research and taking notes. If you do not know where you got an idea or a piece of information, do not use it in your paper until you find out. (*See 11b, pp. 74–75.*)

- When you take notes, be sure to put quotation marks around words, phrases, or sentences taken verbatim from a source. If you use any of those words, phrases, or sentences when summarizing or paraphrasing the source, put them in quotation marks. Changing a word here and there while keeping a source's sentence structure or phrasing constitutes plagiarism, even if you credit the source for the ideas. (*See 11b, pp. 76–77 for an example.*)

11c
research

- Cite the source of all ideas, opinions, facts, and statistics that are not common knowledge: information that readers in a field would know about from a wide range of general resources.

- Choose an appropriate documentation style, and use it consistently and properly. (*See 12c, pp. 84–85.*)

All written materials, including student papers, letters, and e-mail, are covered by copyright, even if they do not bear an official copyright symbol. A copyright grants its owner exclusive rights to the use of a protected work, including reproducing, distributing, and displaying the work. Determine that you have used copyrighted material fairly by considering the following four questions:

- **What is the purpose of the use?** Educational, nonprofit, and personal use are more likely to be considered fair than commercial use.

- **What is the nature of the work being used?** In most cases, imaginative and unpublished materials can be used only if you have the permission of the copyright holder.

- **How much of the copyrighted work is being used?** The use of a small portion of a text for academic purposes is more likely to be considered fair than the use of a whole work for commercial purposes.

- **What effect would this use have on the market for the original?** The use of a work is usually considered unfair if it would hurt sales of the original.

11d Taking stock

Assess the research you have done and synthesize what you have learned. Your credibility depends on the relevance and reliability of your sources as well as the scope and depth of your reading and observation.

As the context and kind of writing change, so too do the requirements for types and numbers of sources. As a general rule, you should consult more than two sources and use only sources that are both reliable and respected by people working in the field. Ask yourself the following questions about the sources you have consulted:

- Are your sources trustworthy? (*See Chapter 9, pp. 65–68, for more on evaluating sources.*)
- Have your sources provided you with a sufficient number of facts, examples, and ideas?
- Have you used sources that examine issues from several different perspectives?

Think about how the sources you have read relate to one another. Ask yourself when, how, and why your sources agree or disagree, and consider where you stand on the issues they raise. Such questions can help you clarify what you have learned from your sources.

You have chosen a research question and have located, read, and evaluated a variety of sources. Now you need a thesis that will allow you to share what you have learned as well as your perspective on the issue.

12a Planning and drafting

Whether your paper is primarily informative, interpretive, or argumentative, keep your purpose and context in mind as you decide on a thesis to support and develop.

- **Decide on a thesis.** Consider the question that originally guided your research as well as the new questions provoked by what you have learned. Revise the wording of your question to make it intriguing as well as suitable (*see Chapter 7, pp. 49–52*) and compose an answer that you can use as your tentative thesis. Many writers find that they can present their thesis or focal question at the end of an introductory paragraph or two.

- **Outline a plan for supporting and developing your thesis.** Guided by your tentative thesis, outline a plan that uses your sources in a purposeful way. Decide on the kind of structure you will use to support your thesis—explanatory, exploratory, or argumentative—and develop your support by choosing facts, examples, and ideas drawn from a variety of sources. (*See Chapters 2–4 in Part 1 for more on explanatory, exploratory, and argumentative structures.*)

■ **Write a draft that you can revise and edit.** When you
have a tentative thesis and a plan, you are ready to write a
draft. As you write beyond the introduction, be prepared to
reexamine and refine your thesis. Often writers will come up
with fresh ideas for their introduction, body paragraphs, or
conclusion as they revise and edit their first draft, one reason
it is important to spend time revising and editing your paper.
(*For help with editing, see Parts 6–8.*)

12b Integrating quotations, paraphrases, and summaries

To support and develop your ideas, use quoted, paraphrased, or summarized material from sources. To do so properly and effectively, follow
these guidelines.

1. Integrating quotations

Use quotations when a source's exact words are important and make
your writing more memorable, fair, or authoritative. Quotations should
be short, enclosed in quotation marks, and well integrated into your
sentence structure, as in the following example from a paper on Louis
Armstrong and his manager Joe Glaser:

In his dedication to the unpublished manuscript "Louis Armstrong and the Jewish Family in New Orleans," Armstrong
calls Glaser "the best friend that I ever had," while in a let-

ter to Max Jones, he writes, "I did not get really happy until
I got with my man—my dearest friend—Joe Glaser" (qtd. in
Jones and Chilton 16).

2. Using brackets within quotations

Sentences that include quotations must make sense grammatically.
Sometimes you may have to adjust a quotation to make it fit properly
into your sentence. Use brackets to indicate any minor adjustments
you have made. For example, *my* has been changed to *his* to make the
quotation fit in the following sentence:

> Armstrong confided to a friend that Glaser's death "broke
> [his] heart" (Bergreen 490).

3. Using ellipses within quotations

Use ellipses to indicate that words have been omitted from the body
of a quotation, but be sure that what you omit does not significantly
alter the source's meaning. (*For more on using ellipses, see Part 8:
Editing for Correctness, pp. 370–76.*)

> As Morgenstern put it, "Joe Glaser . . . proved to be the right
> man at the right time" (128).

4. Using block format for longer quotations

Quotations longer than four lines should be used rarely; used too frequently, they break up your text and make your reader impatient. If
you do include a longer quotation, put it in block format (*see Part 8:
Editing for Correctness, pp. 362–69*). Be careful to integrate it into

your paper: Tell your readers why you want them to read the block
quotation, and afterwards, comment on it.

12c
research

5. Using signal phrases to introduce quotations and paraphrases

When you are integrating someone else's thoughts or words into your
writing, use a **signal phrase** that indicates whom you are quoting.
Besides crediting others for their work, signal phrases can make ideas
more interesting by giving them a human face. To keep things interesting, vary your signal phrases. Instead of using the verbs *says* and
writes again and again, consider using *acknowledges, asserts, claims,
concludes, emphasizes, explains, expresses, notes, points out, proves, reports, responds, shows,* or *suggests:*

> *As Bergreen points out,* Armstrong easily reached difficult high
> notes, the F's and G's that stymied other trumpeters (248).

12c Documenting your sources

www.mhhe.com/
wi
To find links to
many of these
style guides,
go to
Research >
Links to
Documentation
Sites

Whenever you use information, ideas, or words from someone else's
work, you must acknowledge that person. The only exception to this
principle is when you use information that is common knowledge, such
as the chemical composition of water or the names of the thirteen original states.

How sources are documented varies by field and discipline. Use the
documentation style that is appropriate for the particular discipline
you are contributing to. If you are not sure which of the styles covered
in this handbook to use, ask your instructor. If you are required to use
an alternative style, consult the list of manuals that follows.

CHARTING the TERRITORY

Style Manuals for Specific Disciplines

12c
sources

DISCIPLINE	POSSIBLE STYLE MANUAL
Chemistry	Dodd, Janet S., ed. *The ACS Style Guide: A Manual for Authors and Editors.* 2nd ed. Washington: American Chemical Society, 1997.
Geology	Bates, Robert L., Rex Buchanan, and Marla Adkins-Heljeson, eds. *Geowriting: A Guide to Writing, Editing, and Printing in Earth Science.* 5th ed. Alexandria: American Geological Institute, 1995.
Government and Law	Garner, Diane L., and Diane H. Smith, eds. *The Complete Guide to Citing Government Information Resources: A Manual for Writers and Librarians.* Rev. ed. Bethesda: Congressional Information Service, 1993.
	Harvard Law Review et al., *The Bluebook: A Uniform System of Citation.* 17th ed. Cambridge: Harvard Law Review Assn., 2000.
Journalism	Goldstein, Norm, ed. *Associated Press Stylebook and Briefing on Media Law.* Revised and updated ed. New York: Associated Press, 2000.
Linguistics	Linguistic Society of America. "LSA Style Sheet." *LSA Bulletin.* Published annually in the December issue.
Mathematics	American Mathematical Society. *AMS Author Handbook: General Instructions for Preparing Manuscripts.* Providence: AMS, 1997.
Medicine	Iverson, Cheryl, ed. *American Medical Association Manual of Style: A Guide for Authors and Editors.* 9th ed. Baltimore: Williams & Wilkins, 1998.
Physics	American Institute of Physics. *Style Manual for Guidance in the Preparation of Papers.* 5th ed. New York: AIP, 1995.
Political Science	American Political Science Association. *Style Manuals for Political Science Papers.* Rev. ed. Washington: APSA, 2001.

The list that follows will help you get started doing research in specific disciplines. Both print and electronic resources are listed because you should use both types in your research. (Print entries precede electronic entries.) *(For a list of online databases, see pp. 58–60.)*

www.mhhe.com/
wi

For an
online list
of discipline-
specific
resources,
go to

Research >
Discipline Specific
Resources

Anthropology

Abstracts in Anthropology
Annual Review of Anthropology
Dictionary of Anthropology
Encyclopedia of World Cultures
American Anthropology Association
    <http://www.aaanet.org>
Artcyclopedia
    <http://www.artcyclopedia.com>
WWW Virtual Library: Anthropology
    <http://vlib.anthrotech.com>

Art and Architecture

Art Abstracts
Art Index
BHA: Bibliography of the History of Art
Encyclopedia of World Art
McGraw-Hill Dictionary of Art
National Anthropological Archives
    <http://www.nmnh.si.edu/naa/>
The Louvre
    <http://www.louvre.fr/louvrea.htm>
The Metropolitan Museum of Art (New York)
    <http://www.metmuseum.org>
The National Gallery (Washington, D.C.)
    <http://www.nga.gov>
Voice of the Shuttle Art History and Architecture
    <http://vos.ucsb.edu/index.asp>

Biology

Biological Abstracts
Biological and Agricultural Index
Encyclopedia of the Biological Sciences
Henderson's Dictionary of Biological Terms
Zoological Record
Biology Online
    <http://www.biology-online.org/>
Harvard University Biology Links
    <http://mcb.harvard.edu/BioLinks.html>
National Science Foundation: Biology
    <http://www.nsf.gov/news/overviews/biology/index.jsp>

13 resources

Business

Accounting and Tax Index
Encyclopedia of Business
  Information Sources
ABI/Inform
Business Periodicals
Business and Industry
Newslink Business Newspapers
  <http://newslink.org/
  biznews.html>

Chemistry

Chemical Abstracts (CASEARCH)
McGraw-Hill Dictionary of
  Chemistry
Van Nostrand Reinhold
  Encyclopedia of Chemistry
American Chemical Society
  <http://www.chemistry.org>
Sheffield ChemDex
  <http://www.chemdex.org>
WWW Virtual Library: Chemistry
  <http://www.liv.ac.uk/chemistry/
  links/links.html>

Classics

Oxford Classical Dictionary
Princeton Encyclopedia of
  Classical Sites
Perseus Digital Library
  <http://www.perseus.tufts.edu>

Communications and Journalism

Mass Media Bibliography
Communication Abstracts
International Encyclopedia of
  Communications
Journalism Abstracts
American Communication
  Association
  <http://www.americancomm.org>
Journalism and Mass
  Communications Abstracts
  <http://www.aejmc.org/abstracts/>
The Poynter Institute
  <http://poynter.org>

Computer Science and Technology

Computer Abstracts
Dictionary of Computing
Encyclopedia of Computer Science
McGraw-Hill Encyclopedia of
  Science and Technology
FOLDOC (Free Online Dictionary
  of Computing)
  <http://wombat.doc.ic.ac.uk/
  foldoc/>
MIT and Artificial Intelligence
  Laboratory for Computer Science
  <http://www.csail.mit.edu/
  index.php>

Cultural Studies, American and Ethnic Studies

Encyclopedia of World Cultures

**13
resources**

*Dictionary of American Negro
   Biography*
*Gale Encyclopedia of Multicultural
   America*
Mexican American Biographies
American Studies Web
   <http://lumenprojects.georgetown.
   edu/asw/>
*National Museum of the American
   Indian*
   <http://www.nmai.si.edu>
*Schomburg Center for Research in
   Black Culture*
   <http://www.nypl.org/research/
   sc/sc.html>
*Smithsonian Center for Folklife and
   Cultural Heritage*
   <http://www.folklife.si.edu/
   index.html>

Economics

EconLit
*PAIS: Public Affairs Information
   Service*
American Economic Association
   <http://www.aeaweb.org>
Internet Resources for Economists
   <http://www.oswego.edu/
   ~economic/econweb.htm>
*Resources for Economists on the
   Internet*
   <http://www.aeaweb.org/RFE>

Education

Dictionary of Education
Education Index
*Encyclopedia of Educational
   Research*
*International Encyclopedia of
   Education*
Resources in Education
The Educator's Reference Desk
   <http://www.eduref.org>
EdWeb
   <http://edwebproject.org>
U.S. Department of Education
   <http://www.ed.gov>

Engineering

Applied Science and Technology Index
Engineering Index
*McGraw-Hill Encyclopedia of
   Engineering*
IEEE Spectrum
   <http://www.spectrum.ieee.org>
WWW Virtual Library: Engineering
   <http://www.eevl.ac.uk/
   wwwvl.html>

Environmental Sciences

Dictionary of the Environment
*Encyclopedia of Energy, Technology,
   and the Environment*
Encyclopedia of the Environment
Environment Abstracts

Environment Index
Envirolink
   <http://envirolink.org>
U.S. Environmental Protection
   Agency
   <http://www.epa.gov>

Film

Dictionary of Film Terms
The Film Encyclopedia
Film Index International
Film Literature Index
Internet Movie Database
   <http://us.imdb.com>

Geography

Geographical Abstracts
Longman Dictionary of Geography
Modern Geography: An Encyclopedic
   Survey
CIA World Factbook
   <http://www.cia.gov/cia/
   publications/factbook/index.html>
Resources for Geographers
   <http://www.colorado.edu/
   geography/virtdept/resources/
   contents.htm>

Geology

Bibliography and Index of Geology
Challinor's Dictionary of Geology
The Encyclopedia of Field and
   General Geology

American Geological Institute
   <http://www.agiweb.org>
U.S. Geological Survey
   <http://www.usgs.gov>

**13
resources**

Health and Medicine

American Medical Association
   Encyclopedia of Medicine
Cumulated Index Medicus
Medical and Health Information
   Directory
Nutrition Abstracts and Reviews
U.S. National Library of Medicine
   <http://www.nlm.nih.gov>
World Health Organization
   <http://www.who.int>

History

America: History and Life
Dictionary of Historical Terms
Encyclopedia of American History
An Encyclopedia of World History
Historical Abstracts
Electronic Documents in History
   <http://www.tntech.edu/history/
   edocs.html>
History Cooperative
   <http://historycooperative.
   press.uiuc.edu>
History World
   <http://www.historyworld.net>

13
resources

NARA Archival Research Catalog
  <www.archives.gov/research/
  arc/index.html>

Languages and Linguistics

Cambridge Encyclopedia of Language
*An Encyclopedic Dictionary of
  Language and Languages*
*International Encyclopedia of
  Linguistics*
*LLBA: Linguistics and Language
  Behavior Abstracts*
MLA International Bibliography
Center for Applied Linguistics
  <http://www.cal.org>
SIL International Linguistics
  <http://www.sil.org/linguistics>

Literature

*Concise Oxford Dictionary of
  Literary Terms*
MLA International Bibliography
*The New Princeton Encyclopedia
  of Poetry and Poetics*
*Electronic Text Center at the
  University of Virginia Library*
  <http://etext.lib.virginia.edu>
Project Gutenberg
  <http://www.gutenberg.org>
Voice of the Shuttle
  <http://vos.ucsb.edu/index.asp>

Mathematics

American Statistics Index
Dictionary of Mathematics

Facts on File
*International Dictionary of
  Applied Mathematics*
Mathematical Reviews (MathSciNet)
American Mathematical Society
  <http://www.ams.org>
Math Forum
  <http://mathforum.com>

Music

Music Index
*New Grove Dictionary of Music and
  Musicians*
New Oxford Companion to Music
New Oxford Dictionary of Music
RILM Abstracts of Musical Literature
All Music
  <http://allmusic.com>

Philosophy

Dictionary of Philosophy
Philosopher's Index
*Routledge Encyclopedia of
  Philosophy*
American Philosophical Association
  <http://www.apa.udel.edu/apa/
  index.html>
EpistemeLinks.com
  <http://www.epistemelinks.com>

Physics

Dictionary of Physics
McGraw-Hill Encyclopedia of Physics
Physics Abstracts

American Institute of Physics
   <http://aip.org>
American Physical Society
   <http://www.aps.org>
Institute of Physics
   <http://iop.org>
PhysicsWeb
   <http://physicsweb.org/>

Political Science

Almanac of American Politics
Congressional Quarterly Almanac
*Encyclopedia of Government and
   Politics*
*International Political Science
   Abstracts*
Political Resources on the Net
   <http://www.politicalresources.
   net>
*Public Affairs Information Service
   (PAIS)*
*Non-Western Sources on
   Contemporary Political Issues*
   <http://library.lib.binghamton.
   edu/subjects/polsci/home.html>
*Thomas: Legislative Information on
   the Internet*
   <http://thomas.loc.gov>
United Nations
   <http://www.un.org>

Psychology

*International Dictionary of
   Psychology*

*International Encyclopedia of
   Psychiatry, Psychology,
   Psychoanalysis, and Neurology*
Psychological Abstracts
American Psychological Association
   <http://www.apa.org>
American Psychological Society
   <http://www.psychologicalscience.
   org>
Encyclopedia of Psychology
   <http://www.psychology.org/>
PsychWeb
   <http://www.psywww.com>

Religion

ATLA Religion
Dictionary of Bible and Religion
Encyclopedia of Religion
Religion Index
Beliefnet
   <http://www.beliefnet.com/>
Religions and Scriptures
   <http://www.wam.umd.edu/
   ~stwright/rel>
Religious and Sacred Texts
   <http://davidwiley.com/
   religion.html>

Sociology

Annual Review of Sociology
Encyclopedia of Social Work
Encyclopedia of Sociology
Sociological Abstracts

**13
resources**

Academic Info Sociology: Databases and Centers
<http://www.academicinfo.net/socdata.html>
American Sociological Association
<http://asanet.org>
The SocioWeb
<http://www.socioweb.com/~markbl/socioweb/indexes>

Theater and Dance

International Encyclopedia of the Dance
McGraw-Hill Encyclopedia of World Drama

American Theater Web
<http://www.americantheaterweb.com/>

Women's Studies

Women Studies Abstracts
Women's Studies: A Guide to Information Sources
Women's Studies Encyclopedia
Feminist Majority Foundation Online
<http://www.feminist.org>
National Women's History Project
<http://www.nwhp.org>

Next to the originator of a good
sentence is the first quoter of it.

—RALPH WALDO EMERSON

PART 3

MLA
Documentation
Style

The charts on pages 94–96 can help you locate the right
example of a works-cited list entry for a particular kind of
source. Answering the questions provided will usually lead
you to the sample entry you need. You can also use the
directory on pages 107–9 in Chapter 15.

Entries in a Works-Cited List: BOOKS (109–18)

❓ *Is your source a complete book or part of a book?*

No   Yes
      ↓

	Go to this entry (or these entries)
Is it a complete book with one named author?	
Is it the only book by this author that you are citing?	1
Are you citing more than one book by this author?	2
Is it a published doctoral dissertation?	32
Is it a complete book with more than one named author?	3
Is it a complete book without a named author?	
Is the author an organization?	4
Is the author anonymous or unknown?	18
Is it a complete book with an editor or a translator?	
Is there an editor only or an editor and an author?	5, 6
Is it an anthology?	7
Is it a translation?	11
Is it the published proceedings of an academic conference?	31
Is it a complete book with an edition, a volume, or a series number?	
Does it have an edition number (e.g., Second Edition)?	12
Is it part of a multivolume work (e.g., Volume 3)?	14
Is it one in a series?	15
Is it a complete book but not the only version?	
Is your book a sacred work (e.g., the Bible)?	13
Is your book a republished work (e.g., a classic novel)?	16
Is the book from a publisher's imprint?	19
Does the book's title include the title of another book?	17
Is your source part of an edited book?	
Is it a work in an anthology or a chapter in an edited book?	7
Are you citing two or more items from the same anthology?	8
Is it a published letter (e.g., part of a published collection)?	39
Is it an article in a reference work (e.g., an encyclopedia)?	9
Is it a preface, an introduction, a foreword, or an afterword?	10

Check the next page or the directory on pages 107–9 or consult your instructor.

Entries in a Works-Cited List: PRINT PERIODICALS OR OTHER PRINT SOURCES (118–24)

? Is your source from a journal, a magazine, or a newspaper?

No Yes
↓

*Go to this entry
(or these entries)*

Is it from an academic journal?	
Are the page numbers continued from one issue to the next?	20
Do the page numbers in each issue start with 1?	21
Is it from a magazine?	
Is the magazine published monthly or weekly?	22, 23
Is your source a letter to the editor?	28
Is it a review (e.g., a review of a book or film)?	26
Is it an interview?	35
Is it from a newspaper?	
Is it an article?	24
Is it a review (e.g., a review of a book or film)?	26
Is it an editorial?	27
Is it a letter to the editor?	28
Is it an interview?	35
Is the author unknown?	25

? Is it a print source but not a book or a periodical article?

No Yes
↓

*Go to this entry
(or these entries)*

Is it published by the government or a nongovernment organization?	
Is it a report or pamphlet from a government agency?	29, 30
Is it a court case or other legal document?	42
Is it an unpublished dissertation or an abstract of a dissertation?	33, 34
Is it a personal letter or a letter from an archive?	40, 41
Is it a map, a chart, a cartoon, or an advertisement?	36–38
Is it stored in an archive?	41

Check the next page or the directory on pages 107–9 or consult your instructor.

Entries in a Works-Cited List: ELECTRONIC OR OTHER NONPRINT SOURCES (124–33)

❓ *Did you find your nonprint source online?*

No   Yes
↓

	Go to this entry (or these entries)
Is it a professional or personal Web site?	44
Is it an article from an online scholarly journal?	46
Is it an article you found through a subscription database service (e.g., EBSCO or ProQuest)?	48
Is it from an online magazine or newspaper?	46
Is it an online book or scholarly project?	
Is it an online book?	45
Is it an online scholarly project?	43
Is it an online communication?	
Is it a posting to a news group or other type of online forum?	49
Is it from a real-time, synchronous forum (e.g., a chat room)?	50
Is it an e-mail communication?	51
Is your source an online graphic, audio, or video file?	52

❓ *Is your source a nonprint source that is not published online?*

No   Yes
↓

	Go to this entry (or these entries)
Is your source stored on a CD-ROM or DVD?	47, 53
Is it a film, DVD, or videotape?	54
Is it a television or radio program?	55
Is it a personal or telephone interview?	59
Is it a sound recording, musical composition, or work of art?	56–58
Is it a lecture or performance?	60, 61

Check the directory on pages 107–9 or consult your instructor.

The documentation style developed by the Modern Language Association (MLA) is used by many researchers in the arts and humanities. The guidelines presented here are based on the sixth edition of Joseph Gibaldi's *MLA Handbook for Writers of Research Papers* (New York: MLA, 2003), updated to reflect the latest changes to MLA style in the third edition of the *MLA Style Manual and Guide to Scholarly Publishing* (New York: MLA, 2008).

MLA documentation style has three parts:

- In-text citations
- List of works cited
- Explanatory notes

In-text citations and a list of works cited are mandatory; explanatory notes are optional. The following is an in-text citation and its corresponding works-cited entry:

IN-TEXT CITATION

As Hennessey explains, record deals were usually negotiated by "white middlemen" (127).

WORKS-CITED ENTRY

Hennessey, Thomas J. *From Jazz to Swing: African-Americans and Their Music 1890-1935*. Detroit: Wayne State UP, 1984. Print.

MLA

www.mhhe.com/
wi

For links to Web sites for documentation styles used in various disciplines, go to

Research > Links to Documentation Sites

MLA in-text citation format requires that you do the following:

- **Name the author,** either in a signal phrase such as *As Hennessey explains* or in a parenthetical citation.

- **Include a page reference** in parentheses. No "p." precedes the page number, and if the author is named in the parentheses, there is no punctuation between the name and page number. You may leave out the page number of a one-page source.

- **Place the citation as close to the material being cited as possible** and before any commas, semicolons, or periods—except in a block quotation, where the citation comes after the period.

MLA In-Text Citations: Directory to Sample Types
(*See pp. 107–33 for works-cited examples*)

MLA

1. Author named in sentence: You can use the last name only, unless two or more of your sources have the same last name.

> As Hennessey explains, record deals were usually negotiated by "white
>
> middlemen" (127).

Note that the parenthetical page citation comes after the closing quotation mark but before the period.

2. Author named in parentheses: If you do not name the source's author in your sentence, then you must provide the name in the parentheses.

> Armstrong easily reached difficult high notes, the F's and G's that
>
> stymied other trumpeters (Bergreen 248).

Note that there is no comma between the author's name and the page number. If you cite two or more distinct pages, however, separate the numbers with a comma: (Bergreen 450, 457).

3. Two or more works by the same author: You must identify which work you are citing, either in your sentence or in an abbreviated form in parentheses.

In *Louis Armstrong, an American Genius,* Collier reports that Glaser paid Armstrong's mortgage, taxes, and basic living expenses (330).

During those years, Glaser paid Armstrong's mortgage, taxes, and basic living expenses (Collier, *Louis Armstrong* 330).

4. Two or more authors of the same work: If a source has up to three authors, you should name them all either in your text, as shown below, or in parentheses: (Jones and Chilton 160, 220).

TWO AUTHORS

According to Jones and Chilton, Glaser's responsibilities included booking appearances, making travel arrangements, and paying the band members' salaries (160, 220).

If the source has more than three authors, either list all the authors or give the first author's last name followed by *et al.,* the abbreviation for the Latin phrase meaning "and others."

MORE THAN THREE AUTHORS

Changes in social regulations are bound to produce new forms of subjectivity (Henriques et al. 275).

5. Authors with the same last name: If two or more of your sources have the same last name, include the first initial of the author you are citing; if the first initial is also shared, use the full first name, as shown at the top of page 101.

In the late nineteenth century, the sale of sheet music spread rapidly in a Manhattan area along Broadway known as Tin Pan Alley (Richard Campbell 63).

6. Organization as author: Treat the organization as the author. If the organization's name is long, put it in a signal phrase.

The Centre for Contemporary Cultural Studies claims that "there is nothing inherently concrete about historiography" (10).

7. Unknown author: Cite a work by its title, using either the full title in a signal phrase or an abbreviated version in the parentheses.

"Squaresville, USA vs. Beatsville" makes the Midwestern small-town home seem boring compared with the West Coast artist's "pad" (31).

The Midwestern small-town home seems boring compared with the West Coast artist's "pad" ("Squaresville" 31).

8. Entire work: When you want to acknowledge an entire work, such as a film, a concert, or a book, it is usually better to do so in your text, not in a parenthetical citation. Be sure to include the work in your list of works cited.

Sidney J. Furie's film *Lady Sings the Blues* presents Billie Holiday as a

beautiful woman in pain rather than as the great jazz artist she was.

9. Web site or other online electronic source: For online
sources, MLA recommends using the guidelines already established
for print sources. If you cannot find the author of an online source,
then identify the source by title. Because most online sources do not
have set page, section, or paragraph numbers, they must usually be
cited as entire works.

In the 1920s, many young black musicians from New Orleans migrated

north to Chicago, hoping for a chance to perform with the best

("Chicago").

**10. Work with numbered paragraphs or sections instead of
pages:** Give the paragraph or screen number(s) after the author's
name and a comma. To distinguish them from page numbers, use the
abbreviation *par(s).* or the type of division, such as *section(s).*

Rothstein suggests that many German Romantic musical techniques

may have originated in Italian opera (par. 9).

11. Work with no page or paragraph numbers: When citing a
source without page, paragraph, or other reference numbers, give the
author's name in your text instead of in a parenthetical citation.

Crouch argues that Armstrong remains a driving force in present-day

music, from country and western music to the chanted doggerel of rap.

12. Multivolume work: When using and citing more than one volume of a multivolume source, include the volume number, followed by a colon, a space, and the page number.

> Schuller argues that even though jazz's traditional framework appears
>
> European, its musical essence is African (1: 62).

However, if you consulted only one volume of a multivolume work, it is unnecessary to cite the volume number in the parenthetical reference. You should include it as part of the works-cited entry (*see p. 115*).

MLA

13. Literary works:
Novels and literary nonfiction books: Include the relevant page number, followed by a semicolon, a space, and the chapter number.

> Louis Armstrong figures throughout Ellison's *Invisible Man,* including
>
> in the narrator's penultimate decision to become a "yes" man who
>
> "undermine[s] them with grins" (384; ch. 23).

If the author is not named in your sentence, add the name in front of the page number: (Ellison 384; ch. 23). If the work has no chapters or numbered sections, just include the page number.

Poems: Use line numbers, not page numbers.

> In "Trumpet Player," Hughes says that the music "Is honey / Mixed with
>
> liquid fire" (lines 19-20). This image returns at the end of the poem, when
>
> Hughes concludes that "Trouble / Mellows to a golden note" (43-44).

Note: The word *lines* (not *l.* or *ll.*) is used in the first citation to establish what the numbers in parentheses refer to; subsequent citations need not use the word *lines.* (*See pp. 363 and 376 for more information about quoting poetry.*)

Plays and long, multisection poems: Use division (act, scene, canto, book, part) and lines, not page numbers. In the following example, notice that arabic numerals are used for act and scene divisions as well as for line numbers: (*Ham.* 2.3.22–27). The same is true for canto, verse, and lines in the following citation of Byron's *Don Juan:* (*DJ* 1.37.4–8).

14. Sacred works: Cite material in sacred works such as the Bible and the Qur'an, or Koran, by book, chapter, and verse, using an appropriate abbreviation when the name of the book is in the parentheses rather than in your sentence.

> As the Bible says, "The wise man knows there will be a time of
>
> judgment" (Eccles. 8.5).

Note that titles of biblical books are not italicized.

15. Indirect source: When you quote or paraphrase a quotation you found in someone else's work, put *qtd. in* (meaning "quoted in") before the name of your source.

> Armstrong confided to a friend that Glaser's death "broke [his] heart"
>
> (qtd. in Bergreen 490).

In your list of works cited, list only the work you consulted, in this case the indirect source by Bergreen.

16. Two or more sources in one citation: Use a semicolon to separate the citations.

Giving up his other business ventures, Glaser now became Armstrong's

exclusive agent (Bergreen 376-78; Collier 273-76; Morgenstern 124-28).

17. Work in an anthology: Give the name of the specific work's author, not the name of the editor of the whole anthology.

When Dexter Gordon threatened to quit, Armstrong offered him a

raise—without consulting with Glaser (Morgenstern 132).

Here, Morgenstern is cited as the source even though his work appears in a collection edited by Marc Miller. Note that the list of works cited must include an entry for Morgenstern (*see p. 141*).

18. Entry in a reference work: Give the title of the entry or the word (for a dictionary entry).

The word sort used to be a printer's term for an individual letter in a

typeface ("Sort").

If the reference work indicates the name of the author, however, give that name in the text.

19. Historical document or legal source: Cite familiar documents such as the Declaration of Independence and the United States Constitution in the text as follows:

Congress has the power under the Constitution to regulate commerce

that involves more than one state (US Const. art. I, sec. 8).

The in-text citation of court cases and acts of Congress should consist of the name of the case (italicized) or act (not italicized or enclosed in quotation marks), treated like a work without an author (see number 7).

20. E-mail, letter, personal interview: Cite by name the person you communicated with, using either a signal phrase or parentheses.

Much to Glaser's surprise, both "Hello, Dolly" and "What a Wonderful

World" became big hits after the rights had been sold (Jacobs).

In the works-cited list, you will need to identify the kind of communication and its date (*see pp. 123, 130, and 133*).

Besides in-text citations, MLA documentation style requires a works-cited page, where readers can find full bibliographic information about the sources you have used. The list of works cited should appear at the end of your paper, beginning on a new page entitled "Works Cited." Include only those sources you cite in your paper, unless your instructor tells you to prepare a "Works Consulted" list.

In order to format works-cited entries correctly, it is important to know what kind of source you are citing. The directory that follows will help you find the appropriate sample to use as your model. As an alternative, you can use the charts on pages 94–96 to help you locate the right example. Answering the questions provided in the charts will usually lead you to the sample entry you need. If you cannot find what you are looking for after consulting the appropriate directory or chart, ask your instructor for help.

To help locate the information you need in an actual source, consult the facsimiles on pages 111, 119, or 129.

MLA

www.mhhe.com/
wi

To download
Bibliomaker
Software for
MLA, go to
Research >
Bibliomaker

MLA Works-Cited Entries: Directory to Sample Types
(See pp. 98–106 for examples of in-text citations.)

Books

MLA

Books

Figure 15.1 on page 111 shows where the elements of a works-cited entry for a book can be found.

1. Book with one author: Italicize the book's title. Conclude with the medium. Notice that in the example the publisher's name, *Wayne State University Press,* is abbreviated to *Wayne State UP.*

Hennessey, Thomas J. *From Jazz to Swing: African-Americans and Their*

Music 1890-1935. Detroit: Wayne State UP, 1984. Print.

2. Two or more works by the same author(s): When you list more than one work by the same author, give the author's name in the first entry only. For the author's other works, replace the name with three hyphens and a period. Alphabetize the works by title.

MLA

Collier, James Lincoln. *Jazz: The American Theme Song.* New York: Oxford

UP, 1993. Print.

---. *Louis Armstrong: An American Genius.* New York: Oxford UP, 1983. Print.

3. Book with two or more authors: Name the authors in the order in which they appear on the title page, putting the last name first for the first author only. When a work has more than three authors, you may list them all or use the abbreviation *et al.* (meaning "and others") to replace the names of all authors except the first.

Davis, Miles, and Quincy Troupe. *Miles: The Autobiography.* New York:

Simon, 1989. Print.

Henriques, Julian, et al. *Changing the Subject: Psychology, Social Regulation,*

and Subjectivity. New York: Methuen, 1984. Print.

4. Organization as author: Consider as an organization any group, commission, association, or corporation whose members are not identified on the title page.

Centre for Contemporary Cultural Studies. *Making Histories: Studies in*

History Writing and Politics. London: Hutchinson, 1982. Print.

5. Book by an editor or editors: Treat the editor as an author but put the abbreviation *ed.* after the name. Use the plural *eds.* when more than one editor is listed, and put only the first editor's name in reverse order.

Miller, Paul Eduard, ed. *Esquire's Jazz Book.* New York: Smith, 1944. Print.

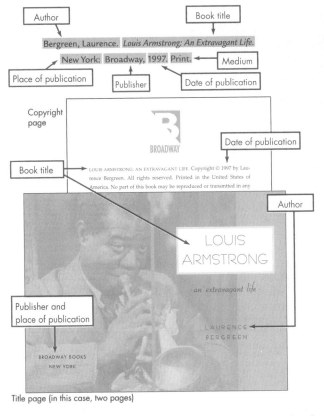

Title page (in this case, two pages)

FIGURE 15.1 The elements of an MLA works-cited entry: books.
Information for a book citation can be found on the book's title and
copyright pages.

GENERAL GUIDELINES for the LIST of WORKS CITED

1. Begin on a new page.
2. Begin with the centered title "Works Cited."
3. Include an entry for every in-text citation.
4. Include author, title, publication data, and medium for each entry, if available. Use a period to set off each of these elements from the others. Leave one space after the periods.
5. Do not number the entries.
6. Put entries in alphabetical order by author's or editor's last name. (If the author is unknown, use the first word of the title, excluding the articles *a, an,* or *the*).
7. Italicize titles of books and periodicals.
8. Capitalize the first and last words as well as all other important words in titles and subtitles. Do not capitalize articles, prepositions, coordinating conjunctions, and the *to* in infinitives.
9. Abbreviate publishers' names and months (*Dec.* rather than *December; Oxford UP* instead of *Oxford University Press*), and include the name of the city in which the publisher is located but not the state: *Danbury: Grolier.* Use *n.p.* in place of publisher or location if unavailable.
10. Do not use *p., pp.,* or *page(s).* When page spans over 100 have the same first digit, use only the last two digits of the second number: 243–47. Use *n. pag.* if the work lacks page or paragraph numbers.
11. Use a hanging indent: Start the first line of each entry at the left margin, and indent all subsequent lines of the entry one-half inch on the computer (or five spaces).
12. Double-space both within entries and between them.

6. Book with an author and an editor: Put the author and title first, followed by *Ed.* (meaning "edited by") and the name of the editor. However, if you cited something written by the editor rather than the author, see number 10.

> Armstrong, Louis. *Louis Armstrong--A Self-Portrait.* Ed. Richard Meryman.
>
> New York: Eakins, 1971. Print.

7. Work in an anthology or chapter in an edited book: List the author and title of the selection, followed by the title of the anthology, the abbreviation *Ed.* for "edited by," the editor's name, publication data, page numbers, and medium.

> Smith, Hale. "Here I Stand." *Readings in Black American Music.*
>
> Ed. Eileen Southern. New York: Norton, 1971. 286-89. Print.

8. Two or more items from one anthology: Include a complete entry for the anthology, beginning with the name of the editor(s). Each selection from the anthology that you are citing should have its own entry in the alphabetical list that includes only the author, title of the selection, editor, and page numbers.

> entry for a selection
> Johnson, Hall. "Notes on the Negro Spiritual." Southern 268-75.
>
> entry for the anthology
> Southern, Eileen, ed. *Readings in Black American Music.* New York:
>
> Norton, 1971. Print.
>
> entry for a selection
> Still, William Grant. "The Structure of Music." Southern 276-79.

9. Article in a reference work: If an entry in an encyclopedia or dictionary is signed, cite the author's name, title of the entry (in quotation marks), title of the reference work (italicized), publication information, and medium. If the entry is not signed, start with the title. (For well-known reference works, such as the *Encyclopædia Britannica,* the place and publisher can be omitted.)

> Robinson, J. Bradford. "Scat Singing." *The New Grove Dictionary of Jazz.*
>
> > Ed. Barry Kernfeld. Vol. 3. London: Macmillan, 2002. 515-16. Print.

10. Preface, foreword, introduction, or afterword: When the writer of the part is different from the author of the book, use the word *By* after the book's title and cite the author's full name. If the writer of the part is the same as the book's author, use only the author's last name after the word *By.*

> Crawford, Richard. Foreword. *The Jazz Tradition.* By Martin Williams.
>
> > New York: Oxford UP, 1993. v-xiii. Print.

> Fowles, John. Preface. *Islands.* By Fowles. Boston: Little, 1978. 1-2. Print.

11. Translation: Cite the work under the author's name, not the translator's. The translator's name goes after the title, with the abbreviation *Trans.* (meaning "translated by").

> Goffin, Robert. *Horn of Plenty: The Story of Louis Armstrong.*
>
> > Trans. James F. Bezov. New York: Da Capo, 1977. Print.

12. Edition other than the first: If you are citing an edition other than the first, include the number of the edition: *2nd ed., 3rd ed.,* and so on. Place the number after the title, or if there is an editor, after that person's name.

Panassie, Hugues. *Louis Armstrong.* 2nd ed. New York: Da Capo, 1980.

Print.

13. Sacred works: Give the version, italicized; the editor's name (if any); and the publication information.

New American Standard Bible. La Habra: Lockman Foundation, 1995. Print.

14. Multivolume work: Your citation should indicate whether you used more than one volume of a multivolume work.

MORE THAN ONE VOLUME USED

Lissauer, Robert. *Lissauer's Encyclopedia of Popular Music in America.* 3 vols.

New York: Facts on File, 1996. Print.

ONLY ONE VOLUME USED

Lissauer, Robert. *Lissauer's Encyclopedia of Popular Music in America.* Vol. 2.

New York: Facts on File, 1996. Print.

15. Book in a series: After the medium, put the name of the series and, if available on the title page, the number of the work.

Floyd, Samuel A., Jr., ed. *Black Music in the Harlem Renaissance.* New York:

Greenwood, 1990. Print. Contributions in Afro-American and

African Studies 128.

16. Republished book: Put the original date of publication, followed by a period, before the current publication data. In the following example, the writer cites a 1974 republication of a book that originally appeared in 1936.

> Cuney-Hare, Maud. *Negro Musicians and Their Music.* 1936.
>
> New York: Da Capo, 1974. Print.

17. Title in a title: When a book's title contains the title of another book, do not italicize the second title. In the following example, the novel *Invisible Man* is not italicized.

> O'Meally, Robert, ed. *New Essays on* Invisible Man. Cambridge:
>
> Cambridge UP, 1988. Print.

18. Unknown author: The citation begins with the title. In the list of works cited, alphabetize the citation by the first important word, not by articles like *A, An,* or *The.*

> *Webster's College Dictionary.* New York: Random; New York:
>
> McGraw, 1991. Print.

Note that this entry includes both of the publishers listed on the dictionary's title page; they are separated by a semicolon.

19. Publisher's imprint: Give the name of the imprint and then the publisher's name, separated by a hyphen.

> Ehrenreich, Barbara. *Nickel and Dimed: On (Not) Getting by in America.*
>
> New York: Metropolitan-Holt, 2001. Print.

Periodicals   Periodicals are published at set intervals, usually four times a year for scholarly journals, monthly or weekly for magazines, and daily or weekly for newspapers. Between the author and the publication data are two titles: the title of the article, in quotation marks, and the title of the periodical, italicized. Figure 15.2 on page 119 shows where the elements of a works-cited entry for a journal article can be found.

MLA

20. Article in a journal paginated by volume: Put the volume number after the title. Place a period after the volume number and follow it with the issue number. In the example, the volume is 27 and the issue is number 2. Give the year of publication in parentheses, followed by a colon, a space, the page numbers of the article, and the medium.

Tirro, Frank. "Constructive Elements in Jazz Improvisation." *Journal of*

   the American Musicological Society 27.2 (1974): 285-305. Print.

21. Article in a journal paginated by issue: Cite journals paginated by issue as you would those paginated by volume.

Aguiar, Sarah Appleton. "'Everywhere and Nowhere': Beloved's 'Wild'

   Legacy in Toni Morrison's *Jazz.*" *Notes on Contemporary Literature*

   25.4 (1995): 11-12. Print.

22. Article in a monthly magazine: Provide the month and year, abbreviating the names of all months except *May, June,* and *July*.

Walker, Malcolm. "Discography: Bill Evans." *Jazz Monthly*

June 1965: 20-22. Print.

23. Article in a weekly magazine: Include the complete date of publication: day, month, and year.

Taylor, J. R. "Jazz History: The Incompleted Past." *Village Voice*

3 July 1978: 65-67. Print.

24. Article in a newspaper: Provide the day, month, and year. If an edition is indicated, specify the edition (*natl. ed.,* for example) and use a comma between the date and the edition. Whenever possible, give the section (*E* in the example) with the page number. If the article appears on nonconsecutive pages, put a plus (+) beside the first page number.

Blumenthal, Ralph. "Satchmo with His Tape Recorder Running."

New York Times 3 Aug. 1999: E1+. Print.

25. Unsigned article: The citation begins with the title and is alphabetized by the first word other than *A, An,* or *The.*

"Squaresville, U.S.A. vs. Beatsville." *Life* 21 Sept. 1959: 31. Print.

FIGURE 15.2 The elements of an MLA works-cited entry: journal articles. Some academic journals, like this one, provide most of the information needed for a citation on the first page of an article as well as, like others, on the cover or contents page. You will need to look at the article's final page for the last page number.

Author

Article title

Edwards, Brent Hayes. "Louis Armstrong and the Syntax of Scat."

Critical Inquiry 28.3 (2002): 618-49. Print.

Journal title

Medium

Volume and
issue number

Year of publication

Page numbers

Author and
article title

Starting
page
number

Journal title,
volume and
issue number,
and year of
publication

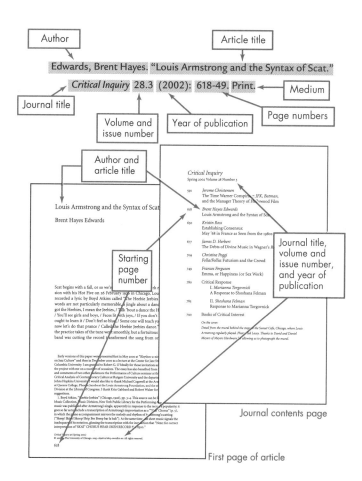

Journal contents page

First page of article

26. Review: Begin with the name of the reviewer and, if there is one, the title of the review. Add *Rev. of* and the title plus the author of the work being reviewed. Notice that the word *by* precedes the author's name.

> Ostwald, David. "All That Jazz." Rev. of *Louis Armstrong:*
>
> *An Extravagant Life,* by Laurence Bergreen. *Commentary*
>
> Nov. 1997: 68-72. Print.

27. Editorial: Treat editorials as articles, but add the word *Editorial* after the title. If the editorial is unsigned, begin with the title.

> Shaw, Theodore M. "The Debate over Race Needs Minority
>
> Students' Voices." Editorial. *Chronicle of Higher Education*
>
> 25 Feb. 2000: A72. Print.

28. Letter to the editor: Include the word *Letter* after the author's name.

> Gaines, William C. Letter. *Smithsonian* Aug. 2005: 12. Print.

Other Print Sources

29. Government document: Begin with either the name of the government and agency or the name of the author of the document. If the government and agency name come first, follow the title of the document with the word *By* for a writer, *Ed.* for an editor, or *Comp.* for a compiler if one is indicated.

> United States. Bureau of National Affairs. *The Civil Rights Act of 1964:*
>
> *Text, Analysis, Legislative History; What It Means to Employers,*

Businessmen, Unions, Employees, Minority Groups. Washington:

BNA, 1964. Print.

30. Pamphlet: Treat as you would a book. If the pamphlet has an
author, list his or her name first; otherwise, begin with the title.

All Music Guide to Jazz. 2nd ed. San Francisco: Miller Freeman, 1996.

Print.

31. Conference proceedings: Cite as you would a book, but include information about the conference if it is not in the title.

Mendel, Arthur, Gustave Reese, and Gilbert Chase, eds. *Papers Read*

at the International Congress of Musicology held at New York September

11th to 16th, 1939. New York: Music Educators' Natl. Conf. for the

Amer. Musicological Soc., 1944. Print.

32. Published dissertation: Cite as you would a book. After the
title, add *Diss.* for "dissertation," the name of the institution, the year
the dissertation was written, and the medium.

Fraser, Wilmot Alfred. *Jazzology: A Study of the Tradition in Which Jazz*

Musicians Learn to Improvise. Diss. U of Pennsylvania, 1983. Ann

Arbor: UMI, 1987. Print.

33. Unpublished dissertation: After the author's name, give the dissertation title in quotation marks, the abbreviation *Diss.,* the institution, the year the dissertation was written, and the medium.

MLA

Reyes-Schramm, Adelaida. "The Role of Music in the Interaction of

Black Americans and Hispanos in New York City's East Harlem."

Diss. Columbia U, 1975. Print.

34. Abstract of a dissertation: Use the format for an unpublished dissertation. After the dissertation date, give the abbreviation *DA* or *DAI* (for *Dissertation Abstracts* or *Dissertation Abstracts International*), then the volume number, issue number, date, page number, and medium.

Quinn, Richard Allen. "Playing Together: Improvisation in Postwar

American Literature and Culture." Diss. U of Iowa, 2000. *DAI* 61.6

(2001): 2305A. Print.

35. Published or broadcast interview: Name the person interviewed and give the title of the interview or *Interview,* the name of the interviewer, the publication information, and the medium.

Armstrong, Louis. "Authentic American Genius." Interview by Richard

Meryman. *Life* 15 Apr. 1966: 92-102. Print.

36. Map or chart: Italicize the title of the map or chart, and add the word *Map* or *Chart* following the title.

Let's Go Map Guide to New Orleans. Map. New York: St. Martin's, 1997.

Print.

37. Cartoon: Include the cartoonist's name, the title of the cartoon (if any) in quotation marks, the word *Cartoon,* the publication information, and the medium.

Myller, Jorgen. "Louis Armstrong's First Lesson." Cartoon. *Melody*

   Maker Mar. 1931: 12. Print.

38. Advertisement: Name the item or organization being advertised, include the word *Advertisement,* and indicate where the ad appeared.

   Hartwick College Summer Music Festival and Institute. Advertisement.

   New York Times Magazine 3 Jan. 1999: 54. Print.

39. Published letter: Treat like a work in an anthology, but include the date. Include the number, if one was assigned by the editor. If you use more than one letter from a published collection, follow the instructions for cross-referencing in number 8.

   Hughes, Langston. "To Arna Bontemps." 17 Jan. 1938. *Arna*

   Bontemps--Langston Hughes Letters 1925-1967. Ed. Charles H.

   Nichols. New York: Dodd, 1980. 27-28. Print.

40. Personal letter: To cite a letter you received, start with the writer's name, followed by the descriptive phrase *Letter to the author* and then the date.

   Cogswell, Michael. Letter to the author. 15 Mar. 2008. MS.

To cite someone else's unpublished personal letter, see the guidelines in number 41.

41. Manuscripts, typescripts, and material in archives: Give the author, a title or description of the material (*Letter, Notebook*), the form (*MS.* if manuscript, *TS.* if typescript), any identifying number, the name and location of the institution housing the material, and the medium.

Glaser, Joe. Letter to Lucille Armstrong. 28 Sept. 1960. MS. Box 3. Louis

Armstrong Archives. Queens College City U of New York, Flushing.

42. Legal source: Name the plaintiff and defendant in a court case, followed by the case number, the court that heard the case, the decision date, publication information (if possible), and the medium.

Ashcroft v. the Free Speech Coalition. 535 US 234-152. Supreme Court

of the US. 2002. Print.

For an act of Congress, give the name of the legislation, followed by its Public Law number, its Statute at Large number, pages, the date it was signed into law, and medium.

Family Entertainment and Copyright Act of 2005. Pub. L. 109-9.27

218 Stat. Apr. 2005. Print.

Electronic Sources

The examples that follow are based on the guidelines for the citation of electronic sources in the sixth edition of the *MLA Handbook for Writers of Research Papers* (2003), updated based on the third edition of the *MLA Style Manual and Guide to Scholarly Publishing* (2008).

Note: The Internet address for an electronic source is its uniform resource locator, or URL. Only include a URL in a citation if the reader may not be able to find the source without it.

43. Online scholarly project:

Entire Web site: Begin with the name of the author or editor, followed by the title of the site and the electronic publication data, which includes, if relevant, the version number, the publisher or sponsor (or *n.p.*), the date of publication or update, and the medium. End with the date you used the project.

> Raeburn, Bruce Boyd, ed. *William Ransom Hogan Archive of New Orleans*
>
> *Jazz*. Tulane U, 30 Oct. 2004. Web. 3 May 2008.

Part of a Web site: When citing one part, document, or page of a project, add the author (if known) and the title of the part in quotation marks. If the author is unknown, start with the title of the part in quotation marks.

> Raeburn, Bruce Boyd. "An Introduction to New Orleans Jazz." *William*
>
> *Ransom Hogan Archive of New Orleans Jazz*. Ed. Bruce Boyd Raeburn.
>
> Tulane U, 30 Oct. 2004. Web. 3 May 2008.

> "Armstrong Biography." *Satchmo.Net: The Official Site for the Louis*
>
> *Armstrong House and Archives*. Queens College City U of New York,
>
> 2003. Web. 3 May 2008.

44. Professional or personal Web site: Name the person responsible for the site, the title of the site (italicized), the publisher or sponsor (or *n.p.*), the date of publication or update, the medium, and the date of access. If no title is available, use a descriptive term such as *Home page* (without italics or quotation marks).

> Henson, Keith. *The Keith Henson Jazzpage.* N.p., 1996. Web.
>
> 3 May 2008.

> Wildman, Joan. *The World of Jazz Improvisation.* U of Wisconsin,
>
> Madison, n.d. Web. 3 May 2008.

If you are citing a home page for a course, substitute the name of the course for the title of the site.

45. Online book:

Entire book: Cite as for print books, including author; title (italicized); editor, translator, or compiler (if any); and publication data for the print version. Add the name of the database or project, medium, and date of access.

> Sandburg, Carl. *Chicago Poems.* New York: Holt, 1916. *Bartleby.com.*
>
> Web. 3 May 2008.

Work in an online book: If you use part of an online book, add the title of the part after the author and put it in quotation marks, unless the part cited is an introduction, foreword, preface, or afterword (*see number 10*).

> Sandburg, Carl. "Chicago." *Chicago Poems.* New York: Holt, 1916.
>
> *Bartleby.com.* Web. 3 May 2008.

46. Article in an online periodical: Provide the writer's name and the title of the work in quotation marks or a descriptive term (*Editorial*). For an online scholarly journal, include the periodical title (italicized), volume and issue numbers, and inclusive page numbers or *n. pag.* Conclude with the medium and access date. For an online magazine or newspaper, give the site title (italicized), publisher, date of publication, medium, and access date.

> "Bulletin Board; Louis Armstrong Centenary." *New York Times.* New York
>
> Times, 7 Nov. 2001. Web. 3 May 2008.
>
> Ross, Michael E. "The New Sultans of Swing." *Salon.* Salon, 18 Apr.
>
> 1996. Web. 3 May 2008.
>
> Schmalfeldt, Janet. "On Keeping the Score." *Music Theory Online* 4.2
>
> (1998): n. pag. Web. 3 May 2008.

47. CD-ROM or DVD: Works on CD-ROM or DVD are usually cited like books or parts of books, but the term *CD-ROM* or *DVD* and the name of the vendor, if different from the publisher, are added after the publication data.

> "Armstrong, (Daniel) Louis 'Satchmo.' " *Microsoft Encarta Multimedia*
>
> *Encyclopedia.* Redmond: Microsoft, 1994. CD-ROM.

48. Work from a library or personal subscription service: For material that you accessed through a library subscription service such as *EBSCO, ProQuest, InfoTrac,* and *Lexis-Nexis,* add the following to your citation: the name of the datebase, the medium, and the date of access. Figure 15.3 shows where the elements of a works-cited entry for an article accessed through *ProQuest* can be found.

> Hardack, Richard. " 'A Music Seeking Its Words': Double-Timing and
>
> Double Consciousness in Toni Morrison's *Jazz*." *Callaloo* 18.2 (1995):
>
> 451-72. *Expanded Academic ASAP*. Web. 3 May 2008.

In the past, America Online offered personal database subscriptions. However, it has stopped doing so, and most subscription databases can be accessed at the library.

FIGURE 15.3 The elements of an MLA works-cited entry: journal article from an online database. A citation for an article obtained from an online subscription database service like *ProQuest* includes information about the database, the medium, and the date of access in addition to information about the print version of the article. Information about the date of access comes from the researcher's notes.

Author, title, and other information
about the print version of the article

Edwards, Brent Hayes. "Louis Armstrong and the Syntax of

Scat." *Critical Inquiry* 28.3 (2002): 618-49. ProQuest

Research Library. Web. 5 May 2008.

Medium | Date of access

Name of
database

MLA

Database title

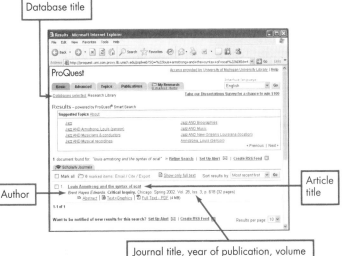

Author

Article
title

Journal title, year of publication, volume
and issue number, and page range
information

49. Online posting: Treat as a Web site. Begin with the author and (in quotation marks) the title or subject line. End with the posting date, the site name, the medium, and the date of access.

> Pomeroy, Leslie K., Jr. "Racing with the Moon." *rec.music.bluenote.*
>
> N.p., 4 May 2008. Web. 6 May 2008.

50. Synchronous communication: Cite the online transcript of a synchronous discussion as you would a Web site. If relevant, the speaker's name can begin the citation.

> Curran, Stuart, and Harry Rusche. "Discussion: Plenary Log 6. Third
>
> Annual Graduate Student Conference in Romanticism." *Prometheus*
>
> *Unplugged: Emory MOO.* Emory U, 20 Apr. 1996. Web. 4 Jan. 1999.

51. E-mail: Include the author; the subject line (if any), in quotation marks; the descriptive term *Message to* plus the name of the recipient, the date of the message, and the medium.

> Hoffman, Esther. "Re: My Louis Armstrong Paper." *Message to* J. Peritz.
>
> 5 Apr. 2008. E-mail.

52. Online graphic, audio, or video file: If a non-Web version exists, base the format of your citation on the closest model. Include the creator's name, the title or description of the source, information about the non-Web version, the title of the Web site or database (italicized), the publication data, the medium, and the date of access. If the source only exists online, cite as part of a Web site (*see no. 43*).

Online film, cited as a film

> *Night of the Living Dead.* Dir. George A. Romero. Image Ten, 1968.
>
> *Internet Archive.* Web. 12 May 2008.

Original video, cited as part of a Web site

> Wesch, Michael. "The machine is us/ing us." *Digital Ethnography.*
>
> Kansas State U, 2007. Web. 12 May 2008.

53. Computer software: Include the title, version, publisher, and date in your text or in an explanatory note. Do not include an entry in the list of works cited.

Audiovisual and Other Nonprint Sources
54. Film, videotape, or DVD: Begin with the title (italicized). For a film, cite the director and the lead actors or narrator (*Perf.* or *Narr.*), followed by the distributor and year. Conclude with the medium (Film, Videocassette, or DVD).

> *Artists and Models.* Dir. Raoul Walsh. Perf. Jack Benny, Ida Lupino, and
>
> Alan Townsend. Paramount, 1937. Film.

55. TV or radio program: Give the episode title (in quotation marks), the program title (italicized), the name of the series (if any), the name of the network, the city, the broadcast date, and the medium.

"The Music of Charlie Parker." *Jazz Set.* WBGO-FM, New York.

2 Dec. 1998. Radio.

56. Sound recording: The entry starts with the composer, conductor, or performer, depending on your focus. Include the work's title (italicized); the artist(s), if not already mentioned; the manufacturer; the date of release, and the medium.

Armstrong, Louis. *Town Hall Concert Plus.* RCA Victor, 1957. LP.

57. Musical composition: Include only the composer and title, unless you are referring to a published score. Published scores are treated like books except that the date of composition appears after the title. Note that the titles of instrumental pieces are italicized only when they are known by name, not just by form and number, or when the reference is to a published score.

Ellington, Duke. *Satin Doll.*

Haydn, Franz Josef. Symphony no. 94 in G Major.

Haydn, Franz Josef. *Symphony No. 94 in G Major.* 1791.

Ed. H. C. Robbins Landon. Salzburg: Haydn-Mozart, 1965. Print.

58. Artwork: Provide the artist's name, the title of the artwork (italicized), the date, the medium, and the institution or private collection and city in which the artwork can be found.

Leonard, Herman. *Louis Armstrong: Birdland 1949*. 1949. Photograph.

Barbara Gillman Gallery, Miami.

If you used a photograph of a work of art from a book, treat it like a work in an anthology (see number 7), but italicize the titles of both the work and the book and include the institution or collection and city where the work can be found prior to information about the book.

59. Unpublished interview: Begin with the person interviewed, followed by *Personal interview* (if you conducted the interview personally) and the date of the interview. (*See number 35 for a published interview.*)

Jacobs, Phoebe. Personal interview. 3 May 2008.

60. Lecture or speech: To cite an oral presentation, give the speaker's name, the title (in quotation marks), the name of the forum or sponsor, the location, the date, and a descriptive label such as *Address* or *Lecture*.

Taylor, Billy. "What Is Jazz?" John F. Kennedy Center for the Performing

Arts, Washington. 14 Feb. 1995. Lecture.

61. Performance: To cite a play, opera, ballet, or concert, begin with the title; followed by the author(s) (*By*); pertinent information about the live performance, such as the director (*Dir.*) and major performers; the site; the city; the performance date, and *Performance*.

Ragtime. By Terrence McNally, Lynn Athrens, and Stephen Flaherty. Dir.

Frank Galati. Ford Performing Arts Center, New York. 11 Nov. 1998.

Performance.

Explanatory notes are used to cite multiple sources for borrowed material or to give readers supplemental information. Their purpose is to avoid distracting readers with an overly long parenthetical citation or an interesting but not directly relevant idea. You can also use explanatory notes to acknowledge people who helped you with research and writing. Explanatory notes can be formatted either as footnotes at the bottom of a manuscript page or as endnotes on a separate page (titled "Notes") before the works-cited list. Identify each note with a raised arabic number in the text.

MLA

TEXT

As a young man during Prohibition, Glaser got caught up in the Chicago underworld.[1]

NOTE

[1]Bergreen 372-76. Even though Ostwald points out a few mistakes in Bergreen's *Louis Armstrong: An Extravagant Life,* I think the book's new information about Glaser is useful and trustworthy.

17 MLA style: Paper format

The following guidelines will help you prepare your research paper in the format recommended by the sixth edition of the *MLA Handbook for Writers of Research Papers.* For sample pages from a research paper using MLA style, see pages 138–41.

MLA

Materials. Before printing your paper, make sure that you have backed up your final draft. Use a high-quality printer and good, white 8½-by-11-inch paper. Choose a standard 11- or 12-point font. Put the printed pages together with a paper clip, not a staple, and do not use a binder unless you have been told to do so by your instructor.

Heading and title. No separate title page is needed. In the upper left-hand corner of the first page, one inch from the top and side, type on separate, double-spaced lines your name, your instructor's name, the course number, and the date. Double-space between the date and the paper's title and the title and the first line of text, as well as throughout your paper. The title should be centered and properly capitalized (*see p. 138*). Do not italicize the title or put it in quotation marks or bold type.

Margins and spacing. Use one-inch margins all around, except for the right-hand top corner, where the page number goes. Your right margin should be ragged (not "justified," or even).

Double-space lines throughout the paper, including quotations, notes, and the works-cited list. Indent the first word of each paragraph one-half inch (or five spaces) from the left margin. For block quotations, indent one inch (or ten spaces) from the left.

Page numbers.   Put your last name and the page number in the upper right-hand corner of the page, one-half inch from the top and flush with the right margin. Most word-processing programs allow you to set up a header so that it will appear on each page automatically.

MLA

Visuals.   Place visuals (tables, charts, graphs, and images) close to the place in your text where you refer to them. Label and number tables consecutively (*Table 1, Table 2*) and give each one an explanatory caption; put this information above the table. The term *Figure* (abbreviated *fig.*) is used to label all other kinds of visuals, except for musical illustrations, which are labeled *Example* (abbreviated *Ex.*). Place figure or example captions below the visuals. Below all visuals, cite the source of the material and provide explanatory notes as needed.

Electronic Submissions.   If you are asked to submit your work electronically, find out which format your instructor prefers. Send the submission to your own e-mail address as well so that you can make sure the paper has been transmitted successfully.

18 Pages from a student paper in MLA style

As a first-year college student, Esther Hoffman wrote a paper about Louis Armstrong and jazz for her composition course. Esther knew little about Armstrong before her instructor took the class to visit the Louis Armstrong Archives. For this paper, Esther did archival research based on what she had learned from consulting online and print sources.

MLA

www.mhhe.com/
wi

For a sample of an entire student paper in MLA style, go to

Research >
Sample Research
Papers

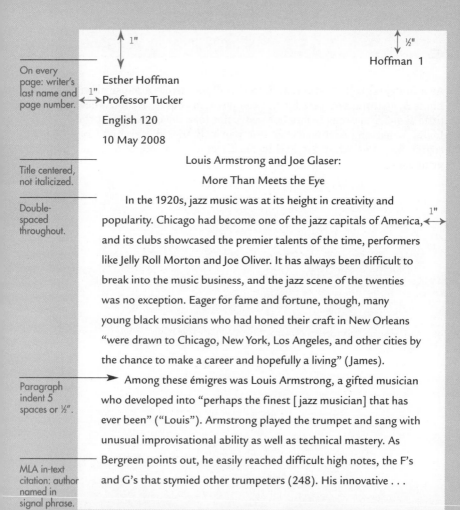

On every page: writer's last name and page number.

Title centered, not italicized.

Double-spaced throughout.

Paragraph indent 5 spaces or ½".

MLA in-text citation: author named in signal phrase.

Esther Hoffman

Professor Tucker

English 120

10 May 2008

Louis Armstrong and Joe Glaser:

More Than Meets the Eye

In the 1920s, jazz music was at its height in creativity and popularity. Chicago had become one of the jazz capitals of America, and its clubs showcased the premier talents of the time, performers like Jelly Roll Morton and Joe Oliver. It has always been difficult to break into the music business, and the jazz scene of the twenties was no exception. Eager for fame and fortune, though, many young black musicians who had honed their craft in New Orleans "were drawn to Chicago, New York, Los Angeles, and other cities by the chance to make a career and hopefully a living" (James).

Among these émigres was Louis Armstrong, a gifted musician who developed into "perhaps the finest [jazz musician] that has ever been" ("Louis"). Armstrong played the trumpet and sang with unusual improvisational ability as well as technical mastery. As Bergreen points out, he easily reached difficult high notes, the F's and G's that stymied other trumpeters (248). His innovative . . .

138

Notes

[1]Bergreen 372-76. Even though Ostwald points out a few mistakes in Bergreen's *Louis Armstrong: An Extravagant Life,* I think the book's new information about Glaser is useful and trustworthy.

    [2]I want to thank George Arevalo of the Louis Armstrong Archives for his help on this project. When I was low on inspiration and in search of some direction, George showed me the two pictures I describe in this paper. Seeing those pictures helped me figure out what I wanted to say--and why I wanted to say it. For introducing me to archival research and to the art of Louis Armstrong, I also want to thank the head of the Louis Armstrong Archives, Michael Cogswell, and my English teacher, Professor Amy Tucker.

Gives supplemental information about key source.

Indent first line 5 spaces or ½".

Acknowledges others who helped.

Works Cited

"Armstrong, (Daniel) Louis 'Satchmo.' " *Microsoft Encarta Multimedia Encyclopedia.* Redmond: Microsoft, 1994. CD-ROM.

Armstrong, Louis. Backstage instructions to Glaser. Apr. 1957. MS. Accessions 1997-26. Louis Armstrong Archives. Queens College City U of New York, Flushing.

---. "Louis Armstrong and the Jewish Family in New Orleans." 31 Mar. 1969. MS. Louis Armstrong Archives. Queens College City U of New York, Flushing.

Bergreen, Laurence. *Louis Armstrong: An Extravagant Life.* New York: Broadway, 1997. Print.

Bogle, Donald. "Louis Armstrong: The Films." *Louis Armstrong: A Cultural Legacy.* Ed. Marc H. Miller. Seattle: U of Washington P and Queens Museum of Art, 1994. 147-79. Print.

Collier, James Lincoln. *Louis Armstrong: An American Genius.* New York: Oxford UP, 1983. Print.

Edwards, Brent Hayes. "Louis Armstrong and the Syntax of Scat." *Critical Inquiry* 28.3 (2002): 618-49. Print.

Glaser, Joe. Letter to Lucille Armstrong. 28 Sept. 1960. MS. Box 3. Louis Armstrong Archives. Queens College City U of New York, Flushing.

New page, title centered.

Entries in alphabetical order.

Source: archival material.

3 hyphens used instead of repeating author's name.

Source: whole book.

Hanging indent ½" or 5 spaces.

Source: journal.

140

Jacobs, Phoebe. Personal interview. 3 May 2008.

James, Gregory N. *The Southern Diaspora: How the Great Migrations of Black and White Southerners Transformed America.* Chapel Hill: U of North Carolina P, 2007. N. pag. Blues, Jazz, and the Great Migration. Web. 7 May 2008.

Jones, Max, and John Chilton. *Louis: The Louis Armstrong Story, 1900-1971.* Boston: Little, 1971. Print.

Morgenstern, Dan. "Louis Armstrong and the Development and Diffusion of Jazz." *Louis Armstrong: A Cultural Legacy.* Ed. Marc H. Miller. Seattle: U of Washington P and Queens Museum of Art, 1994. 95-145. Print.

Ostwald, David. "All That Jazz." Rev. of *Louis Armstrong: An Extravagant Life,* by Laurence Bergreen. *Commentary* Nov. 1997: 68-72. Print.

Pollack, Bracha. "A Man ahead of His Time." 1997. MS.

Robinson, J. Bradford. "Scat Singing." *The New Grove Dictionary of Jazz.* Ed. Barry Kernfeld. Vol. 3 London: Macmillan, 2002. 515-16. Print.

Source: personal interview.

Source: Web document.

Source: selection in an edited book.

Source: review in a monthly magazine.

Source: unpublished paper.

Take the whole range of imaginative literature, and we are all wholesale borrowers. In every matter that relates to invention, to use, or beauty or form, we are borrowers.

—WENDELL PHILLIPS

APA Documentation Style

The charts on pages 143–45 can help you locate the right example of a reference-list entry for a particular kind of source. Answering the questions provided will usually lead you to the sample entry you need. You can also use the directory on pages 153–54.

Entries in a List of References: BOOKS (155-58)

Is your source a complete book or part of a book?

No Yes

	Go to this entry
Is it a complete book with one named author?	
Is it the only book by this author that you are citing?	1
Are you citing more than one book by this author?	4
Is it a complete book with more than one named author?	2
Is it a complete book without a named author or editor?	
Is the author an organization?	3
Is the author unknown?	9
Is it a complete book with an editor or a translator?	
Is there an editor instead of an author?	5
Is it a translation?	7
Is it a complete book with an edition or a volume number?	
Does it have an edition number (e.g., Second Edition)?	10
Is it part of a multivolume work (e.g., Volume 3)?	11
Is it a republished work (e.g., a classic study)?	12
Is your source a work from an anthology	
or a chapter in an edited book?	6
Is it an article in a reference work (e.g., an encyclopedia)?	8
Is it a published presentation from a conference?	23

Check the next page or the directory on pages 153–54 or consult your instructor.

Entries in a List of References: PRINT PERIODICALS OR OTHER PRINT SOURCES (159–65)

❓ *Is your source from a journal, a magazine, or a newspaper?*

No   Yes
↓

	Go to this entry
Is it from an academic journal?	
Are the page numbers continued from one issue to the next?	13
Do the page numbers in each issue of the journal start with 1?	14
Is it a review (e.g., a review of a book)?	20
Is it a published presentation from a conference?	23
Is it from a monthly or weekly magazine?	
Is it an article?	16
Is it an editorial or a letter to the editor?	18
Is it a review (e.g., a review of a book)?	20
Is it from a newspaper?	
Is it an article?	17
Is it an editorial or a letter to the editor?	18
Is it a review (e.g., a review of a book)?	20
Is the author unknown?	19
Are you citing two or more articles published in the same year by the same author?	15

❓ *Is it a print source but not a book or a periodical article?*

No   Yes
↓

	Go to this entry
Is it published by the government or a nongovernment organization?	
Is it a government document?	21
Is it a report, a working paper, or a conference presentation?	22, 23
Is it an unpublished work?	
Is it an unpublished conference presentation?	23
Is it an unpublished dissertation or a dissertation abstract?	24

Check the next page or the directory on pages 153–54 or consult your instructor

Entries in a List of References: ELECTRONIC OR OTHER NONPRINT SOURCES (165–69)

? *Did you find your nonprint source online?*

No **Yes**
↓

	Go to this entry
Is it an article or abstract?	
Does it have a DOI?	27
Does it not have a DOI?	28
Is it from a personal or organizational Web site?	
Is it an entire online document?	29
Is it a portion of an online document?	30
Is it a posting to an online forum?	31
Is it an entry from a blog?	33
Is it an audio podcast?	34
Is it an online video?	35

? *Is your source a nonprint source that is **not** published online?*

No **Yes**
↓

	Go to this entry
Is it a film, DVD, videotape, or audio recording?	25
Is it a television program?	26
Is it computer software?	32

↓

Check the directory on pages 153–54 or consult your instructor.

APA

Instructors of courses in the social sciences and business usually prefer a documentation style that emphasizes the author and the year of publication.

The American Psychological Association (APA) has developed a widely used version of the author-year style; the information in Chapters 19–22 is based on the fifth edition of its *Publication Manual* (Washington: APA, 2001) and the *APA Style Guide to Electronic References* (2007). For updates to the APA documentation system, check the APA-sponsored Web site at <http://www.apastyle.org>.

APA documentation style has two mandatory parts:

- In-text citations
- List of references

The following is an in-text citation and its corresponding reference-list entry:

IN-TEXT CITATION

According to Bentley and Ziegler (2006), the European Union is the "most strongly integrated" economic alliance in the modern world (p. 1137).

REFERENCE-LIST ENTRY

Bentley, J. H. & Ziegler, H. F. (2006). *Traditions and encounters: A global perspective on the past* (Vol. 2). New York: McGraw-Hill.

When you use ideas, information, or words from a source, APA in-text citation format requires that you do the following:

- **Identify the author(s) of the source,** either in the sentence or in a parenthetical citation.

- **Indicate the year of publication of the source** following the author's name, either in parentheses if the author's name is part of the sentence, or if the author is not named in the sentence, after the author's name and a comma in a parenthetical citation.

- **Include a page reference for a quotation or a specific piece of information.** Put a *p.* before the page number. If the author is named in the text, the page number appears in the parenthetical citation following the borrowed material. Page numbers are not necessary when you are summarizing the source as a whole or paraphrasing an idea found throughout a work. (*For more on quotations, paraphrases, and summaries, see Part 2: Researching, pp. 73–80.*)

APA In-Text Citations: Directory to Sample Types

(*See pp. 152–69 for examples of reference-list entries.*)

APA

1. Author named in your sentence: When the author is named in a signal phrase, follow the name with the year of publication (in parentheses).

According to Eidson (1992), several political parties vie for power at

every level during regularly scheduled elections.

2. Author named in parentheses: If you do not name the source's author in your sentence, then you must include the name in parentheses, followed by the date and, if you are giving a quotation or a specific piece of information, the page number. The name, date, and page number are separated by commas.

This safety net plus the free market comprise what Germany calls a

"social market" economy (Eidson, 1992, p. 122).

3. Two to five authors: If a source has five or fewer authors, name all of them the first time you cite the source.

As Calhoun, Light, and Keller (1997) point out, "Income-based

rankings are not necessarily a measure of development" (p. 468).

If you put the names of the authors in parentheses, use an ampersand (&) instead of *and*.

Although income-based rankings are important, they "are not

necessarily a measure of development" (Calhoun, Light, & Keller,

1997, p. 468).

After the first time you cite a work by three or more authors, use the first author's name plus *et al.* Always use both names when citing a work by two authors.

Another key factor is income distribution within countries

(Calhoun et al., 1997, p. 470).

4. Six or more authors: In all in-text citations, give the first author's name plus *et al.* In the reference list, however, provide the first six authors' names, followed by *et al.* for all others.

As Barbre et al. (1989) have argued, using personal narratives enables

researchers to connect the individual and the social.

5. Organization as author: Treat the organization as the author and spell out its name the first time the source is cited. If the organization is well known, you may use an abbreviation thereafter.

The Deutsche Bank's Economics Department (1991) identified a

handful of key problems raised by efforts to rebuild eastern Europe.

Public service announcements were used to inform parents of these

findings (National Institute of Mental Health [NIMH], 1991).

In subsequent citations only the abbreviation and the date need to be given: (*NIMH, 1991*), as long as you are sure that readers will know what the abbreviation stands for.

APA

6. Unknown author: When no author or editor is listed, use the first one or two important words of the title. Use quotation marks for titles of articles or chapters and italics for titles of books or reports.

> The transformation of women's lives has been hailed as "the single
>
> most important change of the past 1,000 years" ("Reflections,"
>
> 1999, p. 77).

7. Two or more authors with the same last name: Always include the appropriate first initial, even when the year of publication differs.

> M. Smith (1988) showed how globalization has restructured both
>
> cities and states.

8. Two or more sources cited at one time: When you are indebted to two or more sources for an idea, cite the authors in the order in which they appear in the list of references. Separate the two sources with a semicolon.

> During World War II, the Nazi regime developed an agrarian ideology
>
> while accelerating the pace of industrial growth (Eidson, 1992;
>
> "Germany," 1995).

9. E-mail, letters, conversations: To cite information received from unpublished forms of personal communication, give the source's initials and last name, and provide as precise a date as possible.

According to A. Tapolcai (personal communication, April 3, 2003),

college-educated Hungarians had long expected this kind of change.

Note: Because readers do not have access to them, you should not include personal communications in your reference list.

10. Indirect source:

When referring to a source that you know only from reading another source, use the phrase *as cited in,* followed by the author of the source you actually read and its year of publication.

A study by Passell (as cited in Calhoun et al., 1997, p. 469) found that

investments in education and technology were lower for countries

that exported natural resources.

Note: The work by Passell would not be included in the reference list, but the work by Calhoun et al. would.

11. Electronic source:

Cite the author's last name and the publication date. If the document is a pdf (portable document format) file with stable page numbers, cite the page number. If the source has paragraph numbers instead of page numbers, use *para.* or ¶ instead of *p.* when citing a specific part of the source.

According to Gordeeva (2000), by the time the Truehand was

disbanded, it had privatized around 14,000 enterprises (para. 2).

Note: If the specific part lacks page or paragraph numbering, cite the heading and the number of the paragraph under that heading where the information can be found. If you cannot find the name of the author, or if the author is an organization, follow the appropriate guidelines for print sources (*see numbers 5 and 6*). If you cannot determine the date, use the abbreviation "n.d." in its place: (*Wilson, n.d.*).

20 APA style: References

www.mhhe.com/
wi
To download
Bibliomaker
software for
APA, go to
Research >
Bibliomaker

APA documentation style requires a list of references where readers can find complete bibliographical information about your sources. The list of references should appear at the end of your paper, beginning on a new page entitled "References."

In order to format entries in a list of references correctly, it is important to know what kind of source you are citing. The directory that follows will help you find the appropriate sample to use as your model. As an alternative, you can use the charts on pages 143–45 to help you locate the right example. If you cannot find what you are looking for after consulting the appropriate directory or chart, ask your instructor for help.

To help locate the information you need in an actual source, consult the facsimiles on pages 157, 161, and 167.

APA Reference Entries: Directory to Sample Types
(See pp. 147–52 for examples of in-text citations.)

GENERAL GUIDELINES for the LIST of REFERENCES in APA STYLE

1. Begin on a new page.
2. Begin with the centered title "References."
3. Include a reference for every in-text citation.
4. Put references in alphabetical order by the author's last name.
5. Give the last name and first or both initials for each author.
6. Put the publication year in parentheses following the author or authors' names.
7. Capitalize only the first word and proper nouns in titles. Also capitalize the first word following the semicolon in a subtitle.
8. Use italics for titles of books but not articles. Do not enclose titles of articles in quotation marks.
9. Include the city and publisher for books. If the city is not well known, include the state, using its two-letter postal abbreviation.
10. Include the periodical name and volume number (both in italics) as well as the page numbers for a periodical article.
11. Separate the author's or authors' names, date (in parentheses), title, and publication information with periods.
12. Begin the first line of each entry flush left, and indent all subsequent lines of an entry one-half inch (five spaces).
13. Double-space both within and between entries (*see pp. 174–75 for an example*).
14. See p. 165 for guidelines on electronic sources.

Books

Figure 20.1 shows where the elements of a reference-list entry for a book can be found.

1. Book with one author:

Brown, J. F. (1991). *Surge to freedom: The end of communist rule in eastern Europe.* Durham, NC: Duke University Press.

2. Book with two or more authors:

Brown, L., Lenssen, N., & Kane, H. (1995). *Vital signs 1995: The trends that are shaping our future.* New York: Norton.

Zelikow, P., & Rice, C. (1995). *Germany unified and Europe transformed: A study in statecraft.* Cambridge, MA: Harvard University Press.

3. Organization as author: When the publisher is the same as the author, use the word "Author" instead of repeating the organization's name as the publisher.

Deutsche Bank, Economics Department. (1991). *Rebuilding eastern Europe.* Frankfurt, Germany: Author.

4. Two or more works by the same author: List the works in publication order, the earliest one first.

Brown, J. F. (1988). *Eastern Europe and communist rule.* Durham, NC: Duke University Press.

Brown, J. F. (1991). *Surge to freedom: The end of communist rule in eastern Europe.* Durham, NC: Duke University Press.

If the works were published in the same year, put them in alphabetical order by title and add a letter (*a, b, c*) to the year so that you can distinguish each entry in your in-text citations; see number 15 for an example related to periodicals.

5. Book with editor(s):   Add (*Ed.*) or (*Eds.*) after the name. If a book lists an author and an editor, treat the editor like a translator (*see number 7*).

Stares, P. B. (Ed.). (1992). *The new Germany and the new Europe.*

Washington, DC: Brookings Institution.

6. Selection in an edited book or anthology: The page numbers of the selection go in parentheses after the book's title.

Kreile, M. (1992). The political economy of the new Germany.

In P. B. Stares (Ed.), *The new Germany and the new Europe*

(pp. 55-92). Washington, DC: Brookings Institution.

7. Translation: After the title of the translation, put the name(s) of the translator(s) in parentheses, followed by the abbreviation *Trans.*

Dostoyevsky, F. (1950). *Crime and Punishment* (C. Garnett, Trans.).

New York: Modern Library. (Original work published 1866)

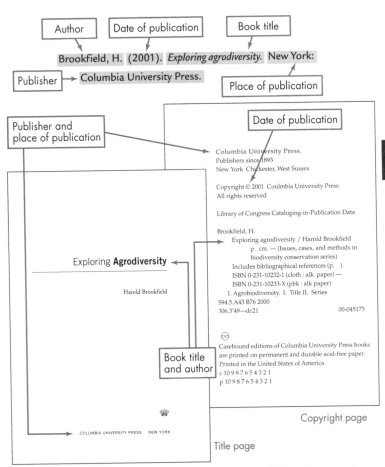

FIGURE 20.1 The elements of an APA reference-list entry: books.
Information for a book citation can be found on the book's title and
copyright pages.

8. Article in a reference work: Begin with the author of the selection, if given. If no author is given, begin with the title of the selection.

Eidson, J. R. (1992). Germans. In *Encyclopedia of world cultures* (Vol. 4,

pp. 121-124). Boston: G. K. Hall.

9. Unknown author or editor: Start with the title. When alphabetizing, use the first important word of the title (excluding articles such as *The, A,* or *An*).

Give me liberty. (1969). New York: World.

10. Second or later edition:

Smyser, W. R. (1993). *The German economy: Colossus at crossroads*

(2nd ed.). New York: St. Martin's Press.

11. One volume of a multivolume work:

Kintner, E. W. (Ed.). (1978). The Clayton Act and amendments.

In *The legislative history of the federal antitrust laws and related*

statutes: The antitrust laws (Vol. 2). New York: Chelsea House.

12. Republished book:

Le Bon, G. (1960). *The crowd: A study of the popular mind.* New York:

Viking. (Original work published 1895)

Note: In-text citations should give both years: "As Le Bon (1895/1960) pointed out. . . ."

Periodicals

Figure 20.2 on page 161 shows where the elements of a reference-list entry for a journal article can be found.

13. Article in a journal paginated by volume: Italicize the title of the periodical and the volume number.

> Arnold, E. (1991). German foreign policy and unification. *International*
>
> *Affairs, 67,* 483-491.

14. Article in a journal paginated by issue: Include the issue number (in parentheses). Notice that the issue number is not italicized as part of the journal's title.

> Lowe, J. H., & Bargas, S. E. (1996). Direct investment positions and
>
> historical-cost basis. *Survey of Current Business, 76*(7), 45-60.

15. Two or more works in one year by the same author: Alphabetize the works by title, and attach a letter to each entry's year of publication, beginning with *a,* then *b,* and so on. In-text citations must use the letter as well as the year so that readers know exactly which work is being cited.

> Agarwal, J. P. (1996a). *Does foreign direct investment contribute to*
>
> *unemployment in home countries?—An empirical survey* (Discussion
>
> Paper No. 765). Kiel, Germany: Institute of World Economics.

Agarwal, J. P. (1996b). Impact of Europe agreements on FDI in

developing countries. *International Journal of Social Economics,*

23(10/11), 150-163.

16. Article in a magazine: After the year, add the month for magazines published monthly or the month and day for magazines published weekly. Note that the volume number is also included.

Klee, K. (1999, December 13). The siege of Seattle. *Newsweek, 134,* 30-35.

17. Article in a newspaper: Use *p.* or *pp.* with the section and page number. List all page numbers, separated by commas, if the article appears on discontinuous pages: *pp. C1, C4, C6.* If there is no identified author, begin with the title of the article.

Andrews, E. L. (1999, February 7). With German craft rules it's hard

just to get work. *The New York Times,* p. A16.

18. Editorial or letter to the editor: In brackets, add to the title a phrase describing the form of the source.

Krugman, P. (2000, July 16). Who's acquiring whom? [Editorial].

The New York Times, Sec. 4, p. 15.

FIGURE 20.2 The elements of an APA reference-list entry: journal articles. In this journal, the information needed for a citation appears on the contents pages and on the first page of an article. Some journals list their contents and publication information on the cover.

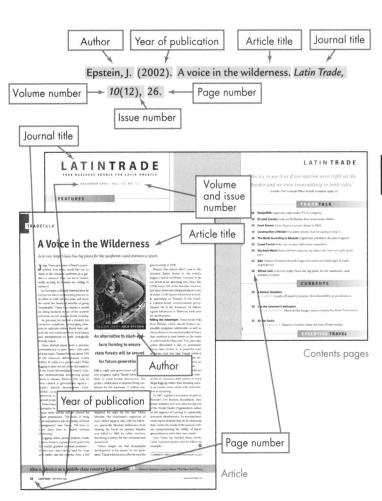

Author · Year of publication · Article title · Journal title

Epstein, J. (2002). A voice in the wilderness. *Latin Trade,*

Volume number · *10*(12), 26. ← Page number

Issue number

Journal title

LATIN TRADE
YOUR BUSINESS SOURCE FOR LATIN AMERICA

DECEMBER 2002 | VOL. 10 NO. 12

FEATURES

Volume and issue number

Article title

LATIN TRADE
We try to see it as if our station were right on the border and we were transmitting to both sides."

TRADE TALK

A Voice in the Wilderness

Acre Gov. Jorge Viana has big plans for the rainforest—and enemies to spare.

An alternative to slash-and-burn farming to ensure state forests will be around for future generation

Article title

Author

Year of publication

Contents pages

Page number

Article

19. Unsigned article: Begin the entry with the title, and alphabetize it by the first important word (excluding articles such as *The, A,* or *An*).

> The biggest anniversary; reflections on a thousand years. (1999,
>
> April 18). *The New York Times Magazine,* 77.

20. Review: If the review is untitled, use a bracketed description in place of a title.

> Bontolft, G. J. (1992). Culture shock in east Germany [Review of the
>
> book *Freedom was never like this: A winter's journey in east Germany*].
>
> *Contemporary Review, 260,* 49-50.

Other Print and Audiovisual Sources

21. Government document: When no author is listed, use the government agency as the author.

> U.S. House Committee on Small Business. (1990). *East Germany's time*
>
> *of crisis.* Washington, D.C.: U.S. Government Printing Office.

22. Report or working paper: If the issuing agency numbered the report, include that number in parentheses after the title.

> Agarwal, J. P. (1996a). *Does foreign direct investment contribute to*
>
> *unemployment in home countries?—An empirical survey* (Discussion
>
> Paper No. 765). Kiel, Germany: Institute of World Economics.

Note: For reports from a deposit service like the *Educational Resources Information Center* (*ERIC*), put the document number in parentheses at the end of the entry.

23. Conference presentation: Treat published conference presentations as a selection in a book (*number 6*), as a periodical article (*numbers 13 or 14*), or as a report (*number 22*), whichever applies. For unpublished conference presentations, provide the author, the year and month of the conference, the title of the presentation, and the presentation's form, forum, and place.

Markusen, J. (1998, June). *The role of multinationals in global economic analysis.* Paper presented at the First Annual Conference in Global Economic Analysis, West Lafayette, IN.

Desantis, R. (1998, June). *Optimal export taxes, welfare, industry concentration and firm size: A general equilibrium analysis.* Poster session presented at the First Annual Conference in Global Economic Analysis, West Lafayette, IN.

24. Unpublished dissertation or dissertation abstract:

Weinbaum, A. E. (1998). Genealogies of "race" and reproduction in transatlantic modern thought (Doctoral dissertation, Columbia University, 1998). *Dissertation Abstracts International, 58,* 229.

If you used the abstract but not the actual dissertation, treat the entry like a periodical article, with *Dissertation Abstracts International* as the periodical.

Weinbaum, A. E. (1998). Genealogies of "race" and reproduction in

transatlantic modern thought. *Dissertation Abstracts International,*

58, 229.

25. Film, DVD, videotape, CD-ROM, or audio recording: Begin with the cited person's name and, if appropriate, a parenthetical notation of his or her role. After the title, identify the medium in brackets, followed by the country and name of the distributor.

Rowling, J. K., Goldenberg, M. (Writers), Yates, D. (Director), & Barron,

D. (Producer). (2007). *Harry Potter and the order of the phoenix* [DVD].

United States: Warner Home Video. (Original release date 2007)

Corigliano, J. (2007). Red violin concerto [Recorded by J. Bell].

Red violin concerto [CD]. New York: Sony Classics.

26. Television program: When citing a single episode, treat the script writer as the author and the producer as the editor of the series.

Weissman, G. (Writer). (2000). Mississippi: River out of control

[Television series episode]. In J. Towers (Producer), *Wrath of God*.

New York: The History Channel.

When citing a whole series or a specific news broadcast, name the producer as author.

Towers, J. (Producer). (2000). *Wrath of God.* New York:

The History Channel.

GUIDELINES for APA ELECTRONIC REFERENCES (from *APA Style Guide to Electronic References* (2007))

Cite online works as you would the same works in another medium, apart from the following considerations:

- Many online journal articles have a Digital Object Identifier (DOI), a unique alphanumeric string. Citations of online documents with DOIs do not require the URL or retrieval date.
- Only include a retrieval date for items that lack a publication date, items that probably will change (such as an in-press article), and reference sources (such as an encyclopedia article).
- Do not include the name of a database or library subscription service in the citation unless the work is only in a few databases or difficult to find in print. If you give the name, omit the URL.
- For online journal articles, always include the issue number.
- Include the URL of the home page for items that require a subscription, appear in reference works, or appear in frames.
- Include the full URL for all other items, except those with a DOI.

Electronic Sources

27. Online article with DOI: If your source has a DOI, include it at the end of the entry; an access date is not needed when a DOI is listed. Always include the issue number. If you found your source via a library database, include the database name only if the source is rare or on just a few databases. If you include the database name, omit the URL.

> Ray, R., Wilhelm, F., & Gross, J. (2008). All in the mind's eye? Anger
>
> rumination and reappraisal. *Journal of Personality and Social*
>
> *Psychology, 94*(1), 133-145. doi:10.1037/0022-3514.94.1.133

28. Online article without DOI: Include the complete URL unless the source is only available via subscription or search, in which case include the home page URL. If your source is not likely to change (such as the final form of a print article), no access date is needed. Always include the issue number. If you found your source via a library database, include the database name only if the source is rare or on just a few databases. If you include the database name, omit the URL.

Journal

> Cook, B. G., & Cook, L. (2004). Bringing science into the classroom
>
> by basing craft on research. *Journal of Learning Disabilities, 37*(3),
>
> 240-247. Retrieved from http://www.ingentaconnect.com/
>
> content/proedcw/jld/2004/00000037/00000003/art00009

Newspaper

> Rohter, L. (2004, December 12). South America seeks to fill the world's
>
> table. *The New York Times.* Retrieved from http://www.nytimes.com

Author, title, and other information about the print version of the article.

Soares-Filho, B., Alencar, A., Nepstad, D., Cerqueira, G., del Carmen
    Vera Diaz, M., Rivero, S., et al. (2004). Simulating the
    response of land-cover changes to road paving and governance
    along a major Amazon highway: the Santarém-Cuiabá corridor.
    Global Change Biology 10(5), 745–764. doi:10.1111/j.1529-
    8817.2003.00769.x

DOI

Author, title, and other information about the print version of the article.

APA

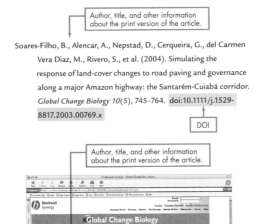

DOI

FIGURE 20.3 The elements of an APA reference-list entry: journal article with DOI.

A citation for the final version of a journal article accessed online does not require a date of access. If the article has a DOI (Digital Object Identifier), the citation does not require a URL. Always include the issue number. Include database information only if the article is rare or available on just a few databases.

29. A Web site document:

Lloyd, J., & Soltani, A. (2001, December). *Report on: Plan Colombia and indigenous peoples.* Retrieved from http://www.amazonwatch.org/ amazon/CO/uwa/reports/plancol_march02.pdf

APA

30. Part of a Web site document:

U.S. Bureau of Oceans and International Environmental and Scientific Affairs. (2007, July 27). Projected greenhouse gas emissions. In *Fourth U.S. climate action report* (chap. 5). Retrieved from http://www.state.gov/documents/organization/89652

31. Online posting to a news group, discussion forum, or mailing list:
Provide the message's author, its date, and the subject line as the title. After the phrase *Message posted to,* give the name of the discussion forum or news group, followed by the address of the message.

Glick, D. (2007, February 10). Bio-char sequestration in terrestrial ecosystems—a review. Message posted to Terra Preta electronic mailing list, archived at http://bioenergylists.org/pipermail/ terrapreta_bioenergylists.org/2007-February/000023.html

32. Computer software:

AllWrite! with Online Handbook. (Version 2.1) (2003). [Software].
New York: McGraw-Hill.

33. Blog posting:

Sulllivan, A. (2007, August 16th). The healthcare debate. Message posted
to http://andrewsullivan.theatlantic.com/the_daily_dish/2007/
week33/index.html

34. Audio podcast:

McDonald, J. (Host). (2008, March 5). *Worldview.* Podcast retrieved
from http://www.npr.org/rss/podcast/podcast_detail.php?siteId
=14537681

35. Online video:

Wesch, M. (2007). The machine is us/ing us [Video file]. Video posted
to http://mediatedcultures.net/ksudigg/?p=84

21 APA style: Paper format

The following guidelines are recommended by the *Publication Manual
of the American Psychological Association,* fifth edition. For sample

pages from a research paper that has been prepared using APA style, see pages 172–75.

Materials. Before printing your paper, make sure that you have stored your final draft on a backup disk. Use a high-quality printer and good white 8½-by-11-inch paper. Choose a standard 11- or 12-point font. Do not justify your text or hyphenate words at the right margin; it should be ragged right.

APA

Title page. The first page of your paper should be a title page. Center the title between the left and right margins in the upper half of the page, and put your name a few lines below the title. Most instructors will also want you to include the course number and title, the instructor's name, and the date. (*See p. 172 for an example.*)

Margins and spacing. Use one-inch margins all around, except for the top right-hand corner, where the page number goes.

Double-space lines throughout the paper, including the abstract (if one is required), within any notes, and in the list of references. Indent the first word of each paragraph one-half inch (or five spaces).

For quotations of more than forty words, use block format and indent five spaces from the left margin. Double-space the quoted lines.

Page numbers and abbreviated titles. All pages, including the title page, should have a number preceded by a short (one- or two-word) version of your title. Put this information in the upper right-hand corner of each page, about one-half inch from the top.

Abstract. Instructors sometimes require an abstract—a 75- to 120-word summary of your paper's thesis, major points, and conclusions.

The abstract appears on its own numbered page, entitled "Abstract," and is placed right after the title page.

Headings. The primary headings should be centered, and all key words in the heading should be capitalized.

Secondary headings should be italicized and should appear flush against the left-hand margin. Do not use a heading for your introduction, however.

Visuals. Place visuals (tables, charts, graphs, and images) close to the place in your text where you refer to them. Label each visual as a table or a figure, and number each kind consecutively (Table 1, Table 2). Provide an informative caption for each visual. Cite the source of the material, preceded by the word *Note* and a period, and provide explanatory notes as needed.

22 Pages from a student paper in APA style

Jennifer Koehler researched and wrote a report on Germany for a course entitled *Business in the Global Environment*. Jennifer consulted a number of online sources in addition to print sources.

www.mhhe.com/wi

For a sample of a complete paper in APA style, go to

Research > Sample Research Papers > APA Style

All pages: short title and page number.

Full title, centered.

Germany's Path to Continuing Prosperity

Jennifer L. Koehler

GLB301 Country Report

Business in the Global Environment

Professor Meznar

November 14, 2001

Germany's Path to Continuing Prosperity

With reunification, Germany faces a major economic challenge. How might a society succeed in combining two completely different economies and cultures bound only by a common language? The German government stepped in to ease the reunification process, but the result was unfortunate: an expensive and intrusive bureaucracy drained Germany's resources and reduced its appeal for corporate investors. A sagging economy followed. Recognizing that its original approaches were not working, Germany decided to pursue a course that would make it more attractive economically. With proper follow-through, the nation can become one of the world's primary sources of direct investment and maintain its status as one of the world's preeminent exporters.

Economic Realities

The German economy is the third largest in the world. Despite this strength, the nation faces a unique problem: how to bring its eastern area up to the western area's standards after forty-five years of Communist rule in the east. According to the *World Factbook,* western Germany accounts for a high percent of overall German GDP and has more per capita income than eastern Germany (Central Intelligence Agency [CIA], 2001).

References

Agarwal, J. P. (1997, April). European integration and German FDI: Implications for domestic investment and central European economies. *National Institute Economic Review.* No. 160.

Bindenagel, J. D. (1997). *Germany—Economic trends.* U.S. Department of Commerce, International Trade Administration. Retrieved November 5, 2001, from DIALOG database. (IT Market IMI970409)

Central Intelligence Agency. (2001). Germany. In *The world factbook.* Retrieved from https://www.cia.gov/library/publications/the-world-factbook/geos/gm.html

Eidson, J. R. (1992). Germans. In *Encyclopedia of world cultures* (Vol. 4, pp. 121-124). Boston: G. K. Hall.

Germany. (1995). In S. P. Parker (Ed.), *World geographical encyclopedia* (Vol. 4, pp. 180-187). New York: McGraw-Hill.

Redman. (1996). *Germany—Balance of payment statistics.* U.S. Department of Commerce, International Trade Administration. Retrieved November 5, 2001, from DIALOG database. (IT Market IM960611.008)

New page, heading centered.

Entries in alphabetical order and double-spaced.

Hanging indent, ½" or 5 spaces.

U.S. Department of State. (2001). *Germany: Economic policy and trade practices, 2000*. Retrieved from http://www.tradeport .org/countries/germany/01grw.html

Nothing gives an author so much pleasure as to find his works respectfully quoted by other learned authors.

—BENJAMIN FRANKLIN

Other
Documentation
Styles

There are many documentation styles besides those developed by the Modern Language Association (*see Part 3*) and the American Psychological Association (*see Part 4*). In this section, we cover the *Chicago Manual* style and the three styles developed by the Council of Science Editors. To find out where you can learn about other style types, consult the list of style manuals on page 85. If you are not sure which style to use, ask your instructor.

**23
Chicago**

www.mhhe.com/
wi
For links to
Web sites for
documentation
styles used in
various
disciplines,
go to
**Research > Links
to Documentation
Sites**

23 Chicago documentation style

The note and bibliography documentation style presented in the fifteenth edition of *The Chicago Manual of Style* (Chicago: University of Chicago Press, 2003) is used in many disciplines, including history, art, philosophy, business, and communications. The Chicago style has three parts:

- Numbered in-text citations
- Numbered footnotes or endnotes
- A bibliography of works consulted

The first two parts are necessary; the third is optional, unless your instructor requires it. For more information on Chicago style, consult

Chicago Chicago Chicago

the *Manual of Style* or go to the University of Chicago Press's Web site at <http://www.Press.uchicago.edu> and click on "*Chicago Manual of Style* Web site."

23a Using numbered in-text citations and notes

Whenever you use information or ideas from a source, indicate what you have borrowed by putting a superscript number in the text ([1]) at the end of the borrowed material. These superscript numbers are placed after all punctuation marks except for the dash.

> As Bergreen points out, Armstrong easily reached difficult high notes, the F's and G's that stymied other trumpeters.[3] And his innovative singing style featured "scat," a technique that combines "nonsense syllables [with] improvised melodies."[4]

Each in-text superscript number must have a corresponding note either at the foot of the page or at the end of the text. Footnotes begin with the number and are single-spaced, with a double space between notes.

If you are using endnotes instead of footnotes, they should begin after the last page of your text on a new numbered page entitled "Notes." Single-space within and double-space between endnotes.

The first time a source is cited in either a footnote or an endnote, include a full citation. Subsequent citations require only the author's name and a page number.

FIRST REFERENCE TO A SOURCE

    3. Laurence Bergreen, *Louis Armstrong: An Extravagant Life* (New York: Broadway Books, 1997), 248.

ENTRY FOR A SOURCE ALREADY CITED

    6. Bergreen, 370.

If the previous reference to this source was several pages ago, include a brief version of the title for clarity.

ENTRY FOR A SOURCE CITED SEVERAL PAGES AGO

    7. Bergreen, *Louis Armstrong,* 370.

If you provide a full footnote for a source and then immediately cite that source again, use the abbreviation *Ibid.* (Latin for "in the same place") and the page number.

    8. Ibid., 370.

23b Preparing a separate bibliography

Some instructors require a separate list of works cited or of works consulted. If you are asked to provide a works-cited list, then do so on a separate, numbered page that has the title "Works Cited." If the list is supposed to include works consulted as well as cited, then title it "Bibliography."

    Bergreen, Laurence. *Louis Armstrong: An Extravagant Life.* New York: Broadway Books, 1997.

www.mhhe.com/
wi
To download
Bibliomaker
software for
Chicago style,
go to
Research >
Bibliomaker

GENERAL GUIDELINES for a BIBLIOGRAPHY or a WORKS-CITED LIST in CHICAGO STYLE

1. Begin on a new page.
2. Begin with the centered title "Works Cited" if you are including only works referred to in your paper. Use the title "Bibliography" if you are including every work you consulted.
3. List sources alphabetically by author's (or editor's) last name.
4. Capitalize the first and last words in titles as well as all important words and words that follow colons.
5. Use a hanging indent: Indent all lines of the entry except the first five spaces, using your word processor's hanging indent function.
6. Use periods between author and title as well as between title and publication data.
7. Single-space each entry; double-space between entries.

23c Using the correct Chicago style for notes and bibliography entries

Chicago Style:
Directory to Sample Note and Bibliography Entries

Print Books
1. Book with one author 182
2. Multiple works by the same author 182
3. Book with two or more authors 183
4. Book with an author and an editor or a translator 183

23c
Chicago

Chicago Chicago Chicago Chicago Chicago

23c
Chicago

Print Books
1. Book with one author:

NOTE

1. James Lincoln Collier, *Louis Armstrong, an American Genius* (New York: Oxford University Press, 1983), 82.

BIBLIOGRAPHY ENTRY

Collier, James Lincoln. *Louis Armstrong, an American Genius.* New York: Oxford University Press, 1983.

2. Multiple works by the same author: After providing complete information in the first footnote, include only a shortened version of the title with the author's last name and the page number in any subsequent footnote. In the bibliography, list entries in either alphabetical order by title or chronological order from earliest to latest. After the first listing, replace the author's name with a "3-em" dash (type three dashes in a row).

NOTES

7. Collier, *Jazz,* 154.
12. Collier, *Louis Armstrong,* 32.

BIBLIOGRAPHY ENTRIES

Collier, James Lincoln. *Jazz: The American Theme Song.* New York: Oxford University Press, 1993.

———. *Louis Armstrong, An American Genius.* New York: Oxford University Press, 1983.

3. Book with two or more authors: In notes, you can name up to three authors. When there are three authors, put a comma after the first name and a comma plus *and* after the second.

NOTE

2. Miles Davis and Quincy Troupe, *Miles: The Autobiography* (New York: Simon & Schuster, 1989), 15.

BIBLIOGRAPHY ENTRY

Davis, Miles, and Quincy Troupe. *Miles: The Autobiography.* New York: Simon & Schuster, 1989.

When more than three authors are listed on the title page, use *and others* or *et al.* after the first author's name in the note.

NOTE

3. Julian Henriques and others, *Changing the Subject: Psychology, Social Regulation, and Subjectivity* (New York: Methuen, 1984), 275.

BIBLIOGRAPHY ENTRY

Henriques, Julian, Wendy Holloway, Cathy Urwin, Couze Venn, and Valerie Walkerdine. *Changing the Subject: Psychology, Social Regulation, and Subjectivity.* New York: Methuen, 1984.

Notice that *and others* or *et al.* is not used in bibliography entries, even when a book has more than three authors.

4. Book with an author and an editor or a translator: Put the author's name first and add the editor's (*ed.*) or translator's (*trans.*) name after the title.

NOTE

    4. Louis Armstrong, *Louis Armstrong--A Self-Portrait,* ed. Richard Meryman (New York: Eakins Press, 1971), 54.

BIBLIOGRAPHY ENTRIES

Armstrong, Louis. *Louis Armstrong--A Self-Portrait.* Edited by Richard Meryman. New York: Eakins Press, 1971.

Goffin, Robert. *Horn of Plenty: The Story of Louis Armstrong.* Translated by James F. Bezov. New York: Da Capo Press, 1977.

5. Book with editor(s):

NOTE

    5. Paul Eduard Miller, ed., *Esquire's Jazz Book* (New York: Smith & Durrell, 1944), 31.

BIBLIOGRAPHY ENTRY

Miller, Paul Eduard, ed. *Esquire's Jazz Book.* New York: Smith & Durrell, 1944.

6. Organization as author:

NOTE

    6. Centre for Contemporary Cultural Studies, *Making Histories: Studies in History Writing and Politics* (London: Hutchinson, 1982), 10.

BIBLIOGRAPHY ENTRY

Centre for Contemporary Cultural Studies. *Making Histories: Studies in History Writing and Politics.* London: Hutchinson, 1982.

7. Work in an anthology or part of an edited book: Begin with the author and title of the specific work or part.

NOTES

     7. Hale Smith, "Here I Stand," in *Readings in Black American Music,* ed. Eileen Southern (New York: Norton, 1971), 287.

     8. Richard Crawford, foreword to *The Jazz Tradition,* by Martin Williams (New York: Oxford University Press, 1993).

BIBLIOGRAPHY ENTRIES

Smith, Hale. "Here I Stand." In *Readings in Black American Music,* edited by Eileen Southern, 286-89. New York: W. W. Norton, 1971.

Crawford, Richard. Foreword to *The Jazz Tradition,* by Martin Williams. New York: Oxford University Press, 1993.

In notes, descriptive terms such as *foreword* and *introduction* are not capitalized. In bibliography entries, descriptive terms *are* capitalized.

8. Letter in a published collection:

NOTE

     9. Langston Hughes to Arna Bontemps, 17 January 1938, in *Arna Bontemps--Langston Hughes Letters 1925-1967,* ed. Charles H. Nichols (New York: Dodd, Mead, 1980), 27-28.

BIBLIOGRAPHY ENTRY

Hughes, Langston. Langston Hughes to Arna Bontemps, 17 January 1938. In *Arna Bontemps--Langston Hughes Letters 1925-1967,* edited by Charles H. Nichols, 27-28. New York: Dodd, Mead, 1980.

9. Article in an encyclopedia or a dictionary: For well-known reference works, publication data can be omitted from a note, but the edition or copyright date should be included. There is no need to include page numbers for entries in reference works that are arranged alphabetically; the abbreviation *s.v.* (meaning "under the word") plus the entry's title can be used instead.

NOTES

10. J. Bradford Robinson, "Scat Singing," in *The New Grove Dictionary of Jazz* (2002).

11. *Encyclopedia Britannica,* 15th ed., s.v. "Jazz."

Reference works are not listed in the bibliography unless they are unusual or crucial to your paper.

BIBLIOGRAPHY ENTRY

Robinson, J. Bradford. "Scat Singing." In *The New Grove Dictionary of Jazz.* Edited by Barry Kernfeld. Vol. 3. London: Macmillan, 2002.

10. Sacred works: Abbreviate the name of the book, and use arabic numbers for chapter and verse. Name the version cited only if it matters. It is not necessary to include the Bible in your bibliography.

NOTE

12. Eccles. 8.5 (Jerusalem Bible).

11. Edition other than the first: Include the number of the edition after the title or, if there is an editor, after that person's name.

NOTE

13. Hugues Panassie, *Louis Armstrong,* 2d ed. (New York: Da Capo Press, 1980), 12.

BIBLIOGRAPHY ENTRY

Panassie, Hugues. *Louis Armstrong.* 2d ed. New York: Da Capo Press, 1980.

12. Multivolume work: Put the volume number, followed by a colon, before the page number.

NOTE

14. Robert Lissauer, *Lissauer's Encyclopedia of Popular Music in America* (New York: Facts on File, 1996), 2:33-34.

BIBLIOGRAPHY ENTRY

Lissauer, Robert. *Lissauer's Encyclopedia of Popular Music in America.* Vol. 2. New York: Facts on File, 1996.

13. Work in a series: Include the name of the series as well as the book's series number.

NOTE

15. Samuel A. Floyd, ed., *Black Music in the Harlem Renaissance,*
Contributions in Afro-American and African Studies, no. 128
(New York: Greenwood Press, 1990), 2.

BIBLIOGRAPHY ENTRY

Floyd, Samuel A., ed. *Black Music in the Harlem Renaissance.*
    Contributions in Afro-American and African Studies, no. 128.
    New York: Greenwood Press, 1990.

14. Unknown author: Cite anonymous works by title and alphabetize them by the first word, ignoring *A, An,* or *The.*

NOTE

16. *The British Album* (London: John Bell, 1790), 2:43-47.

BIBLIOGRAPHY ENTRY

The British Album. Vol. 2. London: John Bell, 1790.

Print Periodicals
15. Article in a journal paginated by volume: When journals
are paginated by yearly volume, your citation should include the following: author, title of article in quotation marks, title of journal, volume number and year, page number(s).

NOTE

17. Frank Tirro, "Constructive Elements in Jazz Improvisation,"
Journal of the American Musicological Society 27 (1974): 300.

BIBLIOGRAPHY ENTRY

Tirro, Frank. "Constructive Elements in Jazz Improvisation." *Journal of the American Musicological Society* 27 (1974): 285-305.

16. Article in a journal paginated by issue: If the periodical is paginated by issue rather than by volume, add the issue number, preceded by the abbreviation *no.*

NOTE

18. Sarah Appleton Aguiar, "'Everywhere and Nowhere': *Beloved*'s 'Wild' Legacy in Toni Morrison's *Jazz*," *Notes on Contemporary Literature* 25, no. 4 (1995): 11.

BIBLIOGRAPHY ENTRY

Aguiar, Sarah Appleton. "'Everywhere and Nowhere': *Beloved*'s 'Wild' Legacy in Toni Morrison's *Jazz*." *Notes on Contemporary Literature* 25, no. 4 (1995): 11-12.

17. Article in a magazine: Identify magazines by week (if available) and month of publication.

NOTE

19. Malcolm Walker, "Discography: Bill Evans," *Jazz Monthly,* June 1965, 22.

BIBLIOGRAPHY ENTRY

Walker, Malcolm. "Discography: Bill Evans." *Jazz Monthly,* June 1965, 20-22.

If the article cited does not appear on consecutive pages, do not put any page numbers in the bibliography entry. You can, however, give specific pages in the note.

NOTE

20. J. R. Taylor, "Jazz History: The Incompleted Past," *Village Voice,* July 3, 1978, 65.

BIBLIOGRAPHY ENTRY

Taylor, J. R. "Jazz History: The Incompleted Past." *Village Voice,* July 3, 1978.

18. Article in a newspaper: Give the section number or title if it is indicated but not the page number. Indicate the edition (for example, *national edition*) before the section number, if applicable.

NOTE

21. Ralph Blumenthal, "Satchmo with His Tape Recorder Running," *New York Times,* August 3, 1999, sec. E.

BIBLIOGRAPHY ENTRY

Blumenthal, Ralph. "Satchmo with His Tape Recorder Running." *New York Times,* August 3, 1999, sec. E.

19. Article with an unknown author: Begin with the title of the periodical, treated as the author.

NOTE

22. *Life,* "Squaresville, U.S.A. vs. Beatsville," September 21, 1959, 31.

BIBLIOGRAPHY ENTRY

Life, "Squaresville, U.S.A. vs. Beatsville," September 21, 1959, 31.

20. Review:

NOTE

23. David Ostwald, "All That Jazz," review of *Louis Armstrong: An Extravagant Life,* by Laurence Bergreen, *Commentary,* November 1997, 72.

BIBLIOGRAPHY ENTRY

Ostwald, David. "All That Jazz." Review of *Louis Armstrong: An Extravagant Life,* by Laurence Bergreen. *Commentary,* November 1997, 68-72.

21. Published interview: Start with the name of the person interviewed.

NOTE

24. Louis Armstrong, "Authentic American Genius," interview by Richard Meryman, *Life,* April 15, 1966, 92.

BIBLIOGRAPHY ENTRY

Armstrong, Louis. "Authentic American Genius." Interview by Richard Meryman. *Life,* April 15, 1966, 92-102.

Online Books and Periodicals   For periodical articles accessed online or through a database, provide page numbers if they are available. If page numbers are not available, you have the option of including an alternate marker such as a paragraph number or a heading. You do not need to provide dates of access unless the site is frequently updated. Dates of access are required for books.

22. Online book:

NOTE

25. Carl Sandburg, *Chicago Poems* (New York: Henry Holt, 1916), http://www.bartleby.com/165/index.html (accessed May 3, 2005).

BIBLIOGRAPHY ENTRY

Sandburg, Carl. *Chicago Poems.* New York: Henry Holt, 1916. http://www.bartleby.com/165/index.html (accessed May 3, 2005).

23. Online journal article:

NOTE

26. Janet Schmalfeldt, "On Keeping the Score," *Music Theory Online* 4, no. 2 (1998), http://smt.ucsb.edu/mto/issues/mto.98.4.2.schmalfeldt.html.

BIBLIOGRAPHY ENTRY

Schmalfeldt, Janet. "On Keeping the Score." *Music Theory Online* 4, no. 2 (1998). http://smt.ucsb.edu/mto/issues/mto.98.4.2.schmalfeldt.html.

24. Online magazine or newspaper article:

NOTES

27. Michael E. Ross, "The New Sultans of Swing," *Salon,* April 18, 1996, http://www.salon.com/weekly/music1.html.

28. Don Heckman, "Jazz, Pop in Spirited Harmony," *Los Angeles Times,* August 10, 2005, http://www.calendarlive.com/music/jazz/cl-et-hancock10aug10,0,7414710.story?coll=cl-home-more-channels (accessed August 12, 2005).

The site is frequently updated, so the access date is included.

BIBLIOGRAPHY ENTRIES

Ross, Michael E. "The New Sultans of Swing." *Salon,* April 18, 1996. http://www.salon.com/weekly/music1.html.

Heckman, Don. "Jazz, Pop in Spirited Harmony." *Los Angeles Times,* August 10, 2005. http://www.calendarlive.com/music/jazz/cl-et-hancock10aug10,0,7414710.story ?coll=cl-home-more-channels (accessed August 12, 2005).

25. Article from an online subscription service:

NOTE

29. Richard Hardack, " 'A Music Seeking Its Words': Double-Timing and Double Consciousness in Toni Morrison's *Jazz," Callaloo* 18 (1995): 453, http://web7.infotrac.galegroup.com.

**23c
Chicago**

BIBLIOGRAPHY ENTRY

Hardack, Richard. "'A Music Seeking Its Words': Double-Timing
and Double Consciousness in Toni Morrison's *Jazz*." *Callaloo* 18
(1995): 451-72. http://web7.infotrac.galegroup.com.

Web Sites and Other Online Resources

Identify as many of the following items as you can: author, title, sponsor, and URL.

26. Web site:

NOTE

30. Kevin Walsh, *Forgotten NY,* http://www.forgotten-ny.com/.

BIBLIOGRAPHY ENTRY

Walsh, Kevin. *Forgotten NY.* http://www.forgotten-ny.com/.

27. Document from a Web site:
Include the author, the title of
the document in quotation marks, the title of the site (in italics), the
sponsor's name, and the URL. If no author is given, treat the sponsor
of the site as the author.

NOTE

31. UNICEF, "Children Living in Poverty," *Childhood under Threat:
The State of the World's Children 2005,* http://www.unicef.org/sow05/
english/poverty.html.

BIBLIOGRAPHY ENTRY

UNICEF. "Children Living in Poverty." *Childhood under Threat: The State of the World's Children 2005.* http://www.unicef.org/sow05/english/ poverty.html.

28. Posting to an online forum: Include the URL for postings that readers can access in an archive. Do not include an online posting in your bibliography.

     32. Don Mopsick, posting to Big Band Music Fans discussion list, March 17, 2000, http://www.remarq.com/list/4755?nav+FIRST&rf+ 1&si+grou.

29. E-mail: Include a note for an e-mail, but do not include an entry in your bibliography.

     33. Anna Morgan, e-mail to author, August 10, 2005.

Other Sources
30. Government document: If it is not already obvious in your text, name the country first.

NOTE

     34. Bureau of National Affairs, *The Civil Rights Act of 1964: Text, Analysis, Legislative History; What It Means to Employers, Businessmen, Unions, Employees, Minority Groups* (Washington, DC: BNA, 1964), 22-23.

BIBLIOGRAPHY ENTRY

U.S. Bureau of National Affairs. *The Civil Rights Act of 1964: Text, Analysis, Legislative History; What It Means to Employers, Businessmen, Unions, Employees, Minority Groups.* Washington, DC: BNA, 1964.

31. Unpublished dissertation or document: Include a description of the document as well as information about where it is available.

NOTES

    35. Adelaida Reyes-Schramm, "The Role of Music in the Interaction of Black Americans and Hispanos in New York City's East Harlem" (PhD diss., Columbia University, 1975), 34-37.

    36. Joe Glaser to Lucille Armstrong, 28 September 1960, Louis Armstrong Archives, Rosenthal Library, Queens College CUNY, Flushing, NY.

BIBLIOGRAPHY ENTRIES

Reyes-Schramm, Adelaida. "The Role of Music in the Interaction of Black Americans and Hispanos in New York City's East Harlem." PhD diss., Columbia University, 1975.

Glaser, Joe. Letter to Lucille Armstrong. Louis Armstrong Archives. Rosenthal Library, Queens College CUNY, Flushing, NY.

32. Unpublished interview: Note the nonprint medium (tape recording, video). Only interviews accessible to your readers are listed in the bibliography (*see number 21*).

NOTE

37. Michael Cogswell, interview by author, tape recording, Louis Armstrong Archives, Queens College CUNY, Flushing, N.Y., March 11, 2001.

33. Source quoted in another source:

NOTE

38. James Fallows, "The Invisible Poor," *New York Times Magazine,* March 19, 2000. Quoted in Barbara Ehrenreich, *Nickel and Dimed: On (Not) Getting By in America* (New York: Henry Holt, 2001), 216.

BIBLIOGRAPHY ENTRY

Fallows, James. "The Invisible Poor." *New York Times Magazine,* March 19, 2000. Quoted in Barbara Ehrenreich, *Nickel and Dimed: On (Not) Getting By in America* (New York: Henry Holt, 2001), 216.

34. Musical score or composition: Treat a published score as a book, and include it in the bibliography.

NOTE

39. Franz Josef Haydn, *Symphony No. 94 in G Major,* ed. H. C. Robbins Landon (Salzburg: Haydn-Mozart Press, 1965), 22.

BIBLIOGRAPHY ENTRY

Haydn, Franz Josef. *Symphony No. 94 in G Major.* Edited by H. C. Robbins Landon. Salzburg: Haydn-Mozart Press, 1965.

For a musical composition, give the composer's name, followed by the title of the work. Put the title in italics unless it names an instrumental work known only by its form, number, and key.

NOTES

40. Duke Ellington. *Satin Doll.*
41. Franz Josef Haydn, Symphony no. 94 in G Major.

35. DVD or videocassette: Provide the original date of release before the publication information if the DVD or videocassette was released in a different year than the theatrical release.

NOTE

42. *Three Kings,* DVD, directed by David O. Russell (1999; Burbank, CA: Warner Home Video, 2000).

BIBLIOGRAPHY ENTRY

Three Kings. DVD. Directed by David O. Russell. 1999; Burbank, CA: Warner Home Video, 2000.

36. Sound recording: Begin with the composer or other person responsible for the content.

NOTE

43. Louis Armstrong, *Town Hall Concert Plus,* RCA INTS 5070.

BIBLIOGRAPHY ENTRY

Armstrong, Louis. *Town Hall Concert Plus.* RCA INTS 5070.

37. Artwork: Begin with the artist's name, and include both the name and location of the institution holding the work. Works of art are usually not included in the bibliography.

NOTE

44. Herman Leonard, *Louis Armstrong: Birdland,* black-and-white photograph, 1956, Barbara Gillman Gallery, Miami.

38. Performance: Begin with the author, director, or performer—whoever is most relevant to your study.

NOTE

45. Terrence McNally, Lynn Athrens, and Stephen Flaherty, *Ragtime,* dir. Frank Galati, Ford Performing Arts Center, New York, November 11, 1998.

BIBLIOGRAPHY ENTRY

McNally, Terrence, Lynn Athrens, and Stephen Flaherty. *Ragtime.*
    Directed by Frank Galati. Ford Performing Arts Center, New York,
    November 11, 1998.

39. CD-ROM or other electronic non-Internet source:

NOTE

46. *Microsoft Encarta Multimedia Encyclopedia,* s.v. "Armstrong, (Daniel) Louis 'Satchmo' " (Redmond, WA: Microsoft, 1994), CD-ROM.

BIBLIOGRAPHY ENTRY

Microsoft Encarta Multimedia Encyclopedia. "Armstrong, (Daniel) Louis
'Satchmo.' " Redmond, WA: Microsoft, 1994, CD-ROM.

23d Sample pages from a student paper in Chicago style

www.mhhe.com/
wi

For a sample
of a complete
paper in
Chicago style,
go to
Research >
Sample Research
Papers > CMS
Style

The following excerpt from Esther Hoffman's paper on Louis Armstrong has been put into Chicago style so that you can see how citation
numbers, endnotes, and bibliography work together.

Chicago style allows you the option of including a title page. If you
do provide a title page, count it as page 1, but do not include the number on the page. Put page numbers in the upper right-hand corner of
the remaining pages, except for the pages with the titles "Notes" and
"Bibliography" or "Works Cited"; on these pages, the number should be
centered at the bottom of the page.

In the 1920s, jazz music was at its height in creativity and popularity. Chicago had become one of the jazz capitals of America, and its clubs showcased the premier talents of the time, performers like Jelly Roll Morton and Joe Oliver. It has always been difficult to break into the music business, and the jazz scene of the twenties was no exception. Eager for fame and fortune, though, many young black musicians who had honed their craft in New Orleans migrated north to Chicago, hoping for a chance to perform with the best.[1]

Among these emigres was Louis Armstrong, a gifted musician who developed into the "first true virtuoso soloist of jazz."[2] Armstrong played the trumpet and sang with unusual improvisational ability as well as technical mastery. As Bergreen points out, he easily reached difficult high notes, the F's and G's that stymied other trumpeters.[3] And his innovative singing style featured "scat," a technique that combines "nonsense syllables [with] improvised melodies."[4] Eventually, Armstrong's innovations became the standard, as more and more jazz musicians took their cue from his style.

Armstrong's beginnings give no hint of the greatness that he would achieve. In New Orleans, he was born into poverty and received little formal education. As a youngster, Armstrong had to

Notes

1. R. D. Frederick, ed., "Chicago; Early 1920s," *Wolverine Antique Music Society,* http://www.shellac.org/wams/wchicag1.html.

2. *Microsoft Encarta Multimedia Encyclopedia,* s.v. "Armstrong, (Daniel) Louis 'Satchmo' " (Redmond, WA: Microsoft, 1994), CD-ROM.

3. Laurence Bergreen, *Louis Armstrong: An Extravagant Life* (New York: Broadway Books, 1997), 248.

4. J. Bradford Robinson, "Scat Singing," in *The New Grove Dictionary of Jazz* (2002).

Bibliography

Armstrong, Louis. "Authentic American Genius." Interview by Richard Meryman. *Life,* April 15, 1966, 92-102.

——. Louis Armstrong Archives, Rosenthal Library, Queens College CUNY, Flushing, NY

——. *Town Hall Concert Plus.* RCA INTS 5070.

Bergreen, Laurence. *Louis Armstrong: An Extravagant Life.* New York: Broadway Books, 1997.

Bogle, Donald. "Louis Armstrong: The Films." In *Louis Armstrong: A Cultural Legacy,* ed. Marc H. Miller, 147-79. Seattle: University of Washington Press and Queens Museum of Art, 1994.

Collier, James Lincoln. *Jazz: The American Theme Song.* New York: Oxford University Press, 1993.

——. *Louis Armstrong, an American Genius.* New York: Oxford University Press, 1983.

Crawford, Richard. Foreword to *The Jazz Tradition,* by Martin Williams. New York: Oxford University Press, 1993.

Davis, Miles, and Quincy Troupe. *Miles: The Autobiography.* New York: Simon & Schuster, 1989.

Frederick, R. D., ed. "Chicago; Early 1920s." *Wolverine Antique Music Society.* http://www.shellac.org/wams/wchicag1.html.

Writer includes *all* sources she consulted, not just those she cited in the body of her paper.

12

The Council of Science Editors (CSE) endorses three documentation styles in the seventh edition of *Scientific Style and Format: The CSE Manual for Authors, Editors, and Publishers* (Reston, VA: CSE, 2006):

- The **name-year style** includes the last name of the author and year of publication in the text. In the list of references, sources are in alphabetical order and unnumbered.

- The **citation-sequence style** includes a superscript number or a number in parentheses in the text. In the list of references, sources are numbered and appear in order of citation.

- The **citation-name style** also uses a superscript number or a number in parentheses in the text. In the list of references, however, sources are numbered and arranged in alphabetical order.

24a In-text citations

Name-year style.   Include the author's last name, the year of publication, and if you are citing a particular passage, the page number(s).

According to Gleeson (1993), a woman loses 35% of cortical bone and 50% of trabecular bone during her lifetime.

Osteoporosis has been defined as "a disease characterized by low bone mass, micro-architectural deterioration of bone tissue, leading to enhanced bone fragility and a consequent increase in fracture risk" (Johnston 1996; p. 30S).

Citation-sequence or citation-name. Insert a superscript number immediately after the relevant name, word, or phrase; and before any punctuation.

> As a group, American women over 45 years of age sustain approximately
>
> 1 million fractures each year, 70% of which are due to osteoporosis.[1]

That number now belongs to that source, and you should use it if you refer to that source again later in your paper.

> According to Gleeson [6], a woman loses 35% of cortical bone and 50%
>
> of trabecular bone over her lifetime.

Credit more than one source at a time by referring to each source's number. If the numbers are not in sequence, separate them with a comma.

> According to studies by Yomo [2], Paleg [3], and others [1,4], barley seed embryos
>
> produce a substance which stimulates the release of hydrolytic enzymes.

If more than two numbers are in sequence, separate them with a hyphen.

> As several others [1-4] have noted, GA has an RNA-enhancing effect.

24b List of references

Every source cited in your paper must correspond to an entry in the references list, which should be prepared according to the guidelines on page 207:

Books and Reports In *name-year style,* include the author(s), last name first; publication year; title; place; and publisher. In *citation-*

sequence or *citation-name style,* include the same information but put the year after the publisher.

1. Book with one author: The number of pages is optional.

NAME-YEAR

Bailey C. 1991. The new fit or fat. Boston (MA): Houghton Mifflin, 167 p.

CITATION-SEQUENCE OR CITATION-NAME

1. Bailey C. The new fit or fat. Boston (MA): Houghton Mifflin; 1991.

CSE LIST of REFERENCES

- Begin on a new page after your text but before any appendices, tables, and figures. Use the centered title "References."
- Include only references that are cited in your paper.
- Start with the author's last name, followed by initials for first and middle names. Add no spaces or periods between initials.
- Abbreviate periodical titles and capitalize major words.
- Use complete book or article titles; capitalize the first word and any proper nouns or proper adjectives.
- Do not use italics, underlining, or quotation marks for titles.
- List the number of pages or screens at the end of the entry if your instructor requires it (see entry 1 on p. 206).

Name-year style:
  * Put the date after the author's name.
  * List the references in alphabetical order, but do not number them.

Citation-sequence style:
  * Put the date after the name of the book publisher or periodical.
  * List and number the references in the order they first appear in the text.

Citation-name style:
  * Put the date after the name of the book publisher or periodical.
  * List and number the references in alphabetical order. Make the numbering of your in-text citations match.

2. Two or more authors: Up to ten authors can be individually listed; if there are more than ten, use the first ten author names with the phrase *et al* (meaning "and others").

NAME-YEAR

Begon M, Harper JL, Townsend CR. 1990. Ecology: individuals, populations, and communities. 2nd ed. Boston (MA): Blackwell.

CITATION-SEQUENCE OR CITATION-NAME

2. Begon M, Harper JL, Townsend CR. Ecology: Individuals, populations, and communities. 2nd ed. Boston (MA): Blackwell; 1990.

3. Book with organization as author: In name-year style, start the entry with the organization's abbreviation but alphabetize the entry by the full name.

NAME-YEAR

[NIH] National Institutes of Health (US). 1993. Clinical trials supported by the National Eye Institute: celebrating vision research. Bethesda (MD): US Department of Health and Human Services.

CITATION-SEQUENCE OR CITATION-NAME

3. National Institutes of Health (US). Clinical trials supported by the National Eye Institute: celebrating vision research. Bethesda (MD): US Department of Health and Human Services; 1993.

4. Chapter in a book:

NAME-YEAR

O'Connell C. 2007. The elephant's secret sense: the hidden life of the wild herds of Africa. New York (NY) : Free Press. Chapter 9, Cracking elephant Morse code; p. 119-126.

CITATION-SEQUENCE OR CITATION NAME

4. O'Connell C. The elephant's secret sense: the hidden life of the wild herds of Africa. New York (NY): Free Press; 2007. Chapter 9, Cracking elephant Morse code; p. 119-126.

5. Book with editor(s):

NAME-YEAR

Wilder E, editor. 1988. Obstetric and gynecologic physical therapy. New York (NY): Churchill Livingstone.

CITATION-SEQUENCE OR CITATION NAME

5. Wilder E, editor. Obstetric and gynecologic physical therapy. New York (NY): Churchill Livingstone; 1988.

6. Selection in an edited book:

NAME-YEAR

Bohus B, Koolhaas JM. 1993. Psychoimmunology of social factors in rodents and other subprimate vertebrates. In: Ader R, Felten DL, Cohen N, editors. Psychoneuroimmunology. San Diego (CA): Academic Press p. 807-830.

CITATION-SEQUENCE OR CITATION NAME

6. Bohus B, Koolhaas JM. Psychoimmunology of social factors in
    rodents and other subprimate vertebrates. In: Ader R, Felten DL,
    Cohen N, editors. Psychoneuroimmunology. San Diego (CA):
    Academic Press;1993. p. 807-830.

Periodicals   Include the author(s); year; title of article; title of
journal (abbreviated); number of the volume, number of the issue;
page numbers, if available (in parentheses). The year goes after the
author(s) in *name-year style* and after the journal title in *citation-
sequence* or *citation-name style*. If you cannot determine the author,
begin with the title.

Note: As with books, up to ten authors can be listed by name.

7. Article in a journal that uses only volume numbers:

NAME-YEAR

Devine A, Prince RL, Bell R. 1996. Nutritional effect of calcium
supplementation by skim milk powder or calcium tablets on total
nutrient intake in postmenopausal women. Am J Clin Nutr. 64: 731-737.

CITATION-SEQUENCE OR CITATION-NAME

7. Devine A, Prince RL, Bell R. Nutritional effect of calcium
    supplementation by skim milk powder or calcium tablets on
    total nutrient intake in postmenopausal women. Am J Clin
    Nutr. 1996;64:731-737.

Books and Reports
1. One author:

1. Bailey C. The new fit or fat. Boston: Houghton Mifflin; 1991. 167 p.

2. Two or more authors: Up to ten authors can be individually listed; if there are more than ten, use the first author's name with the phrase *and others*.

2. Begon M, Harper JL, Townsend CR. Ecology: Individuals, populations, and communities. 2nd ed. Boston: Blackwell; 1990. 945 p.

3. Organization as author:

3. National Institutes of Health. Clinical trials supported by the National Eye Institute: celebrating vision research. Bethesda (MD): US Dept. of Health and Human Services; 1993. 112 p.

4. Chapter in a book: Note that the author of the chapter and the book are the same. Consult number 6 below when the authors are not the same person.

4. Castro J. The American way of health: how medicine is changing and what it means to you. Boston: Little, Brown; 1994. Chapter 9, Why doctors, hospitals, and drugs cost so much; p 131-53.

5. Book with editor(s):

5. Ader R, Felten DL, Cohen N, editors. Psychoneuroimmunology. San Diego (CA): Academic Pr; 1993. 1218 p.

- List the publisher or [publisher unknown].
- To include extent for a document without page numbers, use designations such as [16 paragraphs] or [4 screens].
- List the URL at the end of the reference.
- List a Digital Object Identifier (DOI) after the URL.

These examples are in the citation-sequence or citation-name style. For name-year style, list the publication date after the author's name.

10. Online journal article: This article has a DOI.

10. Shah NP, Tran C, Lee FY, Chen P, Norris D, Sawyers CL. Overriding imatinib resistance with a novel ABL kinase inhibitor. Science [Internet]. 2004 [cited 2008 Apr 22];305(5682):399-401. Available from: http://www.sciencemag.org/cgi/content/full/ 305/5682/399 doi:10.1126/science.1099480

11. Online book (monograph):

11. Kohn LT, Corrigan JM, Donaldson MS, editors. To err is human: building a safer health system [Internet]. Washington (DC): National Academy Press; 2000 [cited 2007 Oct 19]. Available from: http://www.nap.edu/books/0309068371/html

12. Material from a Web site:

12. Hutchinson JR. Vertebrate flight [Internet]. Berkeley (CA): University of California; c1994-2008. [modified 2005 Sep 29; cited 2008 Jan 15]. Available from: http://www.ucmp.berkeley.edu/vertebrates/flight/ flightintro.html

13. Material from a library or subscription database: CSE does not specify a format. This model gives the information for a print article, with database title, publication information, and URL.

13. Baccarelli A, Zanobetti A, Martinelli I, Grillo P, Lifang H, Lanzani G, Mannucci PM, Bertazzi PA, Schwartz, J. Air pollution, smoking, and plasma homocysteine. Environ Health Perspect. [Internet]. 2007 [cited 2007 Oct 23];115(2):176-181. Health Source: Nursing/ Academic Edition. Birmingham (AL): EBSCO. Available from: http://search.ebscohost.com

24c Sample references list: CSE name-year system

References

Anderson A. 1991. Early bird threatens archaeopteryx's perch. Science. 253(5015):35.

Goslow GE, Dial KP, Jenkins FA. 1990. Bird flight: insights and complications. Bioscience. 40(2):108-116.

Liem K, Bernis W, Walker W, and Grande L. 2001. Functional anatomy of the vertebrates: an evolutionary perspective. New York (NY): Harcourt College Publishers. p. 92-96.

Hutchinson JR. Vertebrate flight [Internet]. c1994-2008. Berkeley (CA): University of California; [modified 2005 Sep 29; cited 2008 Jan 15]. Available from: http://www.ucmp.berkeley.edu/vertebrates/ flight/flightintro.html)

24d Sample references list: CSE citation-name system

Citation-sequence would look the same, but entries would be in order of citation.

References

1. Anderson A. Early bird threatens archaeopteryx's perch. Science. 1991;253(5015):35.

2. Goslow GE, Dial KP, Jenkins FA. Bird flight: insights and complications. Bioscience. 1990;40(2):108-116.

3. Liem K, Bernis W, Walker W, and Grande L. Functional anatomy of the vertebrates: an evolutionary perspective. New York (NY): Harcourt College Publishers; 2001. p. 92-96.

4. Hutchinson JR. Vertebrate flight [Internet]. Berkeley (CA): University of California; c1994-2008 [modified 2005, Sept 29; cited 2008 Jan 15]. Available from: http://www.ucmp.berkeley .edu/vertebrates/flight/flightintro.html

I . . . believe that words *can* help us move or keep us paralyzed, and that our choices of language and verbal tone have something—a great deal—to do with how we live our lives and whom we end up speaking with and hearing. . . .

—ADRIENNE RICH

PART

6

Editing
for Clarity

215

A sentence does not have to be short and simple to be concise. Instead, every word in it must count.

25a Eliminating redundancies and unnecessary modifiers

www.mhhe.com/
wi

For information
on and practice
eliminating
redundancies,
go to

Editing >
Eliminating
Redundancies

Be on the lookout for redundancies such as *first and foremost, full and complete, past history,* and *blue in color.*

➤ Students living ~~in close proximity~~ in the dorms need

to cooperate ~~together if they want~~ to live in harmony.

Usually, modifiers such as *very, rather,* and *really* and intensifiers such as *absolutely, definitely,* and *incredibly* can be deleted.

➤ The ending ~~definitely~~ shocked us ~~very much~~.

25b Replacing wordy phrases

Make your sentences more concise by replacing wordy phrases with appropriate one-word alternatives.

➤ ~~It is necessary at this point in time that tests~~ be run ^{*Tests must now*}
~~for the purposes of measuring~~ the switch's strength. ^{*to measure*}

Wordy Phrases	**Concise Alternatives**
at that point in time	then
at this point in time	now
due to the fact that	because
for the reason that	because
in close proximity to	near
in order to	to
in spite of the fact that	although
in the event that	if
in the not-too-distant future	soon
is able to	can
is necessary that	must

25c Editing roundabout sentences

Eliminate expletive constructions like *there is, there are,* and *it is,* replace the static verbs *be* and *have* with active verbs, and beware of overusing nouns derived from verbs.

➤ ~~There are~~ The stylistic similarities between "This Lime-Tree
Bower" and "Tintern Abbey/" ~~which are indications of the~~ indicate
~~influence~~ influenced that Coleridge ~~had on~~ Wordsworth.

➤ The film *JFK,* ~~which was~~ directed by Oliver Stone, revived

interest in the conspiracy theory.

25c
W

IDENTIFY AND EDIT
Wordy Sentences

W

To make your writing concise, ask yourself these questions
as you edit your writing:

? 1. *Do any sentences contain wordy or empty phrases such as* at this point in
time? *Do any of them contain redundancies or other unnecessary
repetitions?*

• ~~The fact is that at this point in time more~~ _{More} women than men _{now}
attend college.

• Total college enrollments have increased steadily ~~upward~~
since the 1940s, but since the 1970s women have enrolled in
greater numbers than men ~~have~~.

? 2. *Can any clauses be reduced to phrases, or phrases to single words?
Can any sentences be combined to reduce repetitive information?*

• ~~Reports that come from college~~ _{College} officials ~~indicate~~ _{report} that
applications from women exceed those from men/~~This~~
~~pattern indicates~~ _{, indicating} that women will continue to outnumber
men in college.

? 3. *Do any sentences include* there is, *or* there are, *or* it is *expressions; weak
verbs; or nouns derived from verbs?*

• In 1970, _{men outnumbered women in college by} ~~there were~~ more than 1.5 million. ~~more men in~~
~~college than women~~.

• This trend ~~is a reflection of~~ _{reflects} broad changes in gender roles
throughout American society.

Often, you can reduce phrases to single words.

➤ **Stone's film *JFK* revived interest in the conspiracy theory.**

Combine short, repetitive sentences.

➤ *Because of a cold front from Canada, the meteorologist on*
   A major storm is expected in the western part of the state/,
   ^   *Channel 7 is predicting a*   ^
   A cold front is coming in from Canada. The meteorologist on
                                with
   Channel 7 is predicting high winds and heavy rain.
                 ^

26 Add missing words.

Do not omit words the reader needs to understand your sentence.

26a Adding needed words to compound structures

For conciseness, words can sometimes be omitted from compound structures: *His anger is extreme and his behavior* [*is*] *violent.* But do not leave out part of a compound structure unless both parts of the compound are the same.

26c
inc

>   *with*
> **The gang members neither cooperated nor listened to**
>   ^
> **the authorities.**

26b Adding the word *that* when needed

Add the word *that* if doing so makes the sentence clearer.

>   *that*
> **The attorney argued men and women should receive equal**
>   ^
> **pay for equal work.**

26c Adding needed words in comparisons

To be clear, comparisons must be complete. Check comparisons to make sure your meaning is clear. In the following example, does the writer mean that she loved her grandmother more than her sister did—or more than she loved her sister? To clarify, add the missing words.

>   *did*
> **I loved my grandmother more than my sister.**
>   ^
>   *I loved*
> **I loved my grandmother more than my sister.**
>   ^

When you use *as* to compare people or things, be sure to use it twice.

>   *as*
> **Napoleon's temper was volatile as a volcano.**
>   ^

Include *other* or *else* to indicate that people or things belong to the group with which the subject is being compared.

➤ *Gone with the Wind* **won more awards than any *other* film in Hollywood history.**

➤ **Professor Koonig wrote more books than anyone *else* in the department.**

26d inc

Complex comparisons may require more than one addition to be clear.

➤ **Smith's book is longer, but his account of the war is** *than Jones's book* **more interesting than Jones's.** *Jones's account.*

26d Adding the articles *a, an,* or *the* where necessary

Omitting an article usually sounds odd, unless the omission occurs in a series of nouns.

➤ **He gave me** *the* **books he liked best.**

➤ **The classroom contained a fish tank, birdcage, and rabbit hutch.**

If the articles in a series are not the same, each one must be included.

➤ **The classroom contained an aquarium,** *a* **birdcage, and** *a* **rabbit hutch.**

(*For more information about the use of articles, multilingual writers should consult Chapter 43, pp. 327–30.*)

Sentences that do not fit together grammatically or logically confuse readers and must be revised.

27a Untangling mixed-up grammar

A sentence should not start one way and then, midway through, change grammatical direction.

➤ ~~For family~~ *Family* members who enjoy one another's company

  often decide on a vacation spot together.

A prepositional phrase cannot be the subject of a sentence. Eliminating the preposition *for* makes it clear that *family members* is the subject of the verb *decide*.

➤ In Mexican culture, ~~when~~ a Curanderos *can be* ~~is~~ consulted

  for ~~can address~~ spiritual or physical illness.

The dependent clause *when a Curanderos is consulted* cannot serve as the subject of the sentence. Transforming the dependent clause into an independent clause with a subject and predicate fixes the problem.

27b Repairing illogical predicates

A sentence's subject and verb must match both logically and grammatically. When they do not, the result is faulty predication.

➤ ~~The best kind of education for me would be a~~ *A* university with

both a school of music and a school of government. ^ *would be best for me*

**27b
mix**

A university is an institution, not a type of education, so the sentence needs revision.

The phrases *is when, is where,* and *the reason is . . . because* usually result in faulty predication.

➤ *the production of carbohydrates from the interaction of*
Photosynthesis is ~~where~~ carbon dioxide, water, and

chlorophyll. ~~interact in the presence of sunlight to form~~

~~carbohydrates.~~

Photosynthesis is a process, not a place.

➤ The reason the joint did not hold is ~~because~~ *that* the coupling

bolt broke.

or

➤ The ~~reason the~~ joint did not hold ~~is~~ because the coupling

bolt broke.

28 Fix confusing shifts.

Revise confusing shifts in point of view, tense, mood, or voice.

28a Fixing shifts in point of view

A writer has three points of view to choose from: first person (*I* or *we*), second person (*you*), and third person (*he, she, it, one,* or *they*). Once you choose a point of view, use it consistently.

➤ **Students will have no trouble getting access to a computer**
   they
   if ~~you~~ arrive at the lab before noon.

Note: When making a general statement about what people should or should not do, use the third person, not the second person.

Do not switch from singular to plural or plural to singular for no reason. When correcting such shifts, choose the plural to avoid using *his or her* or introducing gender bias. (*See Part 7: Editing for Grammar Conventions, p. 327.*)

   People are
➤ **~~A person is~~ often assumed to be dumb if they are attractive**

   and smart if they are unattractive.

28b Fixing shifts in tense

Verb tenses show the time of an action in relation to other actions. You should choose a time frame—present, past, or future—and use it

224

CHARTING the TERRITORY

Present Tense and Literary Works

By convention, the present tense is used to write about the content of literary works. Be careful not to shift out of the present tense as you move from one sentence to another.

➤ **David Copperfield observes other people with a fine**

and sympathetic eye. He describes villains such as

Mr. Murdstone and heroes such as Mr. Micawber in

unforgettable detail. But Copperfield ~~was~~ *is* not himself

an especially interesting person.

consistently, changing tense only when the meaning of your text requires you to do so.

➤ **The wind was blowing a hundred miles an hour when**
   suddenly there ~~is~~ *was* a big crash, and a tree ~~falls~~ *fell* into the

   living room.

➤ **She has admired many strange buildings at the university**
   but ~~thought~~ *thinks* that the new Science Center ~~looked~~ *looks* completely

   out of place.

IDENTIFY AND EDIT
Confusing Shifts

shift

28b
shift

To avoid confusing shifts, ask yourself these questions as
you edit your writing:

? *1. Does the sentence shift from one point of view to another? For example,
does it shift from third person to second?*

> ◆ Over the centuries, millions of laborers helped build and
> maintain the Great Wall of China, and ~~if you were one, you~~ *most of them*
> ~~probably~~ suffered great hardship as a result.

? *2. Are the verbs in your sentence consistent in the following ways:*

> *In tense (past, present, or future)?*
> ◆ Historians call the period before the unification of China the
> Warring States period. It ~~ends~~ *ended* when the ruler of the Ch'in
> state conquered the last of his independent neighbors.
>
> *In mood (statements vs. commands or hypothetical conditions)?*
> ◆ If a similar wall ~~is~~ *were* built today, it would cost untold amounts
> of time and money.
>
> *In voice (active vs. passive)?*
> ◆ The purpose of the wall was to protect against invasion, but
> *it also promoted* commerce. ~~was promoted by it also.~~

28c Avoiding unnecessary shifts in mood and voice

Verbs have a mood and a voice. There are three basic moods: the **indicative,** used to state or question facts, acts, and opinions; the **imperative,** used to give commands or advice; and the **subjunctive,** used to express wishes, conjectures, and hypothetical conditions. Unnecessary shifts in mood can confuse and distract your readers.

➤ If he ~~goes~~ *could go* to night school, he would take a course in

accounting.

Most verbs have two voices. In the **active voice,** the subject does the acting; in the **passive voice,** the subject is acted upon. Do not shift abruptly from one voice to the other.

➤ The Impressionist painters hated black. ~~Violet,~~ *They favored violet,* green, blue,

pink, and red. ~~were favored by them.~~

28c
shift

www.mhhe.com/
wi
For information
on shifts in verb
tense and voice,
go to
Editing > Verb and
Voice Shifts

29 Use parallel constructions.

Parallel constructions present equally important ideas in the same grammatical form.

29a
//

> At Gettysburg in 1863, Lincoln said that the Civil War was being fought to make sure that government *of the people, by the people,* and *for the people* might not perish from the earth.

Correct items in a series or paired ideas that do not have the same grammatical form by making them parallel. Put items at the same level in an outline or items in a list in parallel form.

www.mhhe.com/
wi

For information and exercises on parallelism, go to

Editing >
Coordination and
Subordination

29a Making items in a series parallel

A list or series of equally important items should be parallel in grammatical structure.

> The Census Bureau classifies people as employed if they
>
> receive payment for any kind of labor, are temporarily
>
> absent from their jobs, or ~~working~~ work at least fifteen hours as
>
> unpaid laborers in a family business.

Parallel construction can make a sentence more forceful and memorable.

> My sister obviously thought that I was too young, too ignorant,
> and ~~a troublemaker.~~ too troublesome.

228

IDENTIFY AND EDIT
Faulty Parallelism

To avoid faulty parallelism, ask yourself these questions as you edit your writing:

? *1. Are the items in a series in parallel form?*

> *glanced angrily at*
> ◆ The senator stepped to the podium, ~~an angry glance~~
>
> ~~shooting toward~~ her challenger, and began to refute his
>
> charges.

? *2. Are paired items in parallel form?*

> *had*
> ◆ She claimed that her challenger ~~had~~ not only ‸accused her
>
> falsely of accepting illegal campaign contributions, but ~~his~~ *also*
> *had himself accepted illegal contributions.*
> ‸~~contributions were from illegal sources also.~~

? *3. Are the items in outlines and lists in parallel form?*

> FAULTY She listed four reasons for voters to send her back
> PARALLELISM to Washington:
> 1. Ability to protect the state's interests
> 2. Her seniority on important committees
> 3. Works with members of both parties to get things done
> 4. Has a close working relationship with the President
>
> REVISED She listed four reasons for voters to send her back
> to Washington:
> 1. *Her ability* to protect the state's interests
> 2. *Her seniority* on important committees
> 3. *Her ability* to work with members of both parties to get
> things done
> 4. *Her* close working *relationship* with the President

29b Making paired ideas parallel

**30a
mm**

Paired ideas connected with a coordinating conjunction (*and, but, or, nor, for, so, yet*), a correlative conjunction (*not only . . . but also, both . . . and, either . . . or, neither . . . nor*), or a comparative expression (*as much as, more than, less than*) must have parallel grammatical form.

➤ Successful teachers must inspire ~~students~~ and ~~challenging them is also important.~~
   (*both*)   (*challenge their students.*)

➤ I dreamed not only of getting the girl but also of the gold medal.
   (*winning*)

➤ The junta preferred to fight rather than ~~compromising.~~
   (*to compromise.*)

30 Fix misplaced and dangling modifiers.

For a sentence to make sense, its parts must be arranged appropriately. When a modifying word, phrase, or clause is misplaced or dangling, readers get confused.

30a Fixing misplaced modifiers

Modifiers should come immediately before or after the words they modify. In the following sentence, the clause *after the police arrested them* modifies *protesters,* not property.

30b
mm

➤ *After the police arrested them, the*
~~The~~ protesters were charged with destroying college
   ^

property. ~~after the police arrested them.~~
        ^

www.mhhe.com/
wi

For information
and exercises
on misplaced
modifiers, go to

Editing >
Misplaced
Modifiers

Prepositional phrases used as adverbs are easy to misplace.

➤ *From the cabin's porch, the*
~~The~~ hikers watched the storm gathering force. ~~from the~~
   ^   ^

~~cabin's porch.~~

30b Clarifying ambiguous modifiers

Adverbs can modify what precedes or follows them. Make sure that the adverbs you use are not ambiguously placed. In the following sentence, what is vehement, the objection or the argument? Changing the position of *vehemently* eliminates this ambiguity.

➤   *vehemently*
   Historians who object to this account ~~vehemently~~ argue
                       ^

   that the presidency was never endangered.

30b
mm

IDENTIFY AND EDIT
Misplaced Modifiers

mm

To avoid misplaced modifiers, ask yourself these questions as you edit your writing:

❓ *1. Are all the modifiers close to the expressions they modify?*

> ◆ ~~People~~ *At the beginning of the Great Depression, people* panicked and all tried to get their money out of the banks at the same time, forcing many banks to close. ~~at the beginning of the Great Depression.~~

❓ *2. Are any modifiers placed in such a way that they modify more than one expression? Pay particular attention to limiting modifiers such as only, even, and just.*

> ◆ President Roosevelt declared a bank holiday, *quickly* ~~quickly~~ helping to restore confidence in the nation's financial system.

> ◆ Congress enacted many programs to combat the Depression *only* ~~only~~ within the first one hundred days of Roosevelt's presidency.

❓ *3. Do any modifiers disrupt the relationships among the grammatical elements of the sentence?*

> ◆ ~~The~~ *Given how entrenched segregation was at the time, the* president's wife, Eleanor, was a surprisingly strong, ~~given how entrenched segregation was at the time,~~ advocate for racial justice in Roosevelt's administration.

Problems occur with limiting modifiers such as *only, even, almost, nearly,* and *just.* Check every sentence that includes one of these modifiers.

AMBIGUOUS	The restaurant *only offers* vegetarian dishes for dinner.
REVISED	The restaurant *offers only* vegetarian dishes for dinner.
	or
	The restaurant *offers* vegetarian dishes *only* at dinner.

30c Moving disruptive modifiers

Separating grammatical elements that belong together, such as a subject and verb, with a lengthy modifying phrase or clause disrupts the connection between the two sentence elements.

> *Despite their similar conceptions of the self,*
> **Descartes and Hume,** ~~despite their similar conceptions~~
>
> ~~of the self,~~ **deal with the issue of personal identity in**
>
> **different ways.**

30d Avoiding split infinitives

An **infinitive** couples the word *to* with the base form of a verb. In a **split infinitive,** one or more words intervene between *to* and the verb form. Avoid splitting infinitives with a modifier unless keeping them together results in an awkward or ambiguous construction.

In the following example, the modifier *successfully* should be moved. The modifier *carefully* should probably stay where it is, however, even though it splits the infinitive *to assess*.

**30e
dm**

> To ~~successfully~~ complete this assignment students have to
> ^{successfully,}
> carefully assess projected benefits in relation to potential
> problems.

30e Fixing dangling modifiers

www.mhhe.com/
wi
For information
and exercises
on dangling
modifiers,
go to
Editing >
Dangling
Modifiers

A **dangling modifier** is a descriptive phrase that implies an actor different from the sentence's subject. When readers try to connect the modifying phrase with the subject, the result may be humorous as well as confusing.

DANGLING MODIFIER *Swimming toward the boat on the horizon,* the crowded beach felt as if it were miles away.

To fix a dangling modifier, you must name its implied actor explicitly, either as the subject of the sentence or in the modifier itself.

REVISED Swimming toward the boat on the horizon, *I* felt as if the crowded beach were miles away.

or

As *I swam* toward the boat on the horizon, the crowded beach seemed miles away.

Simply moving a dangling modifier won't fix the problem. To make the meaning clear, you must make the implied actor in the modifying phrase explicit.

IDENTIFY AND EDIT
Dangling Modifiers

dm

**30e
dm**

To avoid dangling modifiers, ask yourself these questions when you see a descriptive phrase at the beginning of a sentence:

❓ 1. What is the subject of the sentence?

> ◆ Snorkeling in Hawaii, ancient sea turtles were an amazing sight.
>
> The subject of the sentence is *sea turtles.*

❓ 2. Could the phrase at the beginning of the sentence possibly describe this subject?

> ◆ Snorkeling in Hawaii, ancient sea turtles were an amazing sight.
>
> No, sea turtles do not snorkel in Hawaii or anywhere else.

❓ 3. Who or what is the phrase really describing? Either make that person or thing the subject of the main clause, or add a subject to the modifier.

>   *we saw*
> ◆ Snorkeling in Hawaii, ancient sea turtles, ~~were~~ an amazing sight.
>   ^
>
> *While we were snorkeling*   *amazed us.*
> ◆ ~~Snorkeling~~ in Hawaii, ancient sea turtles ~~were an amazing sight.~~
>   ^   ^

<table>
<tr><td>DANGLING
MODIFIER</td><td>*After struggling for weeks in the wilderness,*
the town pleased them mightily.</td></tr>
</table>

31
coord/sub

Moving the dangling modifier to the end of the sentence won't change its unintended meaning.

REVISED   After struggling for weeks in the wilderness, *they* were pleased to come upon the town.

or

After *they had struggled* for weeks in the wilderness, the town was a pleasing sight.

31 Use coordination and subordination effectively.

www.mhhe.com/
wi

For information
and exercises
on coordination
and
subordination,
go to

Editing >
Coordination and
Subordination

Coordination and subordination allow you to combine and develop ideas in ways that readers can follow and understand.

Coordination gives two or more ideas equal weight. To coordinate parts within a sentence, join them with a coordinating conjunction (*and, but, or, for, nor, yet,* or *so*). To coordinate two or more sentences, use a comma plus a coordinating conjunction, or insert a semicolon.

➤ **The auditorium was huge, *and* the acoustics were terrible.**

➤ The tenor bellowed loudly, *but* no one in the back could hear him.

➤ Jones did not agree with her position on health care; *nevertheless,* he supported her campaign for office.

Note: When a semicolon is used to coordinate two sentences, it is often followed by a conjunctive adverb such as *moreover, nevertheless, however, therefore,* or *subsequently.*

Subordination makes one idea depend on another and is therefore used to combine ideas that are not of equal importance. Subordinate clauses start with a relative pronoun (*who, whom, that, which, whoever, whomever, whose*) or a subordinating conjunction such as *after, although, because, if, since, when,* or *where.*

➤ The blue liquid, *which will be added to the beaker later,* must be kept at room temperature.

➤ Christopher Columbus discovered the New World in 1492, *although he never understood just what he had found.*

➤ *After writing the opening four sections,* Wordsworth put the work aside for two years.

Note: Commas often set off subordinate ideas, especially when the subordinate clause or phrase opens the sentence. (*For more on using commas, see Part 8: Editing for Correctness, pp. 336–52.*)

If you do not fix the following problems with coordination and subordination, your readers will have difficulty following your train of thought.

31a Avoiding coordination for ideas of unequal importance

31c
sub

Coordination should be used only when two or more ideas deserve equal emphasis: *Smith supports bilingual education, but Johnson does not.* Subordination, not coordination, should be used to indicate information of secondary importance and to show its logical relation to the main idea.

> *When the*
> ➤ ~~The~~ police arrived, ~~and~~ the burglars ran away.

31b Keeping major ideas in main clauses

Major ideas belong in main clauses, not in subordinate clauses or phrases. The writer revised the following sentence because the subject of the paper was definitions of literacy, not who values literacy.

> *Highly valued by busiesspeople as well as academics, literacy*
> ➤ ~~Literacy, which~~ has been defined as the ability to talk
>
> intelligently about many topics/. ~~is highly valued by~~
>
> ~~businesspeople as well as academics.~~

31c Avoiding excessive subordination

When a sentence seems overloaded, separate it into two or more sentences.

➤ **Big-city mayors,** ~~who are supported by public funds,~~ **should**

be cautious about spending taxpayers' money for personal

needs, ~~such as home furnishings,~~ **especially when municipal**

budget shortfalls have caused extensive job layoffs/.

They risk *by using public funds for home furnishings.*
angering city workers and the general public/

**32a
var**

32 Vary your sentences.

Enliven your prose by using a variety of sentence patterns.

www.mhhe.com/
wi
For information
and exercises
on sentence
variety, go to
Editing >
Sentence Variety

32a Varying sentence openings

When all the sentences in a passage begin with the subject, you risk losing your readers' attention. Vary your sentences by moving a modifier to the beginning. The modifier may be a single word, a phrase, or a clause.

Eventually,
➤ **Armstrong's innovations** ~~eventually~~ **became the standard.**

32b
var

In at least two instances, this
➤ ~~This~~ money-making strategy backfired. ~~in at least two~~
   ^   ^
~~instances.~~

After Glaser became his manager,
➤ Armstrong no longer had to worry about business. ~~after~~
   ^   ^
~~Glaser became his manager.~~

A **participial phrase** begins with an *-ing* verb (*driving*) or a past participle (*moved, driven*) and is used as a modifier. You can often move it to the beginning of a sentence for variety, but make sure that the phrase describes the explicit subject of the sentence or you will end up with a dangling modifier (*see pp. 234–36*).

Pushing the other children aside,
➤ Joseph, ~~pushing the other children aside,~~ demanded that the
         ^
teacher give him a cookie first.

Stunned by the stock market crash, many
➤ ~~Many~~ brokers, ~~stunned by the stock market crash,~~
   ^
committed suicide.

32b Varying sentence length and structure

Short, simple sentences will keep your readers alert if they occur in a context that also includes longer, complex sentences. Do not overuse one kind of sentence structure. Are most of your sentences short and simple? A series of short sentences can make writing so choppy that meaning gets lost.

CHOPPY   My cousin Jim is not an accountant. But he does my taxes every year. He suggests various deductions. These deductions reduce my tax bill considerably.

You can use subordination to combine a series of short, choppy sentences and form a longer, more meaningful sentence. Put the idea you want to emphasize in the main clause.

32b
var

REVISED   Even though he is not an accountant, my cousin Jim does my taxes every year, suggesting various deductions that reduce my tax bill considerably.

If a series of short sentences includes two major ideas of equal importance, use coordination for the two major ideas and subordinate the secondary information.

CHOPPY   Bilingual education is designed for children. The native language of these children is not English. Smith supports expanding bilingual education. Johnson does not support expanding bilingual education.

REVISED   Smith supports bilingual education for children whose native language is not English; Johnson, however, does not support bilingual education.

If most of your sentences are long and complex, put at least one of your ideas into a short, simple sentence. Your goal is to achieve a good mix.

DRAFT   I dived quickly into the sea. I peered through my mask at the watery world. It turned darker. A school of fish went by. The distant light glittered on their bodies, and I stopped swimming. I waited to see if the fish might be chased by a shark. I was satisfied that there was no shark and continued down.

32c
var

REVISED   I dived quickly into the sea, peering through my mask
at a watery world that turned darker as I descended.
A school of fish went by, the distant light glittering on
their bodies. I stopped swimming and waited. Perhaps
the fish were being chased by a shark? Satisfied that
there was no shark, I continued down.

(*For more on coordination and subordination, see pp. 236–39.*)

32c Including a few cumulative and periodic sentences

Cumulative sentences, which add a series of descriptive participial
or absolute phrases to the basic subject-plus-verb pattern, make writing more forceful.

➤ **The motorcycle spun out of control, <u>plunging down the
ravine, crashing through the fence,</u> and <u>coming to rest on
its side.</u>**

Cumulative sentences can also add details.

➤ **Wollstonecraft headed for France, <u>her soul determined to
be free, her mind committed to reason, her heart longing
for love.</u>**

Another way to increase the force of your writing is to use a few
periodic sentences. In a **periodic sentence,** the key word, phrase, or
idea appears at the end.

➤ **In 1946 and 1947, young people turned away from the
horrors of World War II and fell in love—with the jukebox.**

32d Trying an occasional inversion, a rhetorical question, or an exclamation

Most sentences are declarative and follow the normal sentence pattern of subject plus verb plus object. Occasionally, though, you might try using an inverted sentence pattern or another sentence type, such as a rhetorical question or an exclamation.

32d var

- **Inversions.** You can create an **inversion** by putting the verb before the subject.

  ➤ **Characteristic of Smith's work are bold design and original thinking.**

  Because many inversions sound odd, they should be used infrequently and carefully.

- **Rhetorical questions.** To get your readers to participate more actively, ask a question. Because you do not expect your audience to answer, this kind of question is called a **rhetorical question.**

  ➤ **Players injured at an early age too often find themselves without a job, without a college degree, and without physical health. Is it any wonder that a few turn to drugs and alcohol, become homeless, or end up in a morgue long before their time?**

  Rhetorical questions work best in the middle or at the end of a long, complicated passage. Sometimes they can help make a transition from one topic to another. Avoid using them more than a few times in a paper, and avoid using them to begin an essay.

■ **Exclamations.** In academic writing, exclamations are rare. If you decide to use one, be sure that you want to express strong emotion and can do so without losing credibility.

33a

➤ Wordsworth completed the thirteen-book *Prelude* in 1805, after seven years of hard work. Instead of publishing his masterpiece, however, he devoted himself to revising it—for 45 years! The poem, in a fourteen-book version, was finally published in 1850, after he had died.

33 Choose active verbs.

Active verbs such as *run, shout, write,* and *think* are more direct and forceful than forms of the *be* verb (*am, are, is, was, were, been, being*) or passive-voice constructions. The more active verbs you use, the clearer your writing will be.

33a Considering alternatives to *be* verbs

Be does a lot of work in English.

BE AS A LINKING VERB

➤ Germany *is* relatively poor in natural resources.

BE AS A HELPING VERB

> Macbeth *was* returning from battle when he met the three witches.

Be verbs are so useful that they get overworked. Watch for weak, roundabout sentences with *be* verbs, and consider replacing those verbs with active verbs.

> The mayor's refusal to meet with our representatives
> *demonstrates*
> ~~is a demonstration of~~ his lack of respect for us.
> ^

33b

33b Preferring the active voice

Verbs can be in the active or passive voice. In the **active voice,** the subject of the sentence acts; in the **passive voice,** the subject is acted upon.

ACTIVE	The Senate finally passed the bill.
PASSIVE	The bill was finally passed by the Senate.

The passive voice downplays the actors as well as the action, so much so that the actors are often left out of the sentence.

PASSIVE	The bill was finally passed.

The active voice is more forceful, and readers usually want to know who or what does the acting.

PASSIVE	Polluting chemicals were dumped into the river.
ACTIVE	Industrial Products Corporation dumped polluting chemicals into the river.

www.mhhe.com/ wi
For information and exercises on the active and passive voices, go to
Editing > Verbs and Verbals

However, when the recipient of the action is more important than the doer of the action, the passive voice is appropriate.

33b

➤ **After her heart attack, my mother was taken to the hospital.**

Mother and the fact that she was taken to the hospital are more important than who took her to the hospital.

CHARTING the TERRITORY

Passive Voice

The passive voice is often used in scientific reports to keep the focus on the experiment and its results rather than on the experimenters.

➤ **After the bacteria were isolated, they were treated carefully with nicotine and were observed to stop reproducing.**

34 Use appropriate language.

Language is appropriate when it fits your topic, purpose, and audience. You can develop a sense of audience through reading how other writers in the field handle your topic.

34a Avoiding slang, regional expressions, and nonstandard English

In college papers, slang terms and the tone that goes with them should be avoided.

SLANG   In *Heart of Darkness,* we hear a lot about a *dude* named Kurtz, but we don't see the *guy* much.

REVISED   In *Heart of Darkness,* Marlow, the narrator, talks almost continually about Kurtz, but we meet Kurtz himself only at the end.

Like slang, regional and nonstandard expressions such as *y'all, hisself,* and *don't be doing that* work fine in conversation but not in college writing.

34b Using an appropriate level of formality

College writing assignments usually call for a style that avoids the extremes of the stuffy and the casual, the pretentious and the chatty. Revise passages that veer toward one extreme or the other.

**34c
d**

| PRETENTIOUS | Romantic lovers are characterized by a pre-occupation with a deliberately restricted set of qualities in the love object that are viewed as means to some ideal end. |
| REVISED | People in love see what they want to see, usually by idealizing the beloved. |

34c Avoiding jargon

When specialists communicate with each other, they often use technical language. **Jargon** is the inappropriate use of specialized or technical language. You should not use language that is appropriate for specialists when you are writing for a general audience.

www.mhhe.com/
wi

For information
and exercises
on avoiding
jargon,
euphemisms,
and
doublespeak,
go to

Editing > Clichés,
Slang, Jargon . . .

| JARGON | An *opposition education theory* holds that children learn Spanish best *under strict discipline conditions.* |
| REVISED | An *alternative theory of education* holds that children learn Spanish best *when strict discipline is enforced.* |

If you need to use technical terms when writing for nonspecialists, be sure to define them.

➤ **Armstrong's innovative singing style featured "scat,"
a technique that combines "nonsense syllables [with]
improvised melodies" (Robinson 515).**

34d Avoiding euphemisms and doublespeak

Euphemisms and doublespeak have one goal: to cover up the truth.

Euphemisms substitute nice-sounding words like *correctional facility* and *passing away* for such harsh realities as *prison* and *death*.

Doublespeak is used to obscure facts and evade responsibility.

**34e
sexist**

DOUBLESPEAK Pursuant to the environmental protection regulations enforcement policy of the Bureau of Natural Resources, special management area land use permit issuance procedures have been instituted.

Avoid using words that evade or deceive.

34e Avoiding biased or sexist language

**www.mhhe.com/
wi**

For information
and exercises
on avoiding
biased or sexist
language, go to
Editing >
Word Choice

1. Biased language
Always review your writing to see if it is unintentionally biased. Be on the lookout for stereotypes that demean, ignore, or patronize people on the basis of gender, race, religion, national origin, ethnicity, physical ability, sexual orientation, occupation, or any other human condition. Revise for inclusiveness.

For example, do not assume that Irish Catholics have large families.

➤ ~~Although the~~ Browns are Irish ~~Catholics, there are only~~ two
   The   *an*   *Catholic family with*

children. ~~in the family.~~

In addition, remember that a positive stereotype is still a stereotype.

➤ ~~Because Asian students are whizzes at math, we~~ all wanted
                                 We

~~them~~ in our study group.
math whizzes

CHARTING the TERRITORY

Biased Language

The American Psychological Association recommends this test:
Substitute your own group for the group you are discussing. If
you are offended by the resulting statement, revise your phrasing to eliminate bias.

2. The generic use of *he* or *man*

Traditionally, the pronoun *he* and the noun *man* have been used to represent either gender. Today, however, the use of *he* or *man* or any other masculine noun to represent people in general is considered offensive.

BIASED	Everybody had his way.
REVISED	We all had our way.
BIASED	It's every man for himself.
REVISED	All of us have to save ourselves.

Follow these simple principles to avoid gender bias in your writing:

■ Replace terms that indicate gender with their genderless
equivalents:

No	Yes
chairman	chair, chairperson
congressman	representative, member of Congress
forefathers	ancestors

man, mankind	people, humans
man-made	artificial
policeman	police officer
spokesman	spokesperson

34e
sexist

- Refer to men and women in parallel ways: *ladies and gentlemen*, *men and women*, *husband and wife*.

BIASED	D. H. Lawrence and Mrs. Woolf met each other, but Lawrence did not like the Bloomsbury circle that revolved around Virginia.
REVISED	D. H. Lawrence and Virginia Woolf met each other, but Lawrence did not like the Bloomsbury circle that revolved around Woolf.

- Replace the masculine pronouns *he, him, his,* and *himself* when they are being used generically to refer to both women and men. One way to replace masculine pronouns is to use the plural.

> *Senators*   *their districts*
> ➤ ~~Each senator~~ returned to ~~his district~~ during the break.

> *Lawyers need*   *their*
> ➤ ~~A lawyer needs~~ to be frank with ~~his~~ clients.

Some writers alternate *he* and *she,* and *him* and *her.* This strategy is effective but distracting. The constructions *his or her* and *he or she* are acceptable as long as they are not used excessively or more than once in a sentence.

**34e
sexist**

> **Each student in the psychology class was to choose
> a book,** ~~according to his or her interests, to~~ **read** ~~the~~
> ^*it*
> ~~book~~ **overnight,** ~~to~~ **do without** ~~his or her normal~~ **sleep,**
> **to write a short summary of** ~~what he or she had read,~~
> ^*the book the next morning,*
> **and then** ~~to~~ **see if he or she dreamed about the book**
> ^
> **the following night.**

The constructions *his/her* and *s/he* are not acceptable.

Note: Using the neuter impersonal pronoun *one* can sometimes help you
avoid masculine pronouns, but it can make your writing sound stuffy.

STUFFY   The American creed holds that if *one* works
              hard, *one* will succeed in life.

REVISED   The American creed holds that those who work
              hard will succeed in life.

(*For more on editing to avoid the generic use of* he, him, his, *or* himself,
see Part 7: Editing for Grammar Conventions, pp. 308–13.)

3. Sexist language
Avoid language that demeans or stereotypes women and men. Women
are usually the explicit targets. For example, many labels and clichés
imply that women are not as able or mature as men. Consider the
meaning of words and phrases like *the fair sex, [acting like a] girl,
poetess,* and *coed.*

To convey your meaning clearly, you need to choose the right words. Is your choice of words as precise as it should be?

35a Choosing words with suitable connotations

Words have denotations and connotations. **Denotations** are the primary meanings of the word. **Connotations** are the feelings and images associated with a word.

As you revise, replace any word whose connotation does not fit what you want to say.

>   *demand*
> **The players' union should ~~request~~ that the NFL amend
> its pension plan.**

If you cannot think of a more suitable word, consult a print or an online thesaurus for **synonyms**—words with similar meanings. Keep in mind, however, that most words have connotations that allow them to work in some contexts but not in others. To find out more about a synonym's connotations, look the word up in a dictionary.

www.mhhe.com/
wi
For information
and exercises
on choosing
the right word,
go to
Editing >
Word Choice

35b Including specific and concrete words

Specific words name particular kinds of things or items, such as *pines* or *college sophomores.*

Concrete words name things we can sense by touch, taste, smell, hearing, and sight, such as *velvet* or *sweater.*

By creating images that appeal to the senses, specific and concrete words make writing more precise.

VAGUE   The trees were affected by the bad weather.

PRECISE   The tall pines shook in the gale.

As you edit, develop specific and concrete details. Also check for overused, vague terms—such as *factor, thing, good, nice,* and *interesting*—and replace them with more specific and concrete words.

➤ **The protesters were charged with ~~things~~ they never ~~did.~~**
crimes ... *committed.*

35c Using standard idioms

Idioms are customary forms of expression. They are not always logical and are hard to translate. Often they involve selecting the right preposition. If you are not sure which preposition to use, look up the main word in a dictionary.

Some verbs, called **phrasal verbs,** include a preposition to make their idiomatic meaning complete:

Henry *made up* with Gloria.
Henry *made off* with Gloria.
Henry *made out* with Gloria.

35d Avoiding clichés

A **cliché** is an overworked expression that no longer creates a vivid picture in a reader's imagination. Rephrase clichés in plain language.

➤ **When John turned his papers in three weeks late, he had to**
accept the consequences.
~~face the music.~~
                ^

                            made some good observations.
➤ **The speaker at our conference** ~~hit the nail on the head.~~
                                              ^

35d
d

www.mhhe.com/
wi
For information
on avoiding
clichés, go to
Editing > Clichés,
Slang, Jargon . . .

The list that follows gives some common clichés to avoid.

Common Clichés

acid test
agony of suspense
beat a hasty
    retreat
beyond the
    shadow of a
    doubt
blind as a bat
calm, cool, and
    collected
cold, hard facts
cool as a
    cucumber
crazy as a loon
dead as a
    doornail
deep, dark secret
depths of despair
few and far
    between

flat as a pancake
gild the lily
give 110 percent
green with envy
heave a sigh of
    relief
hit the nail on
    the head
last but not least
the other side of
    the coin
pale as a ghost
pass the buck
pretty as a
    picture
quick as a flash
rise to the
    occasion

sadder but wiser
shoulder to the
    wheel
sink or swim
smart as a whip
sneaking
    suspicion
straight and
    narrow
tempest in a
    teapot
tired but happy
tried and true
ugly as sin
untimely death
white as a sheet
worth its weight
    in gold

35f
d

35e Using suitable figures of speech

Figures of speech make writing vivid by supplementing the literal meaning of words. A **simile** is a comparison that contains the word *like* or *as*.

➤ **His smile was like the sun peeking through after a rainstorm.**

A **metaphor** is an implied comparison. It treats one thing or action as if it were something else.

➤ **The critic's slash-and-burn review devastated the cast.**

Because it is compressed, a metaphor is often more forceful than a simile.

Only compatible comparisons make prose vivid. Be careful not to mix metaphors.

MIXED	His presentation of the plan was so *crystal clear* that in a *burst of speed* we decided *to come aboard*.
REVISED	His clear presentation immediately convinced us to support the plan.

35f Avoiding the misuse of words

Avoid mistakes in your use of new terms and unfamiliar words. Consult a dictionary whenever you include an unfamiliar word in your writing.

exhibited
➤ The aristocracy ~~exuded~~ numerous vices, including greed
    licentiousness.
    and ~~license.~~
        ^

36 Glossary of Usage

The following words and expressions are often confused, misused, or considered nonstandard. This list will help you use these words precisely.

www.mhhe.com/
wi
For an online
glossary of
usage, go to
Editing >
Word Choice

a, an Use *a* with a word that begins with a consonant sound: *a cat, a dog, a one-sided argument, a house.* Use *an* with a word that begins with a vowel sound: *an apple, an X ray, an honor.*

accept, except *Accept* is a verb meaning "to receive willingly": *Please accept my apologies. Except* is a preposition meaning "but": *Everyone except Julie saw the film.*

adapt, adopt *Adapt* means "to adjust or become accustomed to": *They adapted to the customs of their new country. Adopt* means "to take as one's own": *We adopted a puppy.*

advice, advise *Advice* is a noun; *advise* is a verb: *I took his advice and deeply regretted it. I advise you to disregard it, too.*

affect, effect As a verb, *affect* means "to influence": *Inflation affects our sense of security.* As a noun, *affect* means "a feeling or an emotion": *To study affect, psychologists probe the unconscious.* As a noun, *effect* means "result":

36 usage

Inflation is one of the many effects of war. As a verb, *effect* means "to make or accomplish": *Inflation has effected many changes in the way we spend money.*

agree to, agree with   *Agree to* means "consent to"; *agree with* means "be in accord with": *They will agree to a peace treaty, even though they do not agree with each other on all points.*

ain't   A slang contraction for *is not, am not,* or *are not, ain't* should not be used in formal writing or speech.

all/all of, more/more of, some/some of   Except before some pronouns, the "of" in these constructions can usually be eliminated: *All France rejoiced. Some students cut class.* But: *All of us wish you well.*

all ready, already   *All ready* means "fully prepared." *Already* means "previously." *We were all ready to go out when we discovered that Jack had already ordered a pizza.*

all right, alright   The spelling *alright* is an alternate, but many educated readers still think it is incorrect in standard written English. *He told me it was all right to miss class tomorrow.*

all together, altogether   *All together* expresses unity or common location; *Altogether* means "completely," often in a tone of ironic understatement. *At the NRA convention, it was altogether startling to see so many guns set out all together in one place.*

allude, elude, refer to   *Allude* means "to refer indirectly": *He alluded to his miserable adolescence. Elude* means "to avoid" or "to escape from": *She eluded the police for nearly two days.* Do not use *allude* to mean "to refer directly": *The teacher referred* [not *alluded*] *to page 468 in the text.*

almost, most   *Almost* means "nearly." *Most* means "the greater part of." Do not use *most* when you mean *almost. He wrote to me about almost* [not *most*] *everything he did. He told his mother about most things he did.*

a lot   *A lot* is always two words. Do not use *alot.*

A.M., AM, a.m.   These abbreviations mean "before noon" when used with numbers: 6 A.M., 6 a.m. Be consistent, and do not use the abbreviations as a synonym for *morning: In the morning* [not *a.m.*], *the train is full.*

among, between   Generally, use *among* with three or more nouns, and *between* with two: *The distance between Boston and Knoxville is a thousand miles. The desire to quit smoking is common among those who have smoked for a long time.*

amoral, immoral   *Amoral* means "neither moral nor immoral" and "not caring about moral judgments." *Immoral* means "morally wrong." *Unlike such amoral natural disasters as earthquakes and hurricanes, war is intentionally violent and therefore immoral.*

**36
usage**

amount, number   Use *amount* for quantities you cannot count; use *number* for quantities you can count. *The amount of oil left underground in the world is a matter of dispute, but the number of countries that profit from oil is well known.*

an   *See* a, an.

anxious, eager   *Anxious* means "fearful": *I am anxious before a test. Eager* signals strong interest or desire: *I am eager to be done with that exam.*

anymore, any more   *Anymore* means "no longer." *Any more* means "no more." Both are used in negative contexts: *I do not enjoy dancing anymore. I do not want any more peanut butter.*

anyone/any one, anybody/any body, everyone/every one, everybody/every body   *Anyone, anybody, everyone,* and *everybody* are indefinite pronouns: *Anybody can make a mistake.* When the pronoun *one* or the noun *body* is modified by the adjective *any* or *every,* the words should be separated by a space: *A good mystery writer accounts for every body that turns up in the story.*

as   Do not use *as* as a synonym for *since, when,* or *because: I told him he should visit Alcatraz since* [not *as*] *he was going to San Francisco. When* [not *as*] *I complained about the meal, the cook said he did not like to eat there himself. Because* [not *as*] *we asked her nicely, our teacher decided to cancel the exam.*

as, like   In formal writing, avoid the use of *like* as a conjunction: *He sneezed as if* [not *like*] *he had a cold. Like* is perfectly acceptable as a preposition that introduces a comparison: *She handled the reins like an expert.*

**36
usage**

at   Avoid the use of *at* to complete the notion of *where*: not *Where is Michael at?* but *Where is Michael?*

awful, awfully   Use *awful* and *awfully* to convey the emotion of terror or wonder (awe-full): *The vampire flew out the window with an awful shriek.* In writing, do not use *awful* to mean "bad" or *awfully* to mean "very" or "extremely."

awhile, a while   *Awhile* is an adverb: *Stay awhile with me. A while* is an article and a noun. Always use *a while* after a preposition: *Many authors are unable to write anything else for a while after they publish their first novel.*

being as, being that   Do not use *being as* or *being that* as synonyms for *since* or *because*: *Because* [not *being as*] *the mountain was there, we had to climb it.*

belief, believe   *Belief* is a noun meaning "conviction"; *believe* is a verb meaning "to have confidence in the truth of": *Her belief that lying was often justified made it hard for us to believe her story.*

beside, besides   *Beside* is a preposition meaning "next to" or "apart from": *The ski slope was beside the lodge. She was beside herself with joy. Besides* is both a preposition and an adverb meaning "in addition to" or "except for": *Besides a bicycle, he will need a tent and a pack.*

better   Avoid using *better* in expressions of quantity: *Crossing the continent by train took more than* [not *better than*] *four days.*

between   See among, between.

bring, take   Use *bring* when an object is being moved toward you, and *take* when it is being moved away: *Please bring me a new disk and take the old one home with you.*

but that, but what   In expressions of doubt, avoid writing *but that* or *but what* when you mean *that*: *I have no doubt that* [not *but that*] *you can learn to write well.*

can, may   *Can* refers to ability; *may* refers to possibility or permission: *I see that you can skateboard without crashing into people, but nevertheless you may not skateboard on the promenade.*

can't hardly   This double negative is ungrammatical and self-contradictory: *I can [not can't] hardly understand algebra. I can't understand algebra.*

capital, capitol   *Capital* refers to a city; *capitol* refers to a building where lawmakers meet: *Protesters traveled to the state capital to converge on the capitol steps. Capital* also refers to wealth or resources.

censor, censure   *Censor* means "to remove or suppress material." *Censure* means "to reprimand formally." *The Chinese government has been censured by the U.S. Congress for censoring newspapers.*

cite, sight, site   The verb *cite* means "to quote or mention": *Be sure to cite all your sources in your bibliography.* As a noun, the word *sight* means "view": *It was love at first sight. Site* is a noun meaning "a particular place": locations on the Internet are referred to as *sites.*

compare to, compare with   Use *compare to* to point out similarities between two unlike things: *She compared his singing to the croaking of a wounded frog.* Use *compare with* for differences or likenesses between two similar things: *Compare Shakespeare's* Antony and Cleopatra *with Dryden's* All for Love.

complement, compliment   *Complement* means "to go well with": *I consider sauerkraut the perfect complement to sausages. Compliment* means "praise": *She received many compliments on her thesis.*

conscience, conscious   The noun *conscience* means "a sense of right and wrong": *His conscience bothered him.* The adjective *conscious* means "awake" or "aware": *I was conscious of a presence in the room.*

continual, continuous   *Continual* means "repeated regularly and frequently": *She continually checked her computer for new e-mail. Continuous* means "extended or prolonged without interruption": *The car alarm made a continuous wail in the night.*

could of, should of, would of   Avoid these ungrammatical forms of *could have, should have,* and *would have.*

**36
usage**

criteria, criterion *Criteria* is the plural form of the Latin word *criterion,* meaning "standard of judgment": *The criteria are not very strict. The most important criterion is whether you can do the work.*

data *Data* is the plural form of the Latin word *datum,* meaning "fact." Although *data* is often used informally as a singular noun, in writing, treat *data* as a plural noun: *The data indicate that recycling has gained popularity.*

differ from, differ with *Differ from* expresses a lack of similarity; *differ with* expresses disagreement: *The ancient Greeks differed less from the Persians than we often think. Aristotle differed with Plato on some important issues.*

different from, different than The correct idiom is *different from.* Avoid *different than: The east coast of Florida is very different from the west coast.*

discreet, discrete *Discreet* means "tactful" or "prudent." *Discrete* means "separate" or "distinct." *What's a discreet way of telling them that these are two discrete issues?*

disinterested, uninterested *Disinterested* means "impartial": *We expect members of a jury to be disinterested. Uninterested* means "indifferent" or "unconcerned": *Most people today are uninterested in alchemy.*

don't, doesn't *Don't* is the contraction for *do not* and is used with *I, you, we, they,* and plural nouns; *doesn't* is the contraction for *does not* and is used with *he, she, it,* and singular nouns: *You don't know what you're talking about. He doesn't know what you're talking about either.*

due to *Due to* is an overworked and often confusing expression when it is used for *because of.* Use *due to* only in expressions of time in infinitive constructions or in other contexts where the meaning is "scheduled": *The plane is due to arrive in one hour. He is due to receive a promotion this year.*

each and every Use one of these words or the other but not both: *Every cow came in at feeding time. Each one had to be watered.*

each other, one another Use *each other* in sentences involving two subjects and *one another* in sentences involving more than two: *Husbands and wives should help each other. Classmates should share ideas with one another.*

eager *See* anxious, eager.

effect *See* affect, effect.

e.g., i.e. The abbreviation *e.g.* stands for the Latin words meaning "for example." The abbreviation *i.e.* stands for the Latin for "that is." *Come as soon as you can, i.e., today or tomorrow. Bring fruit with you, e.g., apples and peaches.* In formal writing, replace the abbreviations with the English words: *Keats wrote many different kinds of lyrics, for example, odes, sonnets, and songs.*

36 usage

either, neither Both *either* and *neither* are singular: *Neither of the two boys has played the game. Either of the two girls is willing to show you the way home. Either* has an intensive use that *neither* does not, and when it is used as an intensive, *either* is always negative: *She told him she would not go either.* (*For* [either . . . or] *and* [neither . . . nor] *constructions, see p. 290.*)

elicit, illicit The verb *elicit* means "to draw out." The adjective *illicit* means "unlawful." *The detective was unable to elicit any information about other illicit activity.*

elude *See* allude, elude, refer to.

emigrate, immigrate *Emigrate* means "to move away from one's country": *My grandfather emigrated from Greece in 1905. Immigrate* means "to move to another country and settle there": *Grandpa immigrated to the United States.*

eminent, imminent, immanent *Eminent* means "celebrated" or "well known": *Many eminent Victorians were melancholy and disturbed. Imminent* means "about to happen" or "about to come": *In August 1939, many Europeans sensed that war was imminent. Immanent* refers to something invisible but dwelling throughout the world: *Medieval Christians believed that God's power was immanent through the universe.*

etc. The abbreviation *etc.* stands for the Latin *et cetera*, meaning "and others" or "and other things." Because *and* is included in the abbreviation, do not write *and etc.* In a series, a comma comes before *etc.*, just as it would before the coordinating conjunction that closes a series: *He brought string, wax, paper, etc.* In most college writing, it is better to end a series of examples with a final example or the words *and so on.*

**36
usage**

everybody/every body, everyone/every one *See* anyone/any one. . .

except *See* accept, except.

expect, suppose *Expect* means "to hope" or "to anticipate": *I expect a good grade on my final paper. Suppose* means "to presume": *I suppose you did not win the lottery on Saturday.*

explicit, implicit *Explicit* means "stated outright." *Implicit* means "implied, unstated." *Her explicit instructions were to go to the party without her, but the implicit message she conveyed was disapproval.*

farther, further *Farther* describes geographical distances: *Ten miles farther on is a hotel. Further* means "in addition" when geography is not involved: *He said further that he didn't like my attitude.*

fewer, less *Fewer* refers to items that can be counted individually; *less* refers to general amounts. *Fewer people signed up for indoor soccer this year than last. Your argument has less substance than you think.*

firstly *Firstly* is common in British English but not in the United States. *First, second, third,* and so on are the accepted forms.

flaunt, flout *Flaunt* means "to wave" or "to show publicly" with a delight tinged with pride and even arrogance: *He flaunted his wealth by wearing overalls lined with mink. Flout* means "to scorn" or "to defy," especially in a public way, seemingly without concern for the consequences: *She flouted the traffic laws by running through red lights.*

former, latter *Former* refers to the first and *latter* to the second of two things mentioned previously: *Mario and Alice are both good cooks; the former is fonder of Chinese cooking, the latter of Mexican.*

further *See* farther, further.

get In formal writing, avoid colloquial uses of *get,* as in *get with it, get it all together, get-up-and-go, get it,* and *that gets me.*

good, well *Good* is an adjective and should not be used in place of the adverb *well: He felt good about doing well on the exam.*

half, a half, half a   Write *half, a half,* or *half a* but not *half of, a half a,* or *a half of*: *Half the clerical staff went out on strike. I want a half-dozen eggs to throw at the actors. Half a loaf is better than none, unless you are on a diet.*

hanged, hung   People are *hanged* by the neck until dead. Pictures and all other things that can be suspended are *hung.*

36 usage

hopefully   *Hopefully* means "with hope." It is often misused to mean "it is hoped": *We waited hopefully for our ship to come in* [not *Hopefully, our ship will come in*].

i.e.   *See* e.g., i.e.

if . . . then   Avoid using these words in tandem. Redundant: *If I get my license, then I can drive a cab.* Better: *If I get my license, I can drive a cab. Once I get my license, I can drive a cab.*

illicit   *See* elicit, illicit.

immigrate   *See* emigrate, immigrate.

imminent   *See* eminent, imminent, immanent.

immoral   *See* amoral, immoral.

implicit   *See* explicit, implicit.

imply, infer   *Imply* means "to suggest something without stating it directly": *By putting his fingers in his ears, he implied that she should stop singing. Infer* means "to draw a conclusion from evidence": *When she dozed off in the middle of his declaration of eternal love, he inferred that she did not feel the same way about him.*

in, in to, into   *In* refers to a location inside something: *Charles kept a snake in his room. In to* refers to motion with a purpose: *The resident manager came in to capture it. Into* refers to movement from outside to inside or from separation to contact: *The snake escaped by crawling into a drain. The manager ran into the wall, and Charles got into big trouble.*

incredible, incredulous   The *incredible* cannot be believed; the *incredulous* do not believe. Stories and events may be *incredible;* people are *incredulous: Nancy told an incredible story of being abducted by a UFO over the weekend. We were all incredulous.*

infer   *See* imply, infer.

inside of, outside of   The "of" is unnecessary in these phrases: *He was outside the house.*

ironically   *Ironically* means "contrary to what was or might have been expected." It should not be confused with *surprisingly,* which means "unexpected," or with *coincidentally,* which means "occurring at the same time or place." *Ironically, his fastball lost speed after his arm healed.*

irregardless   This construction is a double negative because both the prefix *ir-* and the suffix *-less* are negatives. Use *regardless* instead.

it's, its   *It's* is a contraction, usually for *it is* but sometimes for *it has: It's often been said that English is a difficult language to learn. Its* is a possessive pronoun: *The dog sat down and scratched its fleas.*

kind(s)   *Kind* is singular: *This kind of house is easy to build. Kinds* is plural and should be used only to indicate more than one kind: *These three kinds of toys are better than those two kinds.*

lay, lie   *Lay* means "to place." Its main forms are *lay, laid,* and *laid.* It generally has a direct object, specifying what has been placed: *She laid her book on the steps and left it there. Lie* means "to recline" and does not take a direct object. Its main forms are *lie, lay,* and *lain: She often lay awake at night.*

less   *See* fewer, less.

like   *See* as, like.

literally   *Literally* means "actually" or "exactly as written": *Literally thousands gathered along the parade route.* Do not use *literally* as an intensive adverb when it can be misleading or even ridiculous, as here: *His blood literally boiled.*

loose, lose   *Loose* is an adjective that means "not securely attached." *Lose* is a verb that means "to misplace." *Better tighten that loose screw before you lose the whole structure.*

may *See* can, may.

maybe, may be *Maybe* is an adverb meaning "perhaps": *Maybe he can get a summer job as a lifeguard. May be* is a verb phrase meaning "is possible": *It may be that I can get a job as a lifeguard, too.*

36 usage

moral, morale *Moral* means "lesson," especially a lesson about standards of behavior or the nature of life: *The moral of the story is do not drink and drive. Morale* means "attitude" or "mental condition": *Office morale dropped sharply after the dean was arrested.*

more/more of *See* all/all of. . . .

more important, more importantly The correct idiom is *more important,* not *more importantly.*

most *See* almost, most.

myself (himself, herself, etc.) Pronouns ending with -*self* refer to or intensify other words: *Jack hurt himself. Standing in the doorway was the man himself.* When you are unsure whether to use *I* or *me, she* or *her, he* or *him* in a compound subject or object, you may be tempted to substitute one of the -*self* pronouns. Don't do it: *The quarrel was between her and me* [not *myself*]. (*For more on pronouns, see Part 7, starting on p. 308.*)

neither *See* either, neither

nohow, nowheres These words are nonstandard for *anyway, in no way, in any way, in any place,* and *in no place.* Do not use them in formal writing.

number *See* amount, number.

off of Omit the *of: She took the painting off the wall.*

one another *See* each other, one another.

outside of *See* inside of, outside of.

plus Avoid using *plus* as a substitute for *and: He had to walk the dog, do the dishes, empty the garbage, and* [not *plus*] *write a term paper.*

practicable, practical *Practicable* is an adjective applied to things that can be done: *A space program that would land human beings on Mars is now* *practicable. Practical* means "sensible": *Many people do not think such a journey is practical.*

precede, proceed   *Precede* means "come before;" *proceed* means "go forward": *Despite the heavy snows that preceded us, we managed to proceed up the hiking trail.*

previous to, prior to   Avoid these wordy and somewhat pompous substitutions for *before.*

principal, principle   *Principal* is an adjective meaning "most important" or a noun meaning "the head of an organization" or "a sum of money": *Our principal objections to the school's principal are that he is a liar and a cheat. Principle* is a noun meaning "a basic standard or law": *We believe in the principles of honesty and fair play.*

proceed   *See* precede, proceed.

raise, rise   *Raise* means "to lift or cause to move upward." It takes a direct object—someone raises something: *I raised the windows in the classroom. Rise* means "to go upward." It does not take a direct object—something rises by itself: *We watched the balloon rise to the ceiling.*

real, really   Do not use the words *real* or *really* when you mean *very: The cake was very* [not *real* or *really*] *good.*

reason . . . is because   This is a redundant expression. Use either *the reason is that* or *because: The reason he fell on the ice is that he cannot skate. He fell on the ice because he cannot skate.*

refer to   *See* allude, elude, refer to.

relation, relationship   *Relation* describes a connection between things: *There is a relation between smoking and lung cancer. Relationship* describes a connection between people: *The brothers have always had a close relationship.*

respectfully, respectively   *Respectfully* means "with respect": *Treat your partners respectfully. Respectively* means "in the given order": *The three Williams she referred to were Shakespeare, Wordsworth, and Yeats, respectively.*

rise   *See* raise, rise.

set, sit *Set* is usually a transitive verb meaning "to establish" or "to place." It takes a direct object, and its principal parts are *set, set,* and *set: DiMaggio set the standard of excellence in fielding. She set the box down in the corner.* *Sit* is usually intransitive, meaning "to place oneself in a sitting position." Its principal parts are *sit, sat,* and *sat: The dog sat on command.*

36
usage

shall, will *Shall* was once the standard first-person future form of the verb *to be* when a simple statement of fact was intended: *I shall be twenty-one on my next birthday.* Today, most writers use *will* in the ordinary future tense for the first person: *I will celebrate my birthday by throwing a big party. Shall* is still used in questions. *Shall we dance?*

should of *See* could of, should of, would of.

site *See* cite, sight, site.

some Avoid using the adjective *some* in place of the adverb *somewhat: He felt somewhat* [not *some*] *better after a good night's sleep.*

some of *See* all/all of. . . .

somewheres Use *somewhere* or *someplace* instead.

stationary, stationery *Stationary* means "standing still": *I worked out on my stationary bicycle. Stationery* is writing paper: *That stationery smells like a rose garden.*

suppose *See* expect, suppose.

sure Avoid confusing the adjective *sure* with the adverb *surely: The dress she wore to the party was surely bizarre.*

sure and *Sure and* is often used colloquially. In formal writing, *sure to* is preferred: *Be sure to* [not *be sure and*] *get to the wedding on time.*

take *See* bring, take.

that, which Many writers use *that* for restrictive (i.e., essential) clauses and *which* for nonrestrictive (i.e., nonessential) clauses: *The bull that escaped from the ring ran through my china shop, which was located in the square. (Also see Commas, pp. 339–44, in Part 8.)*

their, there, they're   *Their* is a possessive pronoun: *They gave their lives.* *There* is an adverb of place: *She was standing there.* *They're* is a contraction of *they are: They're reading more poetry this semester.*

this here, these here, that there, them there   When writing, avoid these nonstandard forms.

to, too, two   *To* is a preposition; *too* is an adverb; *two* is a number: *The two of us got lost too many times on our way to his house.*

try and   *Try to* is the standard form: *Try to* [not *try and*] *understand.*

uninterested   *See* disinterested, uninterested.

use, utilize   *Utilize* seldom says more than *use,* and the simpler term is almost always better: *We must learn how to use the computer's zip drive.*

verbally, orally   To say something *orally* is to say it aloud: *We agreed orally to share credit for the work, but when I asked her to confirm it in writing, she refused.* To say something *verbally* is to use words: *His eyes flashed anger, but he did not express his feelings verbally.*

wait for, wait on   People *wait for* those who are late; they *wait on* tables.

weather, whether   The noun *weather* refers to the atmosphere: *She worried that the weather would not clear up in time for the victory celebration.* *Whether* is a conjunction referring to a choice between alternatives: *I can't decide whether to go now or next week.*

well   *See* good, well.

whether   *See* weather, whether.

which, who, whose   *Which* is used for things, and *who* and *whose* for people: *My fountain pen, which I had lost last week, was found by a child who had never seen one before, whose whole life had been spent with ballpoints.*

will   *See* shall, will.

would of   *See* could of, should of, would of.

your, you're   *Your* is a possessive pronoun: *Is that your new car?* *You're* is a contraction of *you are: You're a lucky guy.*

There is a core simplicity to the English language and its American variant, but it's a slippery core.

—STEPHEN KING

Editing for Grammar Conventions

A word group that begins with a capital letter and ends with a period may not be a complete sentence. A complete sentence meets all three of the following requirements:

37
frag

www.mhhe.com/
wi
For information
and exercises
on sentence
fragments,
go to
Editing >
Sentence
Fragments

- **A sentence names a *subject*,** the who or what that the sentence is about.
- **A sentence has a complete *verb* that indicates tense, person, and number.**
- **A sentence includes at least one independent *clause*.** An independent clause has a subject and a complete verb and does not begin with a subordinating word such as *although, because, since, that, unless, which,* or *while.*

In the following example, the first word group meets all three requirements and is a complete sentence. Although the second word group has a subject and a complete verb, they are part of a dependent clause that begins with the subordinating word *that.* Because the second word group does not have an independent clause with a subject and a complete verb, it is not a complete sentence.

POSSIBLE FRAGMENT	Pool hustlers deceive their opponents in many ways. For example, deliberately putting so much spin on the ball that it jumps out of the intended pocket.

You can fix fragments in one of two ways: either transform them into sentences or attach them to a nearby independent clause.

IDENTIFY AND EDIT
Fragments

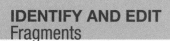

frag

**37
frag**

1. Do you see a complete verb?

Yes	No → FRAGMENT

FRAGMENT	For example, the concept of zero.
	subj verb
SENTENCE	For example, they were among the first to develop the concept of zero.

2. Do you see a subject?

Yes	No → FRAGMENT

FRAGMENT	Developed the concept of zero, for example.
	subj verb
SENTENCE	They developed the concept of zero, for example.

3. Do you see only a dependent clause?

No	Yes → FRAGMENT

FRAGMENT	Because they were among the earliest people to develop the concept of zero.
SENTENCE	The Mayas deserve a place in the history of mathematics because they were among the earliest people to develop the concept of zero.

SENTENCE

➤ Pool hustlers deceive their opponents in many ways. For
    they
example, deliberately put~~ting~~ so much spin on the ball that
      ^
it jumps out of the intended pocket.

➤ Pool hustlers deceive their opponents in many ways/,
   for example, by
~~For example,~~ deliberately putting so much spin on the
    ^
ball that it jumps out of the intended pocket.

CHARTING the TERRITORY

Intentional Fragments

Advertisers often use attention-getting fragments: "Nothing but
Net." "Because you're worth it." Occasionally, you may want to
use a sentence fragment for stylistic reasons. Keep in mind,
however, that advertising and college writing have different contexts and purposes. In formal writing, use deliberate sentence
fragments sparingly.

37a Repairing dependent-clause fragments

Fragments often begin with a subordinating word such as *although,
because, even though, since, so that, whenever,* or *whereas.* Usually, a
fragment that begins with a subordinating word can be attached to a
nearby independent clause.

37a
frag

➤ **None of the thirty-three subjects indicated any concern about**
  the amount or kind of fruit the institution served/, ~~Even~~ *even*
  though all of them identified diet as an important issue.

Sometimes it is better to transform such a fragment into a complete
sentence by deleting the subordinating word.

**37b
frag**

➤ **The solidarity of our group was undermined in two ways.**
  Participants
  ~~When participants~~ **either disagreed about priorities or**
  advocated significantly different political strategies.

37b Repairing phrase fragments

Often unintentional fragments are **phrases,** word groups that lack a
subject or a complete verb or both and usually function as modifiers
or nouns. Phrase fragments frequently begin with **verbals**—words derived from verbs, such as *putting* or *to put.*

| | That summer, we had the time of our lives. |
| **FRAGMENT** | *Fishing in the early morning, splashing in the lake after lunch, exploring the woods before dinner, and playing Scrabble until bedtime.* |

One way to fix this fragment is to transform it into an independent
clause with its own subject and verb:

> *We fished*
> That summer, we had the time of our lives. ~~Fishing~~ in the
> *splashed*   ^   *explored*
> early morning, ~~splashing~~ in the lake after lunch, ~~exploring~~
>   ^   *played*
> the woods before dinner, and ~~playing~~ Scrabble until bedtime.
>   ^

Another way to fix the problem is to attach the fragment to the part of the previous sentence that it modifies (in this case, *the time of our lives*):

>   *fishing*
> That summer, we had the time of our lives/, ~~Fishing~~ in the
>   ^
> early morning, splashing in the lake after lunch, exploring
>
> the woods before dinner, and playing Scrabble until bedtime.

Phrase fragments can also begin with one-word prepositions such as *as, at, by, for, from, in, of, on,* or *to.* To correct these, it is usually easiest to attach them to a nearby sentence.

> Impressionist painters often depicted their subjects in
>   *at*
> everyday situations/, ~~At~~ a restaurant, perhaps, or by the
>   ^
> seashore.

37c Repairing other types of fragments

Word groups that start with transitions or with words that introduce examples, appositives, lists, and compound predicates can also cause problems.

1. Word groups that start with transitions

Some fragments start with two- or three-word prepositions that function as transitions, such as *as well as, as compared with, except for, in addition to, in contrast with, in spite of,* and *instead of.*

➤ **For sixty-five years, the growth in consumer spending has**
  been both steep and steady/, ~~As~~ as compared with the growth
  in gross domestic product (GDP), which has fluctuated
  significantly.

37c
frag

2. Words and phrases that introduce examples

It is always a good idea to check word groups beginning with *for example, like, specifically,* or *such as.*

➤ **Elizabeth I of England faced many dangers as a princess. For**
  example, ~~falling~~ she fell out of favor with her sister, Queen Mary,
  and ~~being~~ was imprisoned in the Tower of London.

3. Appositives

An **appositive** is a noun or noun phrase that renames a noun or pronoun.

➤ **In 1965, Lyndon Johnson increased the number of troops in**
  Vietnam/, ~~A~~ a former French colony in southeast Asia.

4. Lists

Usually, you can connect a list to the preceding sentence using a colon. If you want to emphasize the list, consider using a dash instead.

➤ **In the 1930s, three great band leaders helped popularize**

jazz/: Louis Armstrong, Benny Goodman, and Duke

Ellington.

5. Compound predicates

A **compound predicate** is made up of at least two verbs as well as their objects and modifiers, connected by a coordinating conjunction such as *and, but,* or *or.* The parts of a compound predicate have the same subject and should be together in one sentence.

➤ **The group gathered at dawn at the base of the mountain/**
  and
  ~~And~~ assembled their gear in preparation for the morning's

climb.

A **comma splice** is a sentence with at least two independent clauses joined by only a comma.

COMMA
SPLICE

Dogs that compete in the annual Westminster Dog Show are already champions, they have each won at least one dog show before arriving at Madison Square Garden.

A **run-on sentence,** sometimes called a **fused sentence,** does not even have a comma between the independent clauses, making it difficult for readers to tell where one clause ends and the next begins.

RUN-ON

From time to time, new breeds enter the ring the Border Collie is a recent addition to the show.

Comma splices and run-ons often occur when clauses are linked with a transitional expression such as *as a result, for example, in addition, in other words,* or *on the contrary* or a conjunctive adverb such as *however, consequently, moreover,* or *nevertheless.* (*See p. 281 for a list of familiar conjunctive adverbs and transitional expressions.*)

www.mhhe.com/
wi
For information
and exercises
on comma
splices and run-
on sentences,
go to

Editing > Comma
Splices or
Editing > Run-on
Sentences

COMMA
SPLICE

Rare books can be extremely valuable, for example, an original edition of Audubon's *Birds of America* is worth thousands of dollars.

RUN-ON

Most students complied with the new policy however a few refused to do so.

Run-ons may also occur when a sentence's second clause either specifies or explains its first clause.

RUN-ON

The economy changed in 1991 corporate bankruptcies increased by 40 percent.

279

You can repair comma splices and run-on sentences in one of five ways:

1. Join the two clauses with a comma and a coordinating conjunction (*and, but, or, nor, for, so, yet*).
2. Join the two clauses with a semicolon.
3. Separate the clauses into two sentences.
4. Turn one of the independent clauses into a dependent clause.
5. Transform the two clauses into a single independent clause.

38b
cs/run-on

38a Joining two clauses with a comma and a coordinating conjunction such as *and* or *but*

Be sure to choose the coordinating conjunction that most clearly expresses the logical relationship between the clauses.

➤ John is a very stubborn person,ᶻ⁰ I had a hard time

convincing him to let me take the wheel.

38b Joining two clauses with a semicolon

A semicolon tells your reader that two clauses are logically connected. However, a semicolon does not spell out the logic of the connection.

➤ Most students complied with the new policy.ᵢ; a few

refused to do so.

To show the logic of the connection, you can add a conjunctive adverb or transitional expression.

➤ **Most students complied with the new policy; _however,_ a few refused.**

Familiar Conjunctive Adverbs and Transitional Expressions

**38b
cs/run-on**

also	incidentally	now
as a result	indeed	nonetheless
besides	in fact	of course
certainly	in other words	on the contrary
consequently	instead	otherwise
finally	in the meantime	similarly
for example	likewise	still
for instance	meanwhile	then
furthermore	moreover	therefore
however	nevertheless	thus
in addition	next	undoubtedly

The conjunctive adverb or transitional expression is followed by a comma when it appears at the beginning of the second clause. It can also appear in the middle of a clause, set off by two commas, or at the end, preceded by a comma.

➤ **Most students complied with the new policy; _, however,_ a few refused.**

➤ **Most students complied with the new policy; a few refused _, however_.**

When the first independent clause introduces or expands on the second one, you can use a colon instead of a semicolon.

➤ **Professor Johnson then revealed his most important point:**

the paper would count for half my grade.

IDENTIFY AND EDIT
Comma Splices and Run-ons

cs   run-on

These questions can help you spot comma splices and run-on sentences:

? *1. Does the sentence contain only one independent clause?*

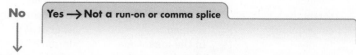

No → | Yes → **Not a run-on or comma splice** |

? *2. Does it contain two independent clauses joined by a comma and a coordinating conjunction such as and, but, or, nor, for, so, or yet?*

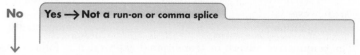

No → | Yes → **Not a run-on or comma splice** |

? *3. Does it contain two independent clauses joined by a semicolon or a semicolon and a transitional expression?*

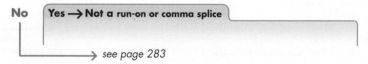

No → | Yes → **Not a run-on or comma splice** |

→ *see page 283*

If your answer to question 3 is no, you have a run-on or comma splice. You can repair it in one of five ways:

No
↓

**38b
cs/run-on**

RUN-ON	├──────── independent clause ─────────┤ Football and most other team sports have a time limit ├── independent clause ──┤ baseball has no time limit.
COMMA SPLICE	Football and most other team sports have a time limit, baseball has no time limit.
REVISED: COMMA AND COORDINATING CONJUNCTION	Football and most other team sports have a time limit, but baseball has no time limit. [See 38a.]
REVISED: SEMICOLON	Football and most other team sports have a time limit; baseball has no time limit. [See 38b.]
REVISED: TWO SENTENCES	Football and most other team sports have a time limit. Baseball has no time limit. [See 38c.]
REVISED: SUBORDINATION	Although football and most other team sports have a time limit, baseball has no time limit. [See 38d.]
REVISED: ONE INDEPENDENT CLAUSE	Baseball, unlike football and most other team sports, has no time limit. [See 38e.]

38d
cs/run-on

38c Separating clauses into two sentences

The simplest way to correct comma splices and run-on sentences is to turn the clauses into separate sentences.

➤ I realized that it was time to choose/ ~~either~~ I had to learn

   how to drive, or I had to move back to the city.

. Either

When the two independent clauses are part of a quotation, with a phrase such as *he said* or *she noted* between them, each clause should be a separate sentence.

➤ "This was the longest day of my life," she said/.
   "Unfortunately,
   ~~"unfortunately,~~ it's not over yet."

38d Turning one of the independent clauses into a dependent clause

Remember that readers will expect subsequent sentences to tell them more about the subject of the main clause.

   Although most
➤ ~~Most~~ students complied with the new policy, ~~however~~ a few

   refused to do so.

38e Transforming two clauses into one independent clause

Transforming two clauses into one clear and correct independent clause is often worth the work.

➤ I realized that it was time ~~to choose/~~ either ~~I had~~ to learn

how to drive or ~~I had~~ to move back to the city.

Sometimes you can change one of the clauses to a phrase and place it next to the word it modifies.

➤ Baseball cards are an obsession among some collectors*, first printed in the nineteenth century,*/~~. the cards were first printed in the nineteenth century.~~

39 Maintain subject-verb agreement.

Verbs must agree with their subjects in **person** (first, second, or third—*I, we; you; he, she, it, they*) and **number** (singular or plural). For regular verbs, the present tense *-s* or *-es* ending is added to the verb if its subject is third-person singular; otherwise, the verb has no ending.

Present Tense Forms of a Regular Verb: *Read*

	SINGULAR	PLURAL
First Person	I *read.*	We *read.*
Second Person	You *read.*	You *read.*
Third Person	He, she, it *reads.*	They *read.*

39
sv agr

www.mhhe.com/
wi
For information
and exercises
on subject-verb
agreement,
go to
**Editing >
Subject-Verb
Agreement**

Note, however, that the verb *be* has irregular forms in both the present and the past tense.

Present Tense and Past Tense Forms of the Irregular Verb *Be*

	SINGULAR	PLURAL
First Person	I *am/was* here.	We *are/were* here.
Second Person	You *are/were* here.	You *are/were* here.
Third Person	He, she, it *is/was* here.	They *are/were* here.

The verbs *have* and *do* have the following forms in the present tense.

Present Tense Forms of the Verb *Have*

	SINGULAR	PLURAL
First Person	I *have.*	We *have.*
Second Person	You *have.*	You *have.*
Third Person	He, she, it *has.*	They *have.*

Present Tense Forms of the Verb *Do* and Its Negative *Don't*

	SINGULAR	PLURAL
First Person	I *do/don't.*	We *do/don't.*
Second Person	You *do/don't.*	You *do/don't.*
Third Person	He, she, it *does/doesn't.*	They *do/don't.*

39a
sv agr

Watch out for mistakes in subject-verb agreement in the situations discussed in the following sections.

39a When a word group separates the subject from the verb

To locate the subject of a sentence, find the verb and then ask the *who* or *what* question about it ("Who is?" "What is?"). Does that subject match the verb in number?

oppose
➤ **The leaders of the trade union ~~opposes~~ the new law.**

The answer to the question "Who opposes?" is *leaders,* a plural noun, so the verb should be in the plural form: *oppose.*

If a word group beginning with *as well as, along with,* or *in addition to* follows a singular subject, the subject does not become plural.

opposes
➤ **My teacher, as well as other faculty members, ~~oppose~~ the**

new school policy.

39a
sv agr

IDENTIFY AND EDIT
Problems with Subject-Verb Agreement

agr

⭐ *1. Find the verb.*

> verb
> PROBLEM SENTENCE   The attorneys for the defense *plans* an afternoon news conference.

Verbs are words that specify action, condition, or state of being.

⭐ *2. Ask the* who *or* what *question to identify the subject.*

> subject   verb
> PROBLEM SENTENCE   The *attorneys* for the defense *plans* an afternoon news conference.

The answer to the question "Who plans?" is *attorneys*.

⭐ *3. Determine the person (first, second, or third) and number (singular or plural) of the subject.*

> subject
> PROBLEM SENTENCE   The *attorneys* for the defense plans an afternoon news conference.

The subject of the sentence—*attorneys*—is third-person plural.

⭐ *4. If necessary, change the verb to agree with the subject.*

>   *plan*
> EDITED PROBLEM SENTENCE   The attorneys for the defense ~~plans~~ an afternoon news conference.

39b Compound subjects

Compound subjects are made up of two or more parts joined by either a coordinating conjunction (*and, or, nor*) or a correlative conjunction (*both . . . and, either . . . or, neither . . . nor*).

1. Most compound subjects are plural.

   PLURAL *The king and his advisers* **were shocked by this turn of events.**

   PLURAL **This poem's** *first line and last word* **have a powerful effect on the reader.**

2. Some compound subjects are singular. Compound subjects should be treated as singular in the following circumstances:

   ▪ When they refer to the same entity:

   ➤ *My best girlfriend and most dependable advisor* **is my mother.**

   ▪ When they are considered as a single unit:

   ➤ **In some ways,** *forty acres and a mule* **continues to be what is needed.**

   ▪ When they are preceded by the word *each* or *every:*

   ➤ *Each* **man, woman, and child** *deserves* **respect.**

3. Some compound subjects can be either plural or singular. Compound subjects connected by *or, nor, either . . . or,* or *neither . . . nor* can take either a singular or a plural verb, depending on the subject that is closest to the verb.

SINGULAR   **Either the children or *their mother is***

                        to blame.

PLURAL   **Neither the experimenter nor *her subjects were***

                        aware of the takeover.

39c   Collective subjects

A **collective noun** names a unit made up of many persons or things, treating it as an entity, such as *audience, family, group,* and *team.*

1. Most often, collective nouns are singular. Words such as *news, physics,* and *measles* are usually singular as well, despite their *-s* ending. Units of measurement used collectively, such as *six inches* or *20%,* are also treated as singular.

    ➤   The *audience is* restless.

    ➤   That *news leaves* me speechless.

    ➤   *One-fourth* of the liquid *was* poured into test tube 1.

2. Some collective subjects are plural. When the members of a group are acting as individuals, the collective subject can be considered plural.

➤ The *group were* passing around a bottle of beer.

You may want to add a modifying phrase that contains a plural noun to make the sentence clearer and avoid awkwardness.

➤ The *group of troublemakers were* passing around

a bottle of beer.

When units of measurement refer to people or things, they are plural.

➤ *One-fourth* of the students in the class *are* failing

the course.

39d Indefinite subjects

Indefinite pronouns do not refer to a specific person or item.

- **Most indefinite pronouns are singular.** The following indefinite pronouns are always singular: *all, anybody, anyone, anything, each, either, everybody, everyone, everything, neither, nobody, no one, none, nothing, one, somebody, someone,* and *something.*

➤ *Everyone* in my hiking club *is* an experienced climber.

None and *neither* are always singular.

➤ In the movie, five men set out on an expedition, but *none returns.*

➤ *Neither sees* a way out of this predicament.

39e
sv agr

▪ **Some indefinite pronouns are always plural.** A handful of indefinite pronouns that mean more than one by definition (*both, few, many, several*) are always plural.

➤ *Both* of us *want* to go to the rally for the environment.

▪ **Some indefinite pronouns can be either plural or singular.** Some indefinite pronouns (*some, any, all, most*) may be either plural or singular depending on whether they refer to a plural or singular noun in the context of the sentence.

➤ *Some* of the *book is* missing, but *all* of the *papers are*

here.

39e When the subject comes after the verb

➤ Out back behind the lean-to *stand an old oak tree and a*

weeping willow.

In sentences that begin with *there is* or *there are,* the subject always follows the verb.

➤ There *is* a worn wooden *bench* in the shade of the two trees.

39f Subject complement

A **subject complement** renames and specifies the sentence's subject. It follows a **linking verb** that joins the subject to its description or definition. In the sentence below, the verb has been changed to agree with *gift,* the subject, instead of *books,* the subject complement.

➤ **One gift that gives her pleasure <del>are</del> books.**
   is

39g Relative pronouns

When a relative pronoun such as *who, which,* or *that* is the subject of a dependent clause, it is taking the place of a noun that appears earlier in the sentence—its **antecedent.** The verb that goes with *who, which,* or *that* needs to agree with this antecedent.

➤ **Measles is a childhood *disease that has* dangerous**

   side effects.

The phrase *one of the* implies more than one and is, therefore, plural. *Only one of the* implies just one, however, and is singular.

PLURAL **Tuberculosis is one of the diseases *that have***

   long, tragic histories in many parts of the world.

SINGULAR **Barbara is the only one of the scientists *who has***

   a degree in physics.

39h Phrases beginning with *-ing* verbs

A **gerund phrase** is an *-ing* verb form followed by objects, complements, or modifiers. When a gerund phrase is the subject in a sentence, it is singular.

39i
sv agr

➤ *Experimenting with drugs is* a dangerous rave practice.

39i Titles of works, names of companies, or words representing themselves

➤ Ernest Hemingway's *For Whom the Bell Tolls is* arguably his darkest work.

➤ *China Airlines is* based in Taiwan.

➤ The phrase *dog days designates* the hottest part of the summer.

40 Check for problems with verbs.

Verbs report action and show time. They change form to indicate person and number, voice and mood.

40a Learning the forms of regular and irregular verbs

**40a
vb**

www.mhhe.com/
wi
For information
and exercises
on verb forms
and tenses,
go to
Editing > Verbs
and Verbals

English verbs have five main forms, except for the verb *be,* which has eight.

- The **base form** is the form you find if you look up the verb in a dictionary. (*For irregular verbs, other forms are given as well. See pp. 296–98 for a list.*)

- The **present tense** form is used to indicate an action occurring at the moment or habitually, as well as to introduce quotations, literary events, and scientific facts (*40e, pp. 302–5 and 40g, p. 306*).

- The **past tense** is used to indicate an action completed at a specific time in the past (*40e, pp. 302–5*).

- The **past participle** is used with *have, has,* or *had* to form the perfect tenses (*40e, pp. 302–5*); with a form of the *be* verb to form the passive voice (*33b, pp. 245–46*); and as an adjective (the *polished* silver).

- The **present participle** is used with a form of the *be* verb to form the progressive tenses (*40e, pp. 302–5*). It can also be used as a noun (the *writing* is finished) and as an adjective (the *smiling* man).

295

Regular verbs always add *-d* or *-ed* to the base verb to form the past tense and past participle. **Irregular verbs,** by contrast, do not form the past tense or past participle in a consistent way. Here are the five principal forms of the regular verb *walk* and the irregular verb *begin* as well as the eight forms of the verb *be*.

40a
vb

Principal Forms of *Walk* and *Begin*

BASE	PRESENT TENSE (THIRD PERSON)	PAST TENSE	PAST PARTICIPLE	PRESENT PARTICIPLE
walk	*walks*	*walked*	*walked*	*walking*
begin	*begins*	*began*	*begun*	*beginning*

Principal Forms of *Be*

BASE	PRESENT TENSE	PAST TENSE	PAST PARTICIPLE	PRESENT PARTICIPLE
be	I *am.* He, she, it *is.* We, you, they *are.*	I *was.* He, she, it *was.* We, you, they *were.*	I have *been.*	I am *being.*

1. A list of common irregular verbs
You can also find the past tense and past participle forms of irregular verbs by looking up the base form in a standard dictionary.

Forms of Common Irregular Verbs

BASE	PAST TENSE	PAST PARTICIPLE
arise	arose	arisen
awake	awoke	awoke/awakened
be	was/were	been

BASE	PAST TENSE	PAST PARTICIPLE
beat	beat	beaten
become	became	become
begin	began	begun
blow	blew	blown
break	broke	broken
bring	brought	brought
buy	bought	bought
catch	caught	caught
choose	chose	chosen
cling	clung	clung
come	came	come
do	did	done
draw	drew	drawn
drink	drank	drunk
drive	drove	driven
eat	ate	eaten
fall	fell	fallen
fight	fought	fought
fly	flew	flown
forget	forgot	forgotten/forgot
forgive	forgave	forgiven
freeze	froze	frozen
get	got	gotten/got
give	gave	given
go	went	gone
grow	grew	grown
hang	hung	hung (for things)
hang	hanged	hanged (for people)
have	had	had

40a
vb

40a
vb

BASE	PAST TENSE	PAST PARTICIPLE
hear	heard	heard
know	knew	known
lose	lost	lost
pay	paid	paid
raise	raised	raised
ride	rode	ridden
ring	rang	rung
rise	rose	risen
say	said	said
see	saw	seen
set	set	set
shake	shook	shaken
sit	sat	sat
spin	spun	spun
steal	stole	stolen
spend	spent	spent
strive	strove/strived	striven/strived
swear	swore	sworn
swim	swam	swum
swing	swung	swung
take	took	taken
tear	tore	torn
tread	trod	trod/trodden
wear	wore	worn
weave	wove	woven
wring	wrung	wrung
write	wrote	written

2. *Went* and *gone, saw* and *seen*

Went and *saw* are the past tense forms of the irregular verbs *go* and *see. Gone* and *seen* are the past participle forms. These verb forms are sometimes confused.

➤ I had ~~went~~ *gone* there yesterday.

➤ We ~~seen~~ *saw* the rabid dog and called for help.

40b
vb

3. Irregular verbs such as *drink* (*drank/drunk*)

For a few irregular verbs, such as *swim* (*swam / swum*), *drink* (*drank / drunk*), and *ring* (*rang / rung*), the difference between the past tense form and the past participle is only one letter. Be careful not to mix up these forms in your writing.

➤ I had ~~drank~~ *drunk* more than eight bottles of water that day.

➤ The church bell had ~~rang~~ *rung* five times before she heard it.

40b Distinguishing between *lay* and *lie, sit* and *set,* and *rise* and *raise*

Even experienced writers confuse the verbs *lay* and *lie, sit* and *set,* and *rise* and *raise.* The correct forms are given below.

Often-Confused Verb Pairs and Their Principal Forms

BASE	PAST	PAST PARTICIPLE	PRESENT PARTICIPLE
lay (to place)	laid	laid	laying
lie (to recline)	lay	lain	lying
sit (to be seated)	sat	sat	sitting
set (to put on a surface)	set	set	setting
rise (to go/get up)	rose	risen	rising
raise (to lift up)	raised	raised	raising

One verb in each of these pairs (*lay, set, raise*) is **transitive,** which means that an object receives the action of the verb. The other verb (*lie, sit, rise*) is **intransitive** and cannot take an object. You should use a form of *lay, set,* or *raise* if you can replace the verb with *place* or *put.*

> direct object
>
> The dog *lays a bone* at your feet, then *lies* down and closes
>
> his eyes.

Lay and *lie* are also confusing because the past tense of the irregular verb *lie* is *lay* (*lie, lay, lain*). To avoid using the wrong form, always double-check the verb *lay* when it appears in your writing.

> laid
> He washed the dishes carefully, then ~~lay~~ them on a
> ^
> clean towel.

40c Adding an -s or -es ending

In the present tense, almost all verbs add an -s or -es ending if the subject is third-person singular. (*See pp. 285–87, for more on standard subject-verb combinations.*) Third-person singular subjects can be nouns (*woman, Benjamin, desk*), pronouns (*he, she, it*), or indefinite pronouns (*everyone*).

40d
vb

> *rises*
> The stock market ~~rise~~ when economic news is good.

If the subject is in the first person (*I*), the second person (*you*), or the third-person plural (*people, they*), the verb does *not* add an -s or -es ending.

> You invest~~s~~ your money wisely.

> People need~~s~~ to learn about companies before buying

> their stock.

40d Adding a -d or an -ed ending

These endings should be included on all regular verbs in the past tense and all past participles of regular verbs.

> *asked*
> The driving instructor ~~ask~~ the student driver to pull over

> to the curb.

> *mixed*
> After we had ~~mix~~ the formula, we let it cool.
>   ^

Also check for missing *-d* or *-ed* endings on past participles used as adjectives.

**40e
vb**

> *concerned*
> The ~~concern~~ parents met with the school board.
>   ^

40e Using tenses accurately

Tenses show the time of a verb's action. English has three basic time frames: present, past, and future, and each tense has simple, perfect, and progressive verb forms to indicate the time span of the actions that are taking place. (*For a review of the present tense forms of a typical verb and of the verbs* be, have, *and* do, *see pp. 285–87; for a review of the principal forms of regular and irregular verbs, which are used to form tenses, see pp. 295–98.*)

1. The simple present and past tenses

The **simple present tense** is used for actions occurring at the moment or habitually. The **simple past tense** is used for actions completed at a specific time in the past.

SIMPLE PRESENT

Every May, she *plans* next year's marketing strategy.

SIMPLE PAST

In the early morning hours before the office opened, she *planned* her marketing strategy.

2. The simple future tense

The **simple future tense,** used for actions that have not yet begun, takes *will* plus the verb.

SIMPLE FUTURE

In May, I *will plan* next year's marketing strategy.

40e
vb

3. The perfect tenses

The **perfect tenses,** used to indicate actions that were or will be completed by the time of another action or a specific time, take a form of *have* (*has, had*) plus the past participle.

PRESENT PERFECT

She *has* already *planned* next year's marketing strategy.

PAST PERFECT

By the time she resigned, Mary *had* already *planned* next year's marketing strategy.

FUTURE PERFECT

By the end of May, she *will have planned* next year's marketing strategy.

When the verb in the past perfect is irregular, be sure to use the proper form of the past participle.

➤ By the time the week was over, both plants had ~~grew~~ *grown*

five inches.

40e
vb

4. Progressive tenses

The progressive forms of the simple and perfect tenses, used to indicate ongoing action, take a form of *be* (*am, are, were*) plus the present participle.

PRESENT PROGRESSIVE

She *is planning* next year's marketing strategy now.

PAST PROGRESSIVE

She *was planning* next year's marketing strategy when she started to look for another job.

FUTURE PROGRESSIVE

During the month of May, she *will be planning* next year's marketing strategy.

5. Perfect progressive tenses

Perfect progressive tenses, used to indicate an action that takes place over a specific period of time, take *have* plus *be* plus the verb. The present perfect progressive tense is used for actions that start in the past and continue to the present; the past and future perfect progressive tenses are used for actions that ended or will end at a specified time or before another action.

PRESENT PERFECT PROGRESSIVE

She *has been planning* next year's marketing strategy since the beginning of May.

PAST PERFECT PROGRESSIVE

She *had been planning* next year's marketing strategy when she was offered another job.

FUTURE PERFECT PROGRESSIVE

By May 18, she *will have been planning* next year's marketing strategy for more than two weeks.

40f Using the past perfect tense

When a past event was ongoing but ended before a particular time or another past event, use the past perfect rather than the simple past.

> ➤ Before the Johnstown Flood occurred in 1889, people in the
> $\overset{had}{}$
>   area expressed their concern about the safety of the dam on
> $\overset{}{\wedge}$
>   the Conemaugh River.

People expressed their concern before the flood occurred.

If two past events happened simultaneously, however, use the simple past, not the past perfect.

> ➤ When the Conemaugh flooded, many people in the area ~~had~~
>   lost their lives.

Research findings are thought of as having been collected at one time in the past. Use the past or present perfect tense to report the results of research:

> ➤ Three of the compounds (nos. 2, 3, and 6) $\overset{responded}{\underset{\wedge}{\text{respond}}}$ positively
>   by turning purple.

40g Using the present tense

If the conventions of a discipline require you to state what your paper does, do so in the present, not the future, tense.

➤ **In this paper, I *describe* the effects of increasing NaCl**

concentrations on the germination of radish seeds.

Here are some other special uses of the present tense.

- By convention, events in a novel, short story, poem, or other literary work are described in the present tense.

  ➤ **Even though Huck's journey down the river ~~was~~ an** *is*

  escape from society, his relationship with Jim ~~was~~ *is*

  a form of community.

- Like events in a literary work, scientific facts are considered to be perpetually present, even though they were discovered in the past.

  ➤ **Mendel discovered that genes ~~had~~ different forms,** *have*

  or alleles.

- The present tense is also used to introduce a quote, paraphrase, or summary of someone else's writing.

  ➤ **William Julius Wilson ~~wrote~~ that "the disappearance** *writes*

  of work has become a characteristic feature of the

  inner-city ghetto" (31).

40h Using complete verbs

With only a few exceptions, all English sentences must contain a main verb along with any helping verbs that are needed to express the tense (*see pp. 302–5*) or voice (*see pp. 245–46*). **Helping verbs** include forms of *be, have,* and *do* and the modal verbs *can, could, may, might, shall, should,* and *will.* Helping verbs can be part of contractions (*He's running, we'd better go*), but they cannot be left out of the sentence entirely.

> *will*
> **They be going on a field trip next week.**
>   ^

A **linking verb,** often a form of *be,* connects the subject to a description or definition of it. Linking verbs can be part of contractions (*She's a student*), but they should not be left out entirely.

> *is*
> **Montreal a major Canadian city.**
>   ^

40i Using the subjunctive mood

The **mood** of a verb indicates the writer's attitude. Use the **indicative mood** to state or to question facts, acts, and opinions (*Our collection is on display. Did you see it?*). Use the **imperative mood** for commands, directions, and entreaties. The subject of an imperative sentence is always *you,* but the *you* is usually understood, not written out (*Shut the door!*). Use the **subjunctive mood** to express a wish, a demand, a request, or a recommendation, or to make a statement contrary to fact (*I wish I were a millionaire*). The mood that writers have the most trouble with is the subjunctive.

Present tense subjunctive verbs do not change form to signal person or number. The only form used is the verb's base form: *find* or *be,* not *finds* or *am, are, is.* The verb *be* has only one past tense form in the subjunctive mood: *were.*

WISH

If only I *were* more prepared for this test.

**41
pn agr** Words such as *ask, insist, recommend, request,* and *suggest* indicate the subjunctive mood; the verb in the *that* clause that follows should be in the subjunctive.

DEMAND

I insist that all applicants *find* their seats by 8:00 a.m.

CONTRARY-TO-FACT STATEMENT

He would not be so irresponsible if his father *were* [not *was*] still alive.

Note: Some common expressions of conjecture are in the subjunctive mood, including *as it were, come rain or shine, far be it from me,* and *be that as it may.*

41 Check for problems with pronouns.

A **pronoun** (*he / him, it / its, they / their*) takes the place of a noun. The noun that the pronoun replaces is called its **antecedent.** In the following sentence, *snow* is the antecedent of the pronoun *it:*

➤ The *snow* fell all day long, and by nightfall *it* was three

feet deep.

Like nouns, pronouns are singular or plural.

SINGULAR

The *house* was dark and gloomy, and *it* sat in a grove of tall cedars.

PLURAL

The *cars* swept by on the highway, all of *them* doing more than sixty-five miles per hour.

A pronoun needs an antecedent to refer to and agree with, and a pronoun must match its antecedent in number (*plural/singular*) and **gender** (*he/his, she/her, it/its*). A pronoun must also be in a form, or case, that matches its function in the sentence.

41a Making pronouns agree with their antecedents

Problems with pronoun-antecedent agreement tend to occur when a pronoun's antecedent is an indefinite pronoun, a collective noun, or a compound noun. Problems may also occur when writers are trying to avoid the generic use of *he*.

1. Indefinite pronouns

Indefinite pronouns such as *someone, anybody,* and *nothing* refer to nonspecific people or things. They sometimes function as antecedents

IDENTIFY AND EDIT
Problems with Gender Bias and Pronoun-Antecedent Agreement

agr

41a
pn agr

Try these three strategies for avoiding gender bias when an indefinite pronoun or generic noun is the antecedent in a sentence:

★ 1. *If possible, change the antecedent to a plural indefinite pronoun or a plural noun.*

> *All*
> ◆ ~~Each~~ of us should decide ~~their~~ *our* vote on issues, not personality.
> ^
> *Responsible citizens decide*
> ◆ ~~The responsible citizen decides~~ their vote on issues, not
> ^
> personality.

★ 2. *Reword the sentence to eliminate the pronoun.*

> ◆ Each of us should ~~decide their~~ vote on issues, not personality.
> *votes*
> ◆ The responsible citizen ~~decides their vote~~ on issues, not
> ^
> personality.

★ 3. *Substitute* he or she *or* his or her *(but never* his/her*) for the singular pronoun to maintain pronoun-antecedent agreement.*

> *his or her*
> ◆ Each of us should decide ~~their~~ vote on issues, not personality.
> ^ *his or her*
> ◆ The responsible citizen decides ~~their~~ vote on issues, not
> ^
> personality.
>
> **Caution:** Use this strategy sparingly. Using *he or she* or *his or her* several times in quick succession makes for tedious reading.

for other pronouns. Most indefinite pronouns are singular (*anybody, anyone, anything, each, either, everybody, everyone, everything, much, neither, nobody, none, no one, nothing, one, somebody, something*).

ALWAYS
SINGULAR
Did *either* of the boys lose *his* bicycle?

**41a
pn agr**

A few indefinite pronouns—*both, few, many,* and *several*—are plural.

ALWAYS
PLURAL
***Both* of the boys lost *their* bicycles.**

The indefinite pronouns *all, any, more, most,* and *some* can be either singular or plural depending on the noun to which the pronoun refers.

PLURAL
The students debated, *some* arguing that *their* assumptions about the issue were more credible than the teacher's.

SINGULAR
The bread is on the counter, but *some* of *it* has already been eaten.

Problems arise when writers attempt to make indefinite pronouns agree with their antecedents without introducing gender bias. There are three ways to avoid gender bias when correcting a pronoun agreement problem such as the following.

FAULTY
None of the great Romantic writers believed that their achievements equaled their aspirations.

1. If possible, change a singular indefinite pronoun to a plural
   pronoun, editing the sentence as necessary.

   > *All*
   > ➤ ~~None~~ of the great Romantic writers believed that
   >   *fell short of*
   > their achievements ~~equaled~~ their aspirations.

41a
pn agr

2. Reword the sentence to eliminate the indefinite pronoun.

   > *The*
   > ➤ ~~None of the~~ great Romantic writers believed that
   >   *did not equal*
   > their achievements ~~equaled~~ their aspirations.

3. Substitute *he or she* or *his or her* (but never *his/her*) for the
   singular pronoun. Change the sentence as necessary to avoid
   using this construction more than once.

   > ➤ None of the great Romantic writers believed that
   >   *his or her   had been realized*
   > ~~their achievements equaled their~~ aspirations.

2. Generic nouns

A **generic noun** represents anyone and everyone in a group—a typical doctor, the average voter. Because most groups consist of both
males and females, using male pronouns to refer to generic nouns is
usually sexist. To fix agreement problems with generic nouns, use one
of the three options suggested above.

> *College students*   *s*
> ➤ A ~~college student~~ should have a mind of their own.
>
>   *an independent point of view.*
> ➤ A college student should have a ~~mind of their own.~~

➤ A college student should have a mind of ~~their~~ own.
his or her

3. Collective nouns
Collective nouns such as *team, family, jury, committee,* and *crowd* are singular unless the people in the group are acting as individuals.

41a
pn agr

➤ All together, the crowd surged through the palace gates,

trampling over everything in ~~their~~ path.
its

➤ The committee left the conference room and returned to

~~its~~ offices.
their

If you are using a collective noun that has a plural meaning, consider adding a plural noun to clarify the meaning: *The committee members . . . returned to their offices.*

4. Compound antecedent
Compound antecedents joined by *and* are almost always plural.

➤ To remove all traces of the crime, James put the book and

the magnifying glass back in ~~its~~ place.
their

When a compound antecedent is joined by *or* or *nor,* the pronoun should agree with the closest part of the compound antecedent. If one part is singular and the other is plural, the sentence will be smoother and more effective if the plural antecedent is closest to the pronoun.

PLURAL **Neither *the child nor the parents* shared *their* food.**

When the two parts of the compound antecedent refer to the same person, or when the word *each* or *every* precedes the compound antecedent, use a singular pronoun.

**41b
ref**

SINGULAR **Being *a teacher and a mother* keeps *her* busy.**

SINGULAR ***Every* poem and letter by Keats has *its* own
special power.**

41b Making pronoun references clear

If a pronoun does not clearly refer to a specific antecedent, readers can become confused.

1. Ambiguous references
If a pronoun can refer to more than one noun in a sentence, the reference is ambiguous. To clear up the ambiguity, eliminate the pronoun and use the appropriate noun.

➤ **The friendly banter between Hamlet and Horatio eventually
provokes ~~him~~ to declare that his world view has changed.**
    Hamlet

Sometimes the ambiguous reference can be cleared up by rewriting the sentence.

➤ Jane Austen ~~and Cassandra~~ corresponded regularly ~~when~~

    When   *was in London, she*   *with Cassandra.*

   ~~she was in London.~~

2. Implied references

The antecedent that a pronoun refers to must be present in the sentence, and it must be a noun or another pronoun, not a word that modifies a noun. Possessives and verbs cannot be antecedents.

➤ In ~~Wilson's~~ essay "When Work Disappears," ~~he~~ proposes a

    his   *Wilson*

   four-point plan for the revitalization of blighted inner-city

   communities.

➤ Every weekday afternoon, my brothers skateboard home

                   their skateboards

   from school, and then they leave ~~them~~ in the driveway.

3. *This, that,* and *which*

The pronouns *this, that,* and *which* are often used to refer to ideas expressed in preceding sentences. To make the sentence containing the pronoun clearer, either change the pronoun to a specific noun or add a specific antecedent or clarifying noun.

➤ As government funding for higher education decreases,

                               these higher costs

   tuition increases. Are we students supposed to accept ~~this~~

   without protest?

➤ **As government funding for higher education decreases,**

 tuition increases. Are we students supposed to accept
 situation
 this without protest?
 ^

4. *You, they,* and *it*

The pronouns *you, they,* and *it* should refer to definite, explicitly stated
antecedents. If their antecedents are unclear, they should be replaced
with appropriately specific nouns, or the sentence should be rewrit-
ten to eliminate the pronoun.

 the government pays
➤ **In some countries such as Canada, ~~they pay~~ for such medical**
 ^

 procedures.

 students
➤ **According to college policy, ~~you~~ must have a permit to park**
 ^

 a car on campus.

 The
➤ **~~In the~~ textbook/ ~~it~~ states that borrowing to fund the purchase**
 ^

 of financial assets results in a double-counting of debt.

41c Choosing the correct pronoun case: for example, *I* vs. *me*

When a pronoun's form, or **case,** does not match its function in a sentence, readers will feel that something is wrong. Most problems with
pronoun case involve the subjective and objective forms.

- Pronouns in the subjective case are used as subjects or subject complements in sentences: *I, you, he, she, it, we, they, who, whoever.*
- Pronouns in the objective case are used as objects of verbs or prepositions: *me, you, him, her, it, us, them, whom, whomever.*

1. Pronouns in compound structures

41c
case

Compound structures (words or phrases joined by *and, or,* or *nor*) can appear as subjects or objects. If you are not sure which form of a pronoun to use in a compound structure, treat the pronoun as the only subject or object, and note how the sentence sounds.

SUBJECT   Angela and ~~me~~ were cleaning up the kitchen.
                                           I

Me [was] cleaning up the kitchen is clearly wrong. The correct form is the subjective pronoun *I.*

OBJECT   My parents waited for an explanation from
                            me
                      John and ~~I~~.

My parents waited for an explanation from I is clearly wrong. The correct form is the objective pronoun *me.*

2. Subject complements

A **subject complement** renames and specifies the sentence's subject. It follows a **linking verb.**

                                               I
SUBJECT   Mark's best friends are Jane and ~~me~~.
COMPLEMENT

You can also switch the order to make the pronoun into the subject: *Jane and I are Mark's best friends.*

IDENTIFY AND EDIT
Problems with Pronoun Case

case

**41c
case**

Follow these steps to decide on the proper form of pronouns in compound structures:

 1. Identify the compound structure (a pronoun and a noun or other pronoun joined by and, but, or, or nor) in the problem sentence.

> compound structure
>
> PROBLEM SENTENCE [Her or her roommate] should call the campus technical support office and sign up for broadband Internet service.
>
> compound structure
>
> PROBLEM SENTENCE The director gave the leading roles to [my brother and I].

2. Isolate the pronoun that you are unsure about, then read the sentence to yourself without the rest of the compound structure. If the result sounds wrong, change the case of the pronoun, and read the sentence again.

> PROBLEM SENTENCE [Her ~~or her roommate~~] should call the campus technical support office and sign up for broadband Internet service.
>
> *Her should call the campus technical support office* sounds wrong. The pronoun should be in the subjective case: *she.*
>
> PROBLEM SENTENCE The director gave the leading roles to [~~my brother and~~ I]
>
> *The director gave the leading roles to I* sounds wrong. The pronoun should be in the objective case: *me.*

3. If necessary, correct the original sentence.

> ◆ She
>   ~~Her~~ or her roommate should call the campus technical support
>   ∧ office and sign up for broadband Internet service.
>
> ◆ The director gave the leading roles to my brother and ~~I~~.
>   me
>   ∧

3. Appositives

Appositives are nouns or noun phrases that rename nouns or pronouns. They appear right after the word they rename and have the same function in the sentence that the word has.

SUBJECTIVE   **The two weary travelers, Ramon and ~~me~~,**
                                               I

                         found shelter in an old cabin.

SUBJECTIVE refers to **41c case**

OBJECTIVE   **The police arrested two protesters, Jane and ~~I~~.** *(me)*

4. *We* or *us*

When *we* or *us* comes before a noun, it has the same function in the sentence as the noun it precedes.

SUBJECTIVE   *(We)* **~~Us~~ students never get to decide such things.**

We renames the subject: *students.*

OBJECTIVE   **Things were looking desperate for ~~we~~ campers.** *(us)*

Us renames the object of the preposition *for: campers.*

5. Comparisons with *than* or *as*

In comparisons, words are often left out of the sentence because the reader can guess what they would be. When a pronoun follows *than* or *as,* make sure you are using the correct form by mentally adding the missing word or words.

➤ **Meg is quicker than she [is].**

➤ **We find ourselves remembering Maria as often as [we remember] her.**

If a sentence with a comparison sounds too awkward or formal, add the missing words: *Meg is quicker than she is.*

41d
case

6. Pronouns as the subject or the object of an infinitive

An **infinitive** is *to* plus the base verb (*to breathe*). A pronoun that functions as the subject or object of an infinitive should be in the objective case.

➤ **We wanted our lawyer and *her* to defend *us* against this unfair charge.**

(subject) *her* (object) *us*

7. Pronouns in front of an -ing noun (a gerund)

When a noun or pronoun appears before a **gerund** (an -*ing* verb form functioning as a noun), it should usually be treated as a possessive.

➤ The ~~animals~~ animals' fighting disturbed the entire neighborhood.

➤ Because of ~~them~~ their screeching, no one could get any sleep.

41d Choosing between *who* and *whom*

The relative pronouns *who, whom, whoever,* and *whomever* are used to introduce dependent clauses and in questions. Their case depends on their function in the dependent clause or question.

- **Subjective:** *who, whoever*
- **Objective:** *whom, whomever*

1. Pronouns in dependent clauses

If the pronoun is functioning as a subject and is performing an action, use *who* or *whoever.* If the pronoun is the object of a verb or preposition, use *whom* or *whomever.*

**41d
case**

SUBJECT	**Henry Ford, *who* started the Ford Motor Company, was autocratic and stubborn.**
OBJECT	**Ford's son Edsel, *whom* the auto magnate treated cruelly, was a brilliant automobile designer.**

2. Pronouns in questions

To choose the correct form for the pronoun, answer the question with a personal pronoun.

SUBJECT	***Who* founded the General Motors Corporation?**

The answer could be *He founded it. He* is in the subjective case, so *who* is correct.

OBJECT	***Whom* did the Chrysler Corporation turn to for leadership in the 1980s?**

The answer could be *It turned to him. Him* is in the objective case, so *whom* is correct.

42 Check for problems with adjectives and adverbs.

Adjectives and **adverbs** are words that qualify—or modify—the meanings of other words. Adjectives modify nouns and pronouns. Adverbs modify verbs, adjectives, and other adverbs.

42a Using adverbs correctly

www.mhhe.com/
wi
For information
and exercises on
adjectives and
adverbs, go to
Editing >
Adjectives and
Adverbs

Adverbs modify verbs, adjectives, other adverbs, and even whole clauses. They tell where, when, why, how, how often, how much, or to what degree.

➤ The authenticity of the document is *hotly* contested.

➤ The water was *brilliant* blue and *icy* cold.

➤ Dickens mixed humor and pathos *better* than any other English writer after Shakespeare.

➤ *Consequently,* Dickens is still read by millions.

Do not substitute an adjective for an adverb. Watch especially for the adjectives *bad, good,* and *real,* which sometimes substitute for the adverbs *badly, well,* and *really* in casual speech.

➤ He plays the role so ~~bad~~ *badly* that it is an insult to Shakespeare.

➤ At times, he gets ~~real~~ *really* close to the edge of the stage.

➤ I've seen other actors play the role ~~good~~, but they were *well*

classically trained.

42b Using adjectives correctly

Adjectives modify nouns and pronouns; they do not modify any other kind of word. Adjectives tell what kind or how many. They may come before or after the noun or pronoun they modify.

➤ The *looming* clouds, *ominous* and *gray,* frightened the children.

Some proper nouns have adjective forms. Proper adjectives, like the proper nouns they are derived from, are capitalized: *America / American.*

In some cases, a noun is used as an adjective without a change in form:

➤ *Cigarette* smoking harms the lungs and is banned in offices.

Occasionally, descriptive adjectives function as if they were nouns:

➤ The *unemployed* should not be equated with the *lazy.*

1. Do not use an adjective when an adverb is needed.

➤ He hit that ball ~~real good.~~ *really well.*

➤ She ~~sure~~ made me work hard for my grade. *certainly*

2. Use adjectives after linking verbs to describe the subject. Descriptive adjectives that modify a sentence's subject but appear after a linking verb are called **subject complements.**

➤ **During the winter, both Emily and Anne *were sick*.**

Linking verbs are related to states of being and the five senses: *appear, become, feel, grow, look, smell, sound,* and *taste.* Verbs related to the senses can be either linking or action verbs, depending on the meaning of the sentence.

	adjective
LINKING	The dog smelled *bad.*
	adverb
ACTION	The dog smelled *badly.*

3. Be aware of adjectives and adverbs that are spelled alike. In most instances, *-ly* endings indicate adverbs; however, words with *-ly* endings can sometimes be adjectives (*the lovely girl*). In standard English, many adverbs do not require the *-ly* ending, and some words are both adjectives and adverbs: *fast, only, hard, right,* and *straight.* Note that *right* also has an *-ly* form as an adverb: *rightly.* When in doubt, consult a dictionary.

42c Using positive, comparative, and superlative adjectives and adverbs

Most adjectives and adverbs have three forms: positive (*dumb*), comparative (*dumber*), and superlative (*dumbest*). The simplest form of the adjective is the positive form.

1. Comparatives and superlatives

Use the comparative form to compare two things and the superlative form to compare three or more things.

➤ **In total area, New York is a *larger* state than Pennsylvania.**

➤ **Texas is the *largest* state in the Southwest.**

42c
ad

2. *-er*/*-est* endings and *more*/*most*

To form comparatives and superlatives of short adjectives, add the suffixes *-er* and *-est* (*brighter*/*brightest*). With longer adjectives (three or more syllables), use *more* or *less* and *most* or *least* (*more dangerous*/*most dangerous*).

➤ **Mercury is the ~~most near~~ planet to the sun.**
    nearest

A few short adverbs have *-er* and *-est* endings in their comparative and superlative forms (*harder*/*hardest*). Most adverbs, however, including all adverbs that end in *-ly,* use *more* or *less* and *most* or *least* in their comparative and superlative forms.

➤ **She sings *more loudly* than we expected.**

Two common adjectives—*good* and *bad*—form the comparative and superlative in an irregular way: *good, better, best* and *bad, worse, worst.*

➤ **He felt ~~badder~~ as his illness progressed.**
    worse

3. Double comparatives and superlatives

Use either an *-er* or an *-est* ending or *more*/*most* to form the comparative or superlative, as appropriate; do not use both.

➤ Since World War II, Britain has been the ~~most~~ closest ally
of the United States.

4. Concepts that cannot be compared

**42d
ad**

Do not use comparative or superlative forms with *absolute* adjectives such as *unique, infinite,* and *impossible.* If something is unique, for example, it is the only one of its kind, making comparison impossible.

➤ You will never find a ~~more~~ *another* ~~unique~~ restaurant ~~than~~ *like* this one.

42d Avoiding double negatives

The words *no, not,* and *never* can modify the meaning of nouns and pronouns as well as other sentence elements.

NOUN	You are *no* friend of mine.
ADJECTIVE	The red house was *not* large.
VERB	He *never* ran in a marathon.

When two negatives are used together, though, they cancel each other out, resulting in a positive meaning. Unless you want your sentence to have a positive meaning *(I am not unaware of your feelings in this matter),* edit by changing or eliminating one of the negative words.

➤ They don't have ~~no~~ *any* reason to go there.

➤ He ~~can't~~ *can* hardly do that assignment.

43
Watch for problems with English grammar of special concern to multilingual writers.

Your native language or even the language of your ancestors may influence the way you use English. The following sections will help you with some common problems encountered by writers whose first language is not English. These sections might help native speakers as well.

43a
art

www.mhhe.com/
wi
For information
and exercises
on problem
areas for
multilingual
writers, go to

Editing >
Multilingual >
ESL Writers

43a Using articles (*a, an,* and *the*) appropriately

Some languages do not use articles at all, and most languages do not use articles in the same way as English. Therefore, articles often cause problems for multilingual writers. In English, there are only three articles: *a, an,* and *the.*

1. Using *a* or *an*

A or *an* refers to one nonspecific person, place, or thing. *A* is used before words that begin with consonant sounds, whether or not the first letter is a vowel (*a European vacation, a country*), and *an* is used before words that begin with vowel sounds, whether or not the first letter is a consonant (*an hour, an opener*)

Count nouns that are singular and refer to a nonspecific person, place, or thing take *a* or *an.* Noncount nouns and plural nouns do not take *a* or *an.* For a list of count and noncount nouns, see the box on page 328.

➤ The manager needs to hire *an* assistant.

➤ We needed to buy a̶ furniture for our apartment.

327

**43a
art**

COUNT AND NONCOUNT NOUNS

A common noun that refers to something specific that can be counted is a **count noun.** Count nouns can be singular or plural, like *cup* or *suggestion* (*four cups, several suggestions*). **Noncount nouns** are nonspecific; these common nouns refer to categories of people, places, or things and cannot be counted. They do not have a plural form. (*The pottery is beautiful. His advice was useful.*)

count nouns	noncount nouns
cars	transportation
computers	Internet
facts	information
clouds	rain
stars	sunshine
tools	equipment
machines	machinery
suggestions	advice
earrings	jewelry
tables	furniture
smiles	happiness

2. Using *the*

The refers to a specific person, place, or thing and can be used with singular or plural nouns. It means "the (these) and no other (none others)." A person, place, or thing is specific if it has already been referred to in a preceding sentence, if it is specified within the sentence itself, or if it is commonly known.

➤ We are trying to solve a difficult problem. *The problem* ~~Problem~~ started

when we planned two meetings for the same day.

➤ *The girl* ~~Girl~~ you have been waiting for is here.

➤ *The moon* ~~Moon~~ is shining brightly this evening.

43a
art

Exception: When a noun represents all examples of something, *the* should be omitted.

➤ *Dogs* ~~The dogs~~ were first domesticated long before recorded

history.

Common nouns that refer to a specific person, place, or thing take *the.* Most proper nouns do not use articles unless they are plural, in which case they take the article *the.* There are some exceptions, however:

- Proper nouns that include a common noun and *of* as part of the title (*the Museum of Modern Art, the Fourth of July, the Statue of Liberty*)
- Names of highways (*the Santa Monica Freeway*)
- Landmark buildings (*the Eiffel Tower*)
- Hotels (*the Marriott Hotel*)
- Cultural and political institutions (*the Metropolitan Opera, the Pentagon*)

- Parts of the globe, names of oceans and seas, deserts, land and water formations (*the West, the Equator, the North Pole, the Mediterranean, the Sahara, the Bering Strait*)
- Countries with more than one word in their names (*the Dominican Republic*)

43b Using helping verbs with main verbs

Verbs change form to indicate person, number, tense, voice, and mood. (*For a detailed discussion of verbs, see Chapter 40.*) To do all this, a **main verb** is often accompanied by one or more **helping verbs** in a **verb phrase.** Helping verbs include forms of *do, have,* and *be* as well as the modal verbs such as *may, must, should,* and *would.*

1. *Do, Does, Did*
The helping verb *do* and its forms *does* and *did* combine with the base form of a verb to ask a question or to emphasize something. It can also combine with the word *not* to create an emphatic negative statement.

QUESTION	*Do* you hear those dogs barking?
EMPHATIC STATEMENT	I *do* hear them barking.
EMPHATIC NEGATIVE	I *do not* want to have to call the police about those dogs.

2. *Have, Has, Had*
The helping verb *have* and its forms *has* and *had* combine with a past participle (usually ending in *-d, -t,* or *-n*) to form the *perfect tenses.* Do

not confuse the simple past tense with the present perfect tense (formed with *have* or *has*), which is distinct from the simple past because the action can continue in the present. (*For a review of perfect tense forms, see Chapter 40, p. 303.*)

SIMPLE PAST	Those dogs *barked* all day.
PRESENT PERFECT	Those dogs *have barked* all day.
PAST PERFECT	Those dogs *had barked* all day.

43b
vb

3. *Be*

Forms of *be* combine with a present participle (ending in *-ing*) to form the *progressive tenses,* which express continuing action. Do not confuse the simple present tense or the present perfect with these progressive forms. Unlike the simple present, which indicates an action that occurs frequently and might include the present moment, the present progressive form indicates an action that is going on right now. In its past form, the progressive tense indicates actions that are going on simultaneously. (*For a review of progressive tense forms, see Chapter 40, pp. 304–5.*)

SIMPLE PRESENT	Those dogs *bark* all the time.
PRESENT PROGRESSIVE	Those dogs *are barking* all the time.
PAST PROGRESSIVE	Those dogs *were barking* all day while I *was trying* to study.

Note: A number of verbs that are related to thoughts, preferences, and ownership are seldom used in the progressive tense in English. These include *appear, believe, know, like, need, own, seem, understand,* and *want.*

Forms of *be* combine with the past participle (which usually ends in *-d, -t,* or *-n*) to form the passive voice, which is often used to express a state of being instead of an action.

BE + PAST PARTICIPLE

PASSIVE   The dogs *were scolded* by their owner.

PASSIVE   I *was satisfied* by her answer.

Intransitive verbs such as *happen* and *occur* cannot appear in the passive voice because they do not take direct objects.

➤ The accident ~~was~~ happened after he returned from his trip.

4. Modals

Other helping verbs, called **modals,** signify the manner, or mode, of an action. Unlike *be, have,* and *do,* one-word modals such as *may, must,* and *will* are almost never used alone as main verbs, nor do they change form to show person or number. Modals do not add *-s* endings, two modals are never used together (such as *might could*), and modals are always followed by the base form of the verb without *to* (*He could be nicer*).

The one-word modals are *can, could, may, might, will, would, shall, should,* and *must.*

                                                  hv   mv

➤ Contrary to press reports, she *will* not *run* for political office.

Note that a negative word such as *not* may come between the helping and the main verb.

Phrasal modals, however, do change form to show time, person, and number. Here are some phrasal modals: *have to, have got to, used to, be supposed to, be going to, be allowed to, be able to.*

➤ Yesterday, I $\overline{was\ going\ to}$ study for three hours.
  hv   mv

➤ Next week, I $\overline{am\ going\ to}$ study three hours a day.
  hv   mv

43c Using complete subjects and verbs

1. Using a complete subject

Every clause in English has a subject, even if it is only a stand-in subject like *there* or *it*. Check your clauses to make sure that each one has a subject.

➤ No one thought the party could end, but ^it^ ended abruptly

   when the stock market crashed.

➤ *There is* general agreement that the crash helped bring on the

   Great Depression.

2. Including a complete verb

Verb structure, as well as where the verb is placed within a sentence, varies dramatically across languages, but in English each sentence needs to include at least one complete verb. The verb cannot be an infinitive—the *to* form of the verb—or an *-ing* form without a helping verb.

NOT COMPLETE	The caterer *to bring* dinner.
COMPLETE VERBS	The caterer *brings* dinner.
	The caterer *will bring* dinner.
	The caterer *is bringing* dinner.

NOT COMPLETE	Children *running* in the park.
COMPLETE VERBS	Children *are running* in the park.
	Children *have been running* in the park.
	Children *will be running* in the park.

43d Using only one subject or object

Watch out for repeated subjects in your clauses.

➤ The celebrity ~~he~~ signed my program.

Watch out as well for repeated objects in clauses that begin with relative pronouns (*that, which, who, whom, whose*) or relative adverbs (*where, when, how*).

➤ Our dog guards the house where we live ~~there~~.

Even if the relative pronoun does not appear in the sentence but is only implied, you should still omit repeated objects.

➤ He is the man I need to talk to ~~him~~.

The relative pronoun *whom* (He is the man *whom* I need to talk to) is implied, so *him* is not needed.

It wasn't a matter of rewriting but simply of tightening up all the bolts.

—MARGUERITE YOURCENAR

PART

8

Editing
for Correctness:

Punctuation, Mechanics, and Spelling

335

You may have been told that commas are used to mark pauses, but that is not an accurate general principle. To clarify meaning, commas are used in the following situations:

- Following introductory elements (*pp. 336–37*)
- After each item in a series and between coordinate adjectives (*pp. 337 and 339*)
- Between coordinated independent clauses (*p. 338*)
- To set off interruptions or nonessential information (*pp. 339–44*)
- To set off direct quotations (*pp. 346–47*)
- In dates, addresses, people's titles, and numbers (*pp. 347–48*)
- To replace an omitted word or phrase or to prevent misreading (*p. 348*)

44a

∧
,

www.mhhe.com/
wi

For information
and exercises
on commas,
go to

Editing >
Commas

44a Using a comma after an introductory word group

A comma both attaches an introductory word, phrase, or clause to and distinguishes it from the rest of the sentence.

➤ **Finally, the car careened to the right, endangering passers-by.**
     ∧

➤ **Reflecting on her life experiences, Washburn attributed her**
                                      ∧

   successes to her own efforts.

➤ **Until he noticed the handprint on the wall, the detective was**

frustrated by the lack of clues.

Do not add a comma after a word group that functions as the subject of the sentence, however.

➤ **Persuading his or her constituents/ is one of a politician's**
most important tasks.

When the introductory phrase is less than five words long and there is no danger of confusion without a comma, the comma can be omitted.

➤ **For several hours we rode on in silence.**

44b Using commas between items in a series

A comma should appear after each item in a series.

➤ **Three industries that have been important to New England**

are shipbuilding, tourism, and commercial fishing.

Commas clarify which items are part of the series.

CONFUSING   For the hiking trip, we needed to pack lunch,
                 chocolate and trail mix.

CLEAR   For the hiking trip, we needed to pack lunch,
                 chocolate, and trail mix.

44b

44c
∧
,

44c Using a comma in front of a coordinating conjunction joining independent clauses

When a coordinating conjunction (*and, but, for, nor, or, so,* or *yet*) is used to join clauses that could each stand alone as a sentence, put a comma before the coordinating conjunction.

➤ **Injuries were so frequent that he began to worry, and his**

   style of play became more cautious.

If the word groups you are joining are not independent clauses, do not add a comma. (*See p. 349.*)

Exception: If you are joining two short clauses, you may leave out the comma unless it is needed for clarity.

➤ **The running back caught the ball and the fans cheered.**

44d Adding a comma between coordinate adjectives

A comma is used between **coordinate adjectives** because these adjectives modify the noun independently.

➤ **This brave, intelligent, persistent woman was the first**

female to earn a Ph.D. in psychology.

If you cannot add *and* between the adjectives or change their order, they are **cumulative adjectives** and should not be separated with a comma or commas (*see p. 350*).

44e
∧
,

44e Using commas to set off nonessential elements

Nonessential, or **nonrestrictive,** words, phrases, and clauses add information to a sentence but are not required for its basic meaning to be understood. Nonrestrictive additions are set off with commas.

NONRESTRICTIVE

Mary Shelley's best-known novel, *Frankenstein or the*

***Modern Prometheus,* was first published in 1818.**

The sentence would have the same basic meaning without the title.

Restrictive words, phrases, and clauses are essential to a sentence because they identify exactly who or what the writer is talking about. Restrictive additions are not set off with commas.

IDENTIFY AND EDIT
Commas with Coordinate Adjectives

∧

Follow these steps if you have trouble determining whether commas should separate two or more adjectives that precede a noun:

44e
∧,

⭐ 1. *Identify the adjectives.*

> PROBLEM SENTENCE Ann is an [excellent art] teacher and a [caring generous] mentor.
>
> Note that nouns such as *art* can also be used as adjectives.

⭐ 2. *Try changing the order of the adjectives or putting the word* and *between them. Then read the adjectives and noun to yourself. How do they sound?*

> PROBLEM SENTENCE Ann is an [art excellent] teacher and a [generous caring] mentor.
>
> We could say that Ann is a generous caring mentor, but it would be awkward to say that she is an art excellent teacher.

> PROBLEM SENTENCE Ann is an [excellent and art] teacher and a [caring and generous] mentor.
>
> We could say that Ann is a caring and generous mentor, but it would be awkward to say that she is an excellent and art teacher.

⭐ 3. *If the phrase sounds wrong, the adjectives are cumulative and don't need a comma between them. If the phrase sounds right, the adjectives are coordinate and require a comma. If need be, correct the original sentence.*

> Ann is an excellent art teacher and a caring, generous mentor.
>
> ∧

RESTRICTIVE

Mary Shelley's novel *Frankenstein or the Modern Prometheus* was first published in 1818.

Without the title, the reader would not know which novel the sentence is referring to.

Three types of additions to sentences often cause problems: adjective clauses, adjective phrases, and appositives.

1. Adjective clauses

44e
∧
ˌ

Adjective clauses begin with a relative pronoun or an adverb—*who, whom, whose, which, that, where,* or *when*—and modify a noun or pronoun within the sentence.

NONRESTRICTIVE

With his tale of Odysseus, *whose journey can be traced on modern maps,* Homer brought accounts of alien and strange creatures to the ancient Greeks.

RESTRICTIVE

The contestant *whom he most wanted to beat* was his father.

Note: Use *that* only with restrictive clauses. *Which* can introduce either restrictive or nonrestrictive clauses. Some writers prefer to use *which* only with nonrestrictive clauses.

2. Adjective phrases

Like an adjective clause, an adjective phrase also modifies a noun or pronoun in a sentence. Adjective phrases begin with a preposition (for example, *with, by, at,* or *for*) or a verbal (a word formed from a verb). Adjective phrases can be either restrictive or nonrestrictive.

IDENTIFY AND EDIT
Commas with Nonrestrictive Words
or Word Groups

∧
⌄

Follow these steps if you have trouble deciding whether a
word or word group should be set off with a comma or commas:

44e
∧
⌄

⭑ 1. *Identify the word or word group that may need to be set off with commas.*
Pay special attention to words that appear between the subject and verb.

> PROBLEM SENTENCE
> subj
> Dorothy Parker [a member of the famous Algonquin
> verb
> Round Table] wrote humorous verse as well as short stories.
>
> PROBLEM SENTENCE
> subj   verb
> Her poem ["One Perfect Rose"] is a lament about a well-
> intentioned gift that falls short.

⭑ 2. *Read the sentence to yourself without the word or word group. Does the*
basic meaning stay the same, or does it change? Can you tell what
person, place, or thing the sentence is about?

> SENTENCE WITHOUT THE WORD GROUP
> Dorothy Parker wrote humorous verse as well as
> short stories.
> The subject of the sentence is identified by name, and the basic
> meaning of the sentence does not change.
>
> SENTENCE WITHOUT THE WORD GROUP
> Her poem is a lament about a well-intentioned gift that
> falls short.
> Without the words "One Perfect Rose," we cannot tell what poem the
> sentence is describing.

3. *If the meaning of the sentence stays the same without the word or word group, set it off with commas. If the meaning changes, the word or word group should not be set off with commas.*

> - Dorothy Parker, a member of the famous Algonquin Round Table, wrote humorous verse as well as short stories.
>
> - Her poem "One Perfect Rose" is a lament about a well-intentioned gift that falls short.
>
>   The sentence is correct. Commas are not needed to enclose "One Perfect Rose."

44e
,

NONRESTRICTIVE

Some people, *by their faith in human nature or their general good will,* bring out the best in others.

The phrase is nonessential because it does not specify which people are being discussed.

RESTRICTIVE

People *fighting passionately for their rights* can inspire others to join a cause.

The phrase indicates which people the writer is talking about.

3. Appositives

Appositives are nouns or noun phrases that rename nouns or pronouns and appear right after the word they rename.

NONRESTRICTIVE

One researcher, *the widely respected R. S. Smith,* has shown that a child's performance on IQ tests can be very inconsistent.

Because *one researcher* already refers to the person at issue, the researcher's name is supplementary but not essential information.

44f

∧
'

RESTRICTIVE

The researcher *R. S. Smith* has shown that a child's performance on IQ tests is not reliable.

The name *R. S. Smith* tells readers which researcher is meant.

44f Using a comma or commas with transitional and parenthetical expressions, contrasting comments, and absolute phrases

1. Transitional expressions

Conjunctive adverbs (*however, therefore, moreover*) and other transitional phrases (*for example, on the other hand*) are usually set off by commas. (*For a list of transitional expressions, see Part 7: Editing for Grammar Conventions, p. 281.*)

➤ Brian Wilson, for example, was unable to cope with the
   ∧   ∧
   pressures of touring with the Beach Boys.

When a transitional expression connects two independent clauses, use a semicolon before and a comma after it.

➤ **The Beatles were a phenomenon when they toured the**

United States in 1964; subsequently, they became the most

successful rock band of all time.

Short expressions such as *also, at least, certainly, instead, of course, then, perhaps,* and *therefore* do not always need to be set off with commas.

44f

➤ **I found my notes and *also* got my story in on time.**

2. Parenthetical expressions

The information that parenthetical expressions provide is relatively insignificant and could easily be left out. Therefore, they are set off with a comma or commas.

➤ **Human cloning, so they say, will be possible within a decade.**

3. Contrasting comments

Contrasting comments beginning with words such as *not, unlike,* or *in contrast to* should be set off with commas.

➤ **Adam Sandler is talented as a comedian, not a tragedian.**

4. Absolute phrases

Absolute phrases usually include a noun (*sunlight*) followed by a participle (*shining*) and are used to modify whole sentences.

➤ The snake slithered through the tall grass, the sunlight
   shining now and then on its green skin.

44g Using a comma or commas to set off words
of direct address, *yes* and *no,* mild interjections,
and tag questions

44h

➤ We have finished this project, Mr. Smith, without any help
   from your foundation.

➤ Yes, I will meet you at noon.

➤ Of course, if you think that's what we should do, then
   we'll do it.

➤ We can do better, don't you think?

44h Using a comma or commas to separate
a direct quotation from the rest of the sentence

➤ Irving Howe declares, "Whitman is quite realistic about the
   place of the self in an urban world" (261).

➤ "Whitman is quite realistic about the place of the self in an
   urban world," declares Irving Howe (261).

A comma is not needed to separate an indirect quotation or a paraphrase from the words that identify its source.

➤ **Irving Howe notes/ that Whitman realistically depicts the urban self as free to wander (261).**

44i Using commas with dates, addresses, titles, and numbers

- **Dates.** Use paired commas in dates when the month, day, and year are included. Do not use commas when the day of the month is omitted or when the day appears before the month.

  ➤ **On March 4, 1931, she traveled to New York.**

  ➤ **She traveled to New York in March 1931.**

  ➤ **She traveled to New York on 4 March 1931.**

- **Addresses.** Use commas to set off the parts of an address or the name of a state, but do not use a comma preceding a zip code.

  ➤ **Here is my address for the summer: 63 Oceanside Drive, Apt. 2A, Surf City, New Jersey 06106.**

- **People's titles or degrees.** Put a comma between the person's name and the title or degree when it comes after the name, followed by another comma.

  ➤ **Luis Mendez, MD, gave her the green light to resume her exercise regimen.**

■ **Numbers.** When a number has more than four digits, use commas to mark off the numerals by hundreds—that is, by groups of three beginning at the right.

➤ **Andrew Jackson received 647,276 votes in the 1828 presidential election.**

If the number is four digits long, the comma is not required.

➤ **The survey had 1856 [or 1,856] respondents.**

Exceptions: Street numbers, zip codes, telephone numbers, page numbers (p. 2304), and years (1828) do not include commas.

44k
no ,

44j Using a comma to take the place of an omitted word or phrase or to prevent misreading

When a writer omits one or more words from a sentence to create an effect, a comma is often needed to make the meaning of the sentence clear for readers.

➤ **Under the tree he found his puppy, and under the car, his cat.**

Commas are also used to keep readers from misunderstanding a writer's meaning when words are repeated or might be misread.

➤ **Many birds that sing, sing first thing in the morning.**

44k Common errors in using commas

A comma used incorrectly can confuse readers. Commas should *not* be used in the following situations.

- To separate major elements in an independent clause

  ➤ **Reflecting on one's life⁄ is necessary for emotional growth.**

    The subject, *reflecting,* should not be separated from the verb, *is.*

  ➤ **Washburn decided⁄ that her own efforts were responsible for her successes.**

    The verb *decided* should not be separated from its direct object, the subordinate clause *that her own efforts were responsible for her successes.*

**44k
no ,**

- Before the first or after the final item in a series

  ➤ **Americans work longer hours than⁄ German, French, or British workers⁄ are expected to work.**

  Note: Commas should never be used after *such as* or *like.* (See p. 351.)

- To separate compound word groups that are not independent clauses

  ➤ **Injuries were so frequent that he became worried⁄ and started to play more cautiously.**

- To set off restrictive elements

  ➤ **The applicants⁄ who had studied for the admissions test⁄ were restless and eager for the exam to begin.**

➤ **The director/ Michael Curtiz/ was responsible for many great films in the 1930s and 1940s, including *Casablanca*.**

Adverb clauses beginning with *after, as soon as, before, because, if, since, unless, until,* and *when* are usually essential to a sentence's meaning and therefore are not usually set off with commas when they appear at the end of a sentence.

RESTRICTIVE   I am eager to test the children's IQ again *because significant variations in a child's test score indicate that the test itself may be flawed.*

Clauses beginning with *although, even though, though,* and *whereas* present a contrasting thought and are usually nonrestrictive.

NONRESTRICTIVE   IQ tests can be useful indicators of a child's abilities, *although they should not be taken as the definitive measurement of a child's intelligence.*

▪ Between cumulative adjectives (see p. 339):

➤ **Three/ well-known/ American writers visited the artist's studio.**

▪ Between adjectives and nouns

➤ **An art review by a celebrated, powerful/ writer would be guaranteed publication.**

▪ Between adverbs and adjectives

> ➤ **The studio was a delightfully/ chaotic environment,
> with canvases everywhere and paints spilled out
> in a fiesta of color.**

▪ After coordinating conjunctions (*and, but, or, nor, for, so, yet*):

> ➤ **The *duomo* in Siena was begun in the thirteenth
> century, and/ it was used as a model for other Italian
> cathedrals.**

**44k
no ,**

▪ After *although, such as,* or *like*

> ➤ **Stage designers can achieve many unusual effects,
> such as/ the helicopter that landed in *Miss Saigon*.**

▪ Before a parenthesis

> ➤ **When they occupy an office cubicle/ (a relatively
> recent invention), workers need to be especially
> considerate of their neighbors.**

▪ With a question mark or an exclamation point

> ➤ **"Where are my glasses?/" she asked in a panic.**

45 Semicolons

Semicolons are used to join ideas that are closely related and grammatically equivalent.

45a Using a semicolon to join independent clauses

45a
;

www.mhhe.com/
wi
For information
and exercises
on semicolons,
go to
Editing >
Semicolons

A semicolon should be used to join two related independent clauses when they are not joined by a comma and a coordinating conjunction (*and, but, or, nor, for, so, yet*). If readers are able to see the relationship between the two without the help of a coordinating conjunction, a semicolon is effective.

➤ Before 8000 BC wheat was not the luxuriant plant it is
   today; it was merely one of many wild grasses that spread
   throughout the Middle East.

Sometimes, the close relationship is a contrast.

➤ Philip had completed the assignment; Lucy had not.

Note: If a comma is used between two clauses without a coordinating conjunction, the sentence is a comma splice, a serious error. If no punctuation appears between the two clauses, the sentence is a run-on. One way to correct a comma splice or a run-on is with a semicolon. (*For more on comma splices and run-on sentences, see Part 7: Editing for Grammar Conventions, pp. 279–85.*)

45b Using semicolons with transitional expressions that connect independent clauses

Transitional expressions, including transitional phrases (*after all, even so, for example*) and conjunctive adverbs (*consequently, however*), indicate the way that two clauses are related to each other. When a transitional expression appears between two clauses, it is preceded by a semicolon and usually followed by a comma. (*For a list of transitional expressions, see Part 7, Editing for Grammar Conventions, p. 281.*)

➤ **Sheila had to wait until the plumber arrived; consequently,**

   she was late for the exam.

The semicolon always appears between the two clauses, even when the transitional expression appears in another position within the second clause. Wherever it appears, the transitional expression is usually set off with a comma or commas.

➤ **My friends are all taking golf lessons; my roommate and I,**

   however, are more interested in tennis.

45c Using a semicolon to separate items in a series when the items contain commas

Because the following sentence contains so many elements, the semicolons are needed for clarity.

➤ The committee included Dr. Curtis Youngblood, the county
medical examiner; Roberta Collingwood, the director of the
bureau's criminal division; and Darcy Coolidge, the chief
of police.

45d Common errors in using semicolons

Watch out for and correct common errors in using the semicolon.

- To join a dependent clause to an independent clause

  ➤ Professional writers need to devote time every day
  to their writing; because otherwise they can lose
  momentum.

  ➤ Although housecats seem tame and lovable;, they can
  be fierce hunters.

- To join independent clauses linked by a coordinating conjunction (*and, but, or, nor, for, so,* or *yet*)

  ➤ Nineteenth-century women wore colorful clothes;, but
  their clothes often look drab in the black-and-white
  photographs of the era.

- To introduce a series or an explanation

➤ My day was planned/: a morning walk, an afternoon in
   ^
the library, dinner with friends, and a great horror

movie.

➤ The doctor finally diagnosed the problem/: a severe
   ^
sinus infection.

46 Colons

A colon draws attention to what it is introducing. It also has other conventional uses.

www.mhhe.com/
wi
For information
and exercises
on colons, go to
Editing > Colons

46a Using colons to introduce lists, appositives, or quotations

Colons are almost always preceded by complete sentences (independent clauses).

LIST   The novel deals with three kinds of futility:
                                                                  ^

pervasive poverty, unrequited love, and

inescapable aging.

APPOSITIVE	**In October 1954, the Northeast was devastated by a ferocious storm: Hurricane Hazel.**
QUOTATION	**He took my hand and said the words I had been dreading: "I really want us to be just friends."**

46c
:

46b Using a colon when a second independent clause elaborates on the first one

The colon can be used to link independent clauses when the second clause restates or elaborates on the first. Use it when you want to emphasize the second clause.

➤ **I can predict tonight's sequence of events: My brother will arrive late, talk loudly, and eat too much.**

Note: When a complete sentence follows a colon, the first word may begin with either a capital or a lowercase letter. Whatever you decide to do, though, you should use the same style throughout your document.

46c Using colons in business letters, to indicate ratios, to indicate times of day, for city and publisher citations in bibliographies, and to separate titles and subtitles

➤ **Dear Mr. Worth:**

➤ **The ratio of armed to unarmed members of the gang was 3:1.**

➤ **He woke up at 6:30 in the morning.**

➤ **New York: McGraw-Hill, 2007**

➤ *Possible Lives: The Promise of Public Education in America*

Note: Colons are often used to separate biblical chapters and verses (John 3:16), but the Modern Language Association (MLA) recommends using a period instead (John 3.16).

46d Common errors in using the colon

46d
:

- Between a verb and its object or complement:

  ➤ **The critical elements in a good smoothie are/ yogurt, fresh fruit, and honey.**

- Between a preposition and its object or objects:

  ➤ **The novel deals with/ pervasive poverty.**

  ➤ **Many feel that cancer can be prevented by a diet of/ fruit, nuts, and vegetables.**

- After *such as, for example,* or *including:*

  ➤ **I am ready for a change, such as/ a trip to the Bahamas or a move to another town.**

Apostrophes show possession and indicate omitted letters in contractions. Apostrophes are used in such a wide variety of ways that they can be confusing. The most common confusion is between plurals and possessives.

47a
ˇ

www.mhhe.com/
wi
For information
and exercises
on apostrophes,
go to
Editing >
Apostrophes

47a Using apostrophes to indicate possession

For a noun to be possessive, two elements are usually required: someone or something is the possessor, and someone, something, or some attribute or quality is possessed.

Note: If you are wondering whether a particular noun should be in the possessive form, reword the sentence using the word *of* (*the bone of the dog*) to make sure that the noun is not plural.

1. Forming possessives with -'s

To form the possessive of all singular nouns, as well as plural nouns that do not end in -*s,* add an apostrophe plus -*s* to the noun.

NOUN/PRONOUN	NUMBER	AS A POSSESSIVE
baby	singular	a baby's smile
hour	singular	an hour's time
men	plural	the men's club
children	plural	the children's papers

Even singular nouns that end in -s form the possessive by adding -'s.

➤ **James's adventure, Ross's flag, Elvis's songs**

If a singular noun with more than two syllables ends in -s and adding -'s would make the word sound awkward, it is acceptable to use only an apostrophe to form the possessive.

➤ **Socrates' students remained loyal to him.**

47a
∨

2. Forming possessives with only an apostrophe
Plural nouns that end in -s take only an apostrophe to form the possessive.

NOUN/PRONOUN	NUMBER	AS A POSSESSIVE
babies	plural	the babies' smiles
companies	plural	the companies' employees
robbers	plural	the robbers' clever plan

3. Showing joint possession
To express joint ownership by two or more people, use the possessive form for the last name only; to express individual ownership, use the possessive form for each name.

➤ **Felicia and Elias's report**

➤ **The city's and the state's finances**

4. Forming the possessive of compound nouns
For compound words, add an apostrophe plus *-s* to the last word in the compound to form the possessive.

➤ **My father-in-law's job**

47b Using an apostrophe and -s with indefinite pronouns

Indefinite pronouns such as *no one, everyone, everything,* and *something* do not refer to a specific person or a specific item. Use *-'s* to form the possessive.

➤ **Well, it is *anybody's* guess.**

47c Using apostrophes to mark contractions

In a contraction, the apostrophe serves as a substitute for omitted letters.

it's	for *it is* or *it has*
weren't	for *were not*

Apostrophes can also substitute for omitted numbers in a year (*The class of '06*).

47d Using an apostrophe with -s to form plural numbers, letters, abbreviations, and words used as words

An apostrophe plus *-s* (*'s*) can be used to show the plural of a number, a letter, or an abbreviation. Underline or italicize single letters but not the apostrophe or the *-s*.

➤ **He makes his 2's look like 5's.**

➤ *Committee* **has two *m*'s, two *t*'s, and two *e*'s.**

➤ **Professor Morris has two Ph.D.'s.**

Exceptions: If an abbreviation does not have periods, the apostrophe is not necessary (*RPMs*). The apostrophe is also not necessary to form the plural of dates (*1990s*).

If a word is used as a word rather than as a symbol of the meaning it conveys, it can be made plural by adding an apostrophe plus *-s*. The word should be italicized or underlined but not the *-s*.

➤ **There are twelve *no*'s in the first paragraph.**

47e Common errors in using apostrophes

Do not use an apostrophe in the following situations.

■ **With a plural noun.** Most often, writers misuse the apostrophe by adding it to a plural noun that is not possessive. The plurals of most nouns are formed by adding *-s: boy / boys; girl / girls; teacher / teachers.* Possessives are formed by adding an apostrophe plus *-s* ('*s*): *boy / boy's; girl / girl's; teacher / teacher's.* The possessive form and the plural form are not interchangeable.

➤ The ~~teacher's~~ *teachers* asked the ~~girl's~~ *girls* and ~~boy's~~ *boys* for their

attention.

■ **With possessive pronouns and contractions.** Be careful not to use a contraction when a possessive is called for, and vice versa. Personal pronouns and the relative pronoun *who* have special possessive forms, which never require apostrophes (*my / mine, your / yours, his, her / hers, it / its, our / ours, their / theirs,* and *whose*). When an apostrophe appears with a pronoun, the apostrophe usually marks omissions in a contraction, unless the pronoun is indefinite. (*See p. 360.*)

> The dog sat down and scratched ~~it's~~ *its* fleas.

Its is a possessive pronoun. *It's* is a contraction for *it is* or *it has:* *It's* [*It + is*] too hot.

> Is that ~~you're~~ *your* new car?

Your is a possessive pronoun; *you're* is a contraction of *you are.*

48 Quotation Marks

www.mhhe.com/ wi For information and exercises on quotation marks, go to

Editing > Quotation Marks

Quotation marks are used to enclose words, phrases, and sentences that are quoted directly; titles of short works such as poems, articles, songs, and short stories; and words and phrases used in a special sense.

48a Using quotation marks to indicate direct quotations

Direct quotations from written material may include whole sentences or only a few words or phrases.

➤ In *Angela's Ashes,* Frank McCourt writes, "Worse than the ordinary miserable childhood is the miserable Irish childhood" (11).

➤ Frank McCourt believes that being Irish worsens what is all too "ordinary"—a "miserable childhood" (11).

Use quotation marks to enclose everything a speaker says in written dialogue. If the quoted sentence is interrupted by a phrase like *he said,* enclose the rest of the quotation in quotation marks.

Do not use quotation marks to set off an indirect quotation, which reports what a speaker said but does not use the exact words.

➤ He said that ⸢he didn't know what I was talking about.⸥

Exception: If you are using a quotation that is longer than four typed lines, set it off from the text as a **block quotation.** A block quotation is *not* surrounded by quotation marks.

> As Carl Schorske points out, the young Freud was passionately interested in classical archeology:
>
>> He cultivated a new friendship in the Viennese professional elite—especially rare in those days of withdrawal—with Emanuel Loewy, a professor of archeology. "He keeps me up till three o'clock in the morning," Freud wrote appreciatively to Fliess. "He tells me about Rome." (273)

Use single quotation marks to set off a quotation within a quotation.

➤ **When the press demanded stronger players and a successful football season, the president of the university said, "I know you're saying to me, 'We want a winning football team.' But I'm telling you this: 'I want an honest football team.' "**

48b Using quotation marks to enclose titles of short works

The titles of long works, such as books, are usually underlined or put in italics. (*See Chapter 53, p. 389.*) The titles of book chapters, essays, most poems, and other short works are usually put in quotation marks. Quotation marks are also used for titles of unpublished works, including student papers, theses, and dissertations.

"The Girl in Conflict" is Chapter 11 of *Coming of Age in Samoa.*

Note: If quotation marks are needed within the title of a short work, use single quotation marks: "The 'Animal Rights' War on Medicine."

48c Using quotation marks to indicate that a word or phrase is being used in a special way

Put quotation marks around a word or phrase that someone else has used in a way that you or your readers may not agree with. Quotation marks used in this way function as raised eyebrows do in conversation and should be used sparingly.

➤ **The "worker's paradise" of Stalinist Russia included slave-labor camps.**

Words cited as words can also be put in quotation marks, although the more common practice is to italicize them.

➤ **The words "compliment" and "complement" sound alike but have different meanings.**

48d
" "

48d Other punctuation with quotation marks

As you edit, check all closing quotation marks and the marks of punctuation that appear next to them to make sure that you have placed them in the right order.

1. Periods and commas

Place the period or comma before the final quotation mark even when the quotation is only one or two words long.

➤ **In *The Atlantic*, Katha Pollitt writes, "The first thing that strikes one about Plath's journals is what they leave out."**

Exception: A parenthetical citation in either MLA or APA style always appears between the closing quotation mark and the period: *"Squaresville, U.S.A. vs. Beatsville" makes the Midwestern small-town home seem boring compared with the West Coast artist's "pad" (31).*

2. Colons and semicolons
Place colons and semicolons after the final quotation mark.

➤ **Dean Wilcox cited the items he called his "daily delights":**
a free parking space for his scooter at the faculty club,
a special table in the club itself, and friends to laugh with
after a day's work.

48d
" "

3. Question marks and exclamation points
Place a question mark or an exclamation point after the final quotation
mark unless the quoted material is itself a question or an exclamation.

➤ **Why did she name her car "Buck"?**

➤ **He had many questions, such as "Can you really do unto**
others as you would have them do unto you?"

4. Dashes
Place a dash outside either an opening or a closing quotation mark,
or both, if it precedes or follows the quotation or if two dashes are used
to set off the quotation.

➤ **One phrase—"time is running out"—haunted me throughout**
my dream.

Place a dash inside either an opening or a closing quotation mark if
it is part of the quotation.

➤ **"Where is the—" she called. "Oh, here it is. Never mind."**

48e Integrating quotations into your sentences

If you introduce a quotation with a complete sentence, you can use a colon before it.

➤ **He was better than anyone else at the job, but he didn't want it: "I don't know what to do," he said.**

If you introduce a direct quotation with *he said, she noted,* or a similar expression, use a comma.

48e
" "

➤ **He said, "She believed I could do it."**

➤ **"She believed I could do it," he said.**

Do not use a comma after expressions such as *he said* or *the researchers note* if an indirect quotation or a paraphrase follows.

➤ **He said/ that he believed he could do it.**

When a quotation is integrated into a sentence's structure, treat the quotation as you would any other sentence element, adding a comma or not as appropriate.

➤ **Telling me that she wanted to "play hooky from her life," she set off on a three-week vacation.**

➤ **He said he had his "special reasons."**

If your quotation begins a sentence, capitalize the first letter after the quotation mark even if the first word does not begin a sentence in the original source. If you change a lowercase letter to a capital letter, enclose it in brackets (*see Chapter 50, p. 381*).

➤ **"The only white people who came to our house were welfare workers and bill collectors," James Baldwin wrote.**

If the sentence you are quoting is interrupted by an expression such as *she said,* begin the sentence with a quotation mark and a capital letter, end the first part of the quotation with a comma and a quotation mark, insert the interrupting words followed by another comma, and then resume the quotation with a lowercase letter.

➤ **"The first thing that strikes one about Plath's journals," writes Katha Pollitt in *The Atlantic,* "is what they leave out."**

If you end one quoted sentence and insert an expression such as *he said* before beginning the next quoted sentence, place a comma at the end of the first quoted sentence and a period after the interruption.

➤ **"There are at least four kinds of doublespeak," William Lutz observes. "The first is the euphemism, an inoffensive or positive word or phrase used to avoid a harsh, unpleasant, or distasteful reality."**

48f Common errors in using quotation marks

Watch out for and correct common errors in using quotation marks.

▪ **To distance yourself from slang, clichés, or trite expressions:** It is best to avoid overused or slang expressions altogether in college writing. If your writing situation permits slang, however, do not enclose it in quotation marks.

WEAK   Californians are so "laid back."

REVISED   Many Californians have a carefree style.

- **For indirect quotations:** Do not use quotation marks for indirect quotations. Watch out for errors in pronoun reference as well. (*See Part 7: Editing for Grammar Conventions, pp. 314–16.*)

  INCORRECT   He wanted to tell his boss that "he needed a vacation."

  CORRECT   He told his boss that his boss needed a vacation.

  CORRECT   He said to his boss, "You need a vacation."

| 48f |
| " " |

- **In quotations that end with a question:** Only the question mark that ends the quoted sentence is needed, even when the entire sentence that includes the quotation is also a question.

  ➤   **What did Juliet mean when she cried, "O Romeo, Romeo! Wherefore art thou Romeo?"?**

- **To enclose the title of your own paper:** Do not use quotation marks around the title of your own essay at the beginning of your paper.

  ➤   **"Edgar Allan Poe and the Paradox of the Gothic"**

49 Other Punctuation Marks

49a The period

Use a period to end all sentences except direct questions or exclamations. Statements that ask questions indirectly end in a period.

➤ **She asked me where I had gone to college.**

49a
.?!

www.mhhe.com/
wi
For information
and exercises
on end
punctuation,
go to
**Editing > End
Punctuation**

A period is conventionally used with the following common abbreviations, which end in lowercase letters.

Mr.	Mrs.	i.e.	Mass.
Ms.	Dr.	e.g.	Jan.

If the abbreviation is made up of capital letters, however, the periods are optional.

RN (or R.N.)	BA (or B.A.)
MD (or M.D.)	PhD (or Ph.D.)

Periods are omitted in abbreviations for organizations, famous people, states in mailing addresses, and acronyms (words made up of initials).

FBI	JFK	MA	NATO
CIA	LBJ	TX	NAFTA

When in doubt, consult a dictionary.

49b The question mark

Use a question mark after a direct question.

➤ **Who wrote *The Old Man and the Sea*?**

Occasionally, a question mark changes a statement into a question.

➤ **You expect me to believe a story like that?**

Do not use a question mark after an indirect quotation, even if the words being indirectly quoted were originally a question.

➤ **He asked her if she would be at home later?.**

49c
.?!

49c The exclamation point

Use exclamation points sparingly to convey shock, surprise, or some other strong emotion.

➤ **Stolen! The money was stolen! Right before our eyes, somebody snatched my purse and ran off with it.**

Using numerous exclamation points throughout a document actually weakens their force. As much as possible, try to convey emotion with your choice of words and your sentence structure instead of with an exclamation point.

➤ **Jefferson and Adams both died on the same day in 1826, exactly fifty years after the signing of the Declaration of Independence!.**

The fact that the sentence reports is surprising enough without the addition of an exclamation point.

www.mhhe.com/
wi
For information
and exercises
on dashes,
go to
Editing > Dashes

49d Dashes

Use a dash or dashes to set off words, phrases, or sentences that deserve special attention. A typeset dash, sometimes called an *em dash,* is a single, unbroken line about as wide as a capital M. Most word-processing programs provide the em dash as a special character. Otherwise, the dash can be made on the keyboard with two hyphens in a row. Do not put a space before or after the dash.

49d

1. To set off parenthetical material, a series, or an explanation

➤ All finite creations—including humans—are incomplete and contradictory.

➤ Coca-Cola, potato chips, and brevity—these are the marks of a good study session in the dorm.

➤ A surprising number of people have taken up birdwatching—a peaceful, relatively inexpensive hobby.

Sometimes a dash is used to set off an independent clause within a sentence. In such sentences, the set-off clause provides interesting information but is not essential to the main assertion.

➤ The first rotary gasoline engine—it was made by Mazda—burned 15% more fuel than conventional engines.

2. To indicate a sudden change in tone or idea

➤ Breathing heavily, the archaeologist opened the old chest in wild anticipation and found—an old pair of socks and an empty soda can.

Note: Used sparingly, the dash can be an effective mark of punctuation, but if it is overused, it can make your writing disjointed.

49e Parentheses

Parentheses should be used infrequently and only to set off supplementary information, a digression, or a comment that interrupts the flow of thought within a sentence or paragraph.

➤ **The tickets (ranging in price from $10 to $50) go on sale Monday morning.**

www.mhhe.com/wi
For information and exercises on parentheses, go to
Editing > Parentheses

When parentheses enclose a whole sentence by itself, the sentence begins with a capital letter and ends with a period before the final parenthesis. A sentence that appears inside parentheses *within a sentence* should neither begin with a capital letter nor end with a period.

➤ **Folktales and urban legends often reflect the concerns of a particular era. (The familiar tale of a cat accidentally caught in a microwave oven is an example of this phenomenon.)**

➤ **John Henry (he was the man with the forty-pound hammer) was a hero to miners fearing the loss of their jobs to machines.**

If the material in parentheses is at the end of an introductory or nonessential word group that is followed by a comma, the comma should be placed after the closing parenthesis. A comma should never appear before the opening parenthesis.

➤ **As he walked past/ (dressed, as always, in his Sunday best),
I got ready to throw the spitball.**

Parentheses are used to enclose numbers or letters that label items
in a list.

➤ **He says the argument is nonsense because (1) university
presidents don't work as well as machines, (2) university
presidents don't do any real work at all, and (3) universities
would be better off if they were run by faculty committees.**

Parentheses also enclose in-text citations in many systems of documenting sources. (*For more on documenting sources, see Parts 3–5.*)

Note: Too many parentheses are distracting to readers. If you find that you
have used a large number of parentheses in a draft, go over it carefully to see
if any of the material within parentheses really deserves more emphasis.

49f Brackets

Brackets set off information you add to a quotation that is not part of
the quotation itself.

➤ **Samuel Eliot Morison has written, "This passage has
attracted a good deal of scorn to the Florentine mariner
[Verrazzano], but without justice."**

Morison's sentence does not include the name of the "Florentine
mariner," so the writer places the name in brackets.

49f
[ ]

Brackets may be used to enclose the word *sic* (Latin for "thus") after a word in a quotation that was incorrect in the original.

➤ **The critic noted that "the battle scenes in *The Patriot* are realistic, but the rest of the film is historically inacurate [sic] and overly melodramatic."**

49g
...

49g Ellipses

Use three spaced periods, called ellipses or an ellipsis mark, to show readers that you have omitted words from a passage you are quoting.

FULL QUOTATION FROM A WORK BY WILKINS

In the nineteenth century, railroads, lacing their way across continents, reaching into the heart of every major city in Europe and America, and bringing a new romance to travel, added to the unity of nations and fueled the nationalist fires already set burning by the French Revolution and the wars of Napoleon.

EDITED QUOTATION

In his account of nineteenth-century society, Wilkins argues that "railroads . . . added to the unity of nations and fueled the nationalist fires already set burning by the French Revolution and the wars of Napoleon."

If you are leaving out the end of a quoted sentence, the three ellipsis points are followed by a period to end the sentence.

EDITED QUOTATION

In describing the growth of railroads, Wilkins pictures them "lacing their way across continents, reaching into the heart of every major city in Europe and America. . . ."

When you need to add a parenthetical reference after the ellipses at the end of a sentence, place it after the quotation mark but before the final period: . . ." (253).

Ellipses are usually not needed to indicate an omission when only a word or phrase is being quoted.

➤ **Railroads brought "a new romance to travel," according to Wilkins.**

To indicate the omission of an entire line or more from the middle of a poem, insert a line of spaced periods.

Ellipses should be used only as a means of shortening a quotation, never as a device for changing its fundamental meaning or for creating emphasis where none exists in the original.

49h Slashes

Use the slash to show divisions between lines of poetry when you quote more than one line of a poem as part of a sentence. Add a space on either side of the slash. When you are quoting four or more lines of poetry, use a block quotation instead. (*See p. 363.*)

➤ **In "The Tower," Yeats makes his peace with "All those things whereof / Man makes a superhuman / Mirror-resembling dream" (163–165).**

The slash is sometimes used between two words that represent choices or combinations. Do not add a space on either side of the slash when it is used in this way.

➤ **The college offers three credit/noncredit courses.**

Some writers use the slash as a marker between the words *and* and *or* or between *he* and *she* or *his* and *her* to avoid sexism. Most writers, however, consider such usage awkward. It is usually better to rephrase the sentence.

50a
cap

50 Capitalization

Many rules for the use of capital letters have been fixed by custom, such as the convention of beginning each sentence with a capital letter, but the rules change all the time. A recent dictionary is a good guide to capitalization.

www.mhhe.com/
wi
For information
and exercises
on
capitalization,
go to
Editing >
Capitalization

50a Proper nouns

Proper nouns are the names of specific people, places, or things, names that set off the individual from the group, such as the name *Jane* instead of the common noun *person*. Capitalize proper nouns, words derived from proper nouns, brand names, abbreviations of capitalized words, and call letters at radio and television stations.

Ronald Reagan
Reaganomics
Apple computer
FBI (government agency)
WNBC (television)

Note: Although holidays and the names of months and days of the week are capitalized, seasons, such as *summer,* are not. Neither are the days of the month when they are spelled out (*the seventh of March*).

50a
cap

TYPES and EXAMPLES of PROPER NOUNS

1. **People:** John F. Kennedy, Ruth Bader Ginsburg, Albert Einstein
2. **Nationalities, ethnic groups, and languages:** English, Swiss, African Americans, Arabs, Chinese, Turkish
3. **Places:** the United States of America, Tennessee, the Irunia Restaurant, the Great Lakes
4. **Organizations and institutions:** Phi Beta Kappa, Republican Party (Republicans), Department of Defense, Cumberland College, the North Carolina Tarheels
5. **Religious bodies, books, and figures:** Jews, Christians, Baptists, Hindus, Roman Catholic Church, the Bible, the Koran or Qur'an, the Torah, God, Holy Spirit, Allah
6. **The genus in scientific names:** *Homo sapiens, H. sapiens, Acer rubrum, A. rubrum*
7. **Days and months:** Monday, Veterans Day, August, the Fourth of July
8. **Historical events, movements, and periods:** World War II, Impressionism, the Renaissance, the Jazz Age

50b   Personal titles

Capitalize titles when they come before a proper name, but do not capitalize them when they appear alone or after the name.

> Every Sunday, *Aunt Lou* tells fantastic stories.
>
> My *aunt* is arriving this afternoon.
>
> The most likely candidate for the Democratic nomination was Grover Cleveland, *governor* of New York.

Exceptions: If the name for a family relationship is used alone (without a possessive such as *my* before it), it should be capitalized.

> I saw *Father* infrequently during the summer months.

> *President of the United States* or the *President* (meaning the chief executive of the United States) is frequently but not always capitalized. Most writers do not capitalize the title *president* unless they are referring to the President of the United States.

50c cap

50c   Titles of creative works

Capitalize the important words in titles and subtitles. Do not capitalize articles (*a, an,* and *the*), the *to* in infinitives, or prepositions and conjunctions unless they begin or end the title or subtitle. Capitalize both words in a hyphenated word. Capitalize the first word after a colon or semicolon in a title.

> **Book:** *Two Years before the Mast*
> **Play:** *The Taming of the Shrew*
> **Building:** the Eiffel Tower

Ship or aircraft: the *Titanic* or the *Concorde*
Painting: the *Mona Lisa*
Article or essay: "On Old Age"
Poem: "Ode on a Grecian Urn"
Music: "The Star-Spangled Banner"
Document: the Bill of Rights
Course: Economics 206: Macro-Economic Analysis

50d Names of areas and regions

Names of geographical regions are generally capitalized if they are
well established, like *the Midwest* and *Central Europe.* Names of directions, as in the sentence *Turn south,* are not capitalized.

CORRECT   *East* meets *West* at the summit.

CORRECT   You will need to go *west* on Sunset.

The word *western,* when used as a general direction or the name of a
genre, is not capitalized. It is capitalized when it is part of the name of
a specific region.

➤ The ~~Western~~ *western* High Noon is one of my favorite movies.

➤ I visited ~~western~~ *Western* Europe last year.

50e Names of races, ethnic groups, and sacred things

The words *black* and *white* are usually not capitalized when they are
used to refer to members of racial groups because they are adjectives
that substitute for the implied common nouns *black person* and *white*

person. However, names of ethnic groups and races are capitalized: *African Americans, Italians, Asians, Caucasians.*

Note: In accordance with current APA guidelines, most social scientists capitalize the terms *Black* and *White,* treating them as proper nouns.

Many religious terms, such as *sacrament, altar,* and *rabbi,* are not capitalized. The word *Bible* is capitalized (though *biblical* is not), but it is never capitalized when it is used as a metaphor for an essential book.

➤ **His book** ***Winning at Stud Poker*** **used to be the** ***bible***
of gamblers.

50f
cap

50f First word of a sentence or quoted sentence

A capital letter is used to signal the beginning of a new sentence. Capitalize the first word of a quoted sentence but not the first word of a quoted phrase.

➤ **Jim, the narrator of** ***My Ántonia,*** **concludes, "Whatever**
we had missed, we possessed together the precious, the
incommunicable past" (324).

➤ **Jim took comfort in sharing with Ántonia "the precious,**
the incommunicable past" (324).

If you need to change the first letter of a quotation to fit your sentence, enclose the letter in brackets.

➤ **The lawyer noted that "[t]he man seen leaving the area after**
the blast was not the same height as the defendant."

If you interrupt the sentence you are quoting with an expression such as *he said,* the first word of the rest of the quotation should not be capitalized.

➤ **"When I come home an hour later," she explained, "the trains are usually less crowded."**

50g First word after a colon

**51
abbr**

If the word group that follows a colon is not a complete sentence, do not capitalize it. If it is a complete sentence, you can capitalize it or not, but be consistent throughout your document.

➤ **The question is serious: do you think this peace will last?**

or

➤ **The question is serious: Do you think this peace will last?**

51 Abbreviations and Symbols

Unless you are writing a scientific or technical report, spell out most terms and titles, except in the following cases.

51a Titles that always precede or follow a person's name

Some abbreviations appear before a person's name (*Mr., Mrs., Dr.*) and some follow a proper name (*Jr., Sr., MD, Esq., PhD*). When an abbreviation follows a person's name, a comma is placed between the name and the abbreviation.

Mrs. Jean Bascom
Elaine Less, CPA, LL.D.

Do not use two abbreviations that represent the same thing: *Dr. Peter Joyce, MD.* Use either *Dr. Peter Joyce* or *Peter Joyce, MD.*
Spell out titles used without proper names.

> Mr. Carew asked if she had seen the d̶r̶. *doctor.*

51b
abbr

www.mhhe.com/
wi
For information
and exercises
on
abbreviations,
go to
**Editing >
Abbreviations**

51b Familiar abbreviations

If you use a technical term or the name of an organization in a report, you may abbreviate it as long as your readers are likely to be familiar with the abbreviation. Abbreviations of three or more capital letters generally do not use periods.

FAMILIAR ABBREVIATION	The EPA has had a lasting impact on the air quality in this country.
UNFAMILIAR ABBREVIATION	After you have completed them, take these *the Human Resources and Education Center.* forms to H̶R̶E̶C̶.

Write out an unfamiliar term or name the first time you use it, and give the abbreviation in parentheses.

➤ **The Student Nonviolent Coordinating Committee (SNCC) was far to the left of other civil rights organizations, and its leaders often mocked the "conservatism" of Dr. Martin Luther King, Jr. SNCC quickly burned itself out and disappeared.**

51b
abbr

Abbreviations or symbols associated with numbers should be used only when accompanying a number: *3 p.m.*, not *in the p.m.; $500,* not *How many $ do you have?* The abbreviation *B.C.* ("Before Christ") follows a date; *A.D.* ("in the year of our Lord") precedes the date. The alternative abbreviations *B.C.E.* ("Before the Common Era") and *C.E.* ("Common Era") can be used instead of *B.C.* or *A.D.,* respectively.

6:00 p.m. or 6:00 P.M. or 6:00 PM
9:45 a.m. or 9:45 A.M. or 9:45 AM
498 B.C. or 498 B.C.E. or 498 BC or 498 BCE
A.D. 275 or 275 C.E. or AD 275 or 275 CE
6,000 rpm
271 cm

CHARTING the TERRITORY

Abbreviations and Symbols

Some abbreviations and symbols may be acceptable in certain contexts, as long as readers will know what they stand for. For example, a medical writer might use *PT* (*physical therapy*) in a medical report or professional newsletter.

CHARTING the TERRITORY

Scientific Abbreviations

Most abbreviations used in scientific or technical writing, such as
those related to measurement, should be given without periods:
mph, lb, dc, rpm. If an abbreviation looks like an actual word,
however, you can use a period to prevent confusion: *in., Fig.*

Note: Be consistent. If you use *a.m.* in one sentence, do not switch to *A.M.* in
the next sentence. If an abbreviation is made up of capital letters, the periods
are optional: *B.C.* or *BC.* (*For more on using periods with abbreviations, see
Chapter 49, p. 370.*)

In charts and graphs, abbreviations and symbols such as = for
equals, in. for *inches,* % for *percent,* and *$* with numbers are acceptable
because they save space.

51c Latin abbreviations

Latin abbreviations can be used in notes or works-cited lists, but in
formal writing it is usually a good idea to avoid even common Latin
abbreviations (*e.g., et al., etc.,* and *i.e.*). Instead of *e.g.,* use *such as* or
for example.

cf.	compare (*confer*)
e.g.	for example, such as (*exempli gratia*)
et al.	and others (*et alii*)

etc.	and so forth, and so on (*et cetera*)
i.e.	that is (*id est*)
N.B.	note well (*nota bene*)
viz.	namely (*videlicet*)

51d Inappropriate abbreviations and symbols

51d
abbr

Days of the week (*Sat.*), places (*TX* or *Tex.*), the word *company* (*Co.*), people's names (*Wm.*), disciplines and professions (*econ.*), parts of speech (*v.*), parts of written works (*ch., p.*), symbols (@), and units of measurement (*lb.*) are all spelled out in formal writing.

➤ The *environmental* (not *env.*) engineers from the Paramus
Water *Company* (not *Co.*) are arriving in *New York City* (not
NYC) this *Thursday* (not *Thurs.*) to correct the problems in
the *physical education* (not *phys. ed.*) building in time for
Christmas (not *Xmas*).

Exceptions: If an abbreviation such as *Inc., Co.,* or *Corp.* is part of a company's official name, then it can be included in formal writing: *Time Inc. announced these changes in late December.* The ampersand symbol (&) can also be used but only if it is part of an official name: *Church & Dwight.*

52a Numerals

In nontechnical writing, spell out numbers up to one hundred and round numbers greater than one hundred.

➤ Approximately *twenty-five* students failed the exam, but more than *two hundred and fifty* passed.

When you are using a great many numbers or when a spelled-out number would require more than three or four words, use numerals.

➤ This regulation affects nearly *10,500* taxpayers, substantially more than the *200* originally projected. Of those affected, *2,325* filled out the papers incorrectly and another *743* called the office for help.

In technical and business writing, use numerals for exact measurements and all numbers greater than ten.

➤ The endosperm halves were placed in each of 14 small glass test tubes.

➤ With its $1.9 trillion economy, Germany has an important trade role to play.

52b
num

www.mhhe.com/
wi
For information
and exercises
on numbers,
go to
Editing >
Numbers

52b Numbers that begin sentences

If a numeral begins a sentence, reword the sentence or spell out the numeral.

➤ *Twenty-five* children are in each elementary class.

52c Conventional uses of numerals

Dates: October 9, 2002; A.D. 1066 (*or* AD 1066)

Time of day: 6 A.M. (*or* AM *or* a.m.), a quarter past eight in the evening, three o'clock in the morning

Addresses: 21 Meadow Road, Apt. 6J

Percentages: 73 percent, 73%

Fractions and decimals: 21.84, 6½

Measurements: 100 mph, 9 kg

Volume, page, chapter: volume 4, chapter 8, page 44

Scenes in a play: *Hamlet,* act 2, scene 1

Scores and statistics: 0 to 3, 98–92, an average age of 35

Amounts of money: $125, $2.25, $2.8 million

53
ital

53 Italics (Underlining)

Italics, a typeface in which the characters slant to the right, are used to set off certain words and phrases. If italics are not available, you can <u>underline</u> words that would be typeset in italics.

53a Titles of works or separate publications

www.mhhe.com/
wi
For information
and exercises
on italics, go to
Editing > Italics

Italicize (or underline) titles of books, magazines, journals, newspapers, comic strips, plays, films, musical compositions, choreographic works, artworks, Web sites, software, long poems, pamphlets, and other long works. In titles of lengthy works, *a, an,* or *the* is capitalized and italicized (underlined) if it is the first word, but *the* is not generally treated as part of the title in names of newspapers and periodicals: the *New York Times.*

**53a
ital**

➤ **Picasso's *Guernica* captures the anguish and despair
of violence.**

➤ **Plays by Shakespeare provide details and story lines
for Verdi's opera *Falstaff,* Cole Porter's musical comedy
Kiss Me, Kate, and Baz Luhrmann's film *Romeo and Juliet.***

Court cases may also be italicized or underlined.

➤ **In *Brown v. Board of Education of Topeka* (1954), the U.S.
Supreme Court ruled that segregation in public schools
is unconstitutional.**

Exceptions: Do not use italics or underlining when referring to the Bible and other sacred books.

Quotation marks are used for the titles of short works—essays, newspaper and magazine articles and columns, short stories, individual episodes of television and radio programs, short poems, songs, and chapters or other book subdivisions. Quotation marks are also used for titles of unpublished works, including student papers, theses, and dissertations. (*See Chapter 48, p. 364, for more on quotation marks with titles.*)

53b Names of ships, trains, aircraft, and spaceships

➤ **The commentators were stunned into silence when the**
Challenger exploded.

53c Foreign terms

➤ **In the Paris airport, we recognized the familiar no smoking**
sign: _Défense de fumer._

Foreign words that have become so common in English that everyone
accepts them as part of the language require no italics or underlining:
rigor mortis, pasta, and sombrero, for example.

53d Scientific names

The scientific (Latin) names of organisms are always italicized.

➤ **Most chicks are infected with _Cryptosporidium baileyi,_**
a parasite typical of young animals.

Note: Although the whole name is italicized, only the genus part of the name
is capitalized.

53e Words, letters, and numbers
referred to as themselves

For clarity, italicize words or phrases used as words rather than for
the meaning they convey. (You may also use quotation marks for this
purpose.) Letters and numbers used alone should also be italicized.

➤ The word *bookkeeper* has three sets of double letters: double
   o, double *k,* and double *e.*

➤ Add a *3* to that column.

53f For emphasis

An occasional word in italics helps you make a point. Too much emphasis, however, may mean no emphasis at all.

WEAK	You don't *mean* that your *teacher* told the whole *class* that *he* did not know the answer *himself*?
REVISED	Your teacher admitted that he did not know the answer? That is amazing.

If you add italics or underlining to a quotation, indicate the change in parentheses following the quotation.

➤ Instead of promising that no harm will come to us, Blake only
   assures us that we "need not *fear* harm" (emphasis added).

**53f
ital**

54 Hyphens

54a To form compound words

A hyphen joins two nouns to make one compound word. Scientists speak of a *kilogram-meter* as a measure of force, and professors of literature talk about the *scholar-poet*. The hyphen lets us know that the two nouns work together as one.

A dictionary is the best resource when you are unsure about whether to use a hyphen. If you cannot find a compound word in the dictionary, spell it as two separate words.

54b
hyph

www.mhhe.com/
wi
For information
and exercises
on hyphens,
go to
Editing >
Hyphens

54b To create compound adjective or noun forms

A noun can also be linked with an adjective, an adverb, or another part of speech to form a compound adjective.

    accident-prone
    quick-witted

Hyphens are also used in nouns designating family relationships and compounds of more than two words:

    brother-in-law
    stick-in-the-mud

Note: Compound nouns with hyphens generally form plurals by adding -*s* or -*es* to the most important word.

    attorney general/attorneys general
    mother-in-law/mothers-in-law

Some proper nouns that are joined to make an adjective are hyphenated: the Franco-Prussian war.

Hyphens often help clarify adjectives that come before the word they modify. Modifiers that are hyphenated when they are placed *before* the word they modify are usually not hyphenated when they are placed *after* the word they modify.

➤ It was a *bad-mannered* reply.

➤ The reply was *bad mannered*.

Do not use a hyphen to connect *-ly* adverbs to the words they modify.

➤ They explored the newly/discovered territories.

In a pair or series of compound nouns or adjectives, add suspended hyphens after the first word of each item.

➤ The child care center accepted three-, four-, and five-year-olds.

54c To spell out fractions and compound numbers

Use a hyphen when writing out fractions or compound numbers from twenty-one to ninety-nine.

> three-fourths of a gallon
> thirty-two

Note: Use a hyphen to show inclusive numbers: *pages 100–40*.

**54c
hyph**

54d To attach some prefixes and suffixes

Use a hyphen to join a prefix and a capitalized word.

➤ **Skipping the parade on the Fourth of July is positively *un-American!***

A hyphen is sometimes used to join a capital letter and a word: *T-shirt, V-six engine.*

The prefixes *ex-, self-,* and *all-* and the suffixes *-elect* and *-odd* (or *-something*) generally take hyphens. However, most prefixes are not attached by hyphens, unless a hyphen is needed to show pronunciation or to reveal a special meaning that distinguishes the word from the same word without a hyphen: *recreate* vs. *re-create.* Check a dictionary to be certain you are using the standard spelling.

➤ **Because he was an *ex-convict,* he was a *nonjudgmental coworker.***

➤ **They were *self-sufficient, antisocial* neighbors.**

54e To divide words at the ends of lines

When you must divide words, do so between syllables, but pronunciation alone cannot always tell you where to divide a word. If you are unsure about how to break a word into syllables, consult your dictionary.

➤ **My writing group had a very fruitful *collab-oration.* [not *colla-boration*]**

Never leave just one or two letters on a line.

➤ **He seemed so sad and vulnerable and so *discon-*** *nected* **from his family. [not *disconnect-ed*]**

Compound words such as *hardworking* should be broken only between the words that form them: *hard-working*. Compound words that already have hyphens, like *brother-in-law,* are broken after the hyphens only.

Note: Never hyphenate an acronym (CIA) or a one-syllable word.

Note: If you need to divide an Internet address between lines, divide it after a slash. Do not divide a word within the address with a hyphen; readers may assume the hyphen is part of the address.

55
sp

55 Spelling

Proofread your writing carefully. Misspellings creep into the prose of even the best writers. Here are some suggestions to help you improve your spelling.

- Use your computer software's spell checker. Remember, though, that a spell checker cannot tell how you are using a particular word. If you write *their* when you should write *there,* the spell checker cannot point out your mistake.

- Become familiar with major spelling rules and commonly misspelled words, and use your dictionary whenever you are unsure about the spelling of a specific word.

www.mhhe.com/
wi
For information
and exercises
on spelling,
go to
Editing >
Spelling

The basic spelling rules that follow will help you become a stronger speller.

1. *i* before *e*

Use *i* before *e* except after *c* or when sounded like *a,* as in *neighbor* and *weigh.*

I BEFORE *E*	believe, relieve, chief, grief, wield, yield
EXCEPT AFTER *C*	receive, deceive, ceiling, conceit
EXCEPTIONS	seize, caffeine, codeine, weird, height

2. Adding suffixes

▪ **Final silent -*e*:** When adding a suffix that begins with a vowel, drop the final silent -*e* from the root word. Keep the final -*e* if the suffix begins with a consonant.

force/forcing   remove/removable
surprise/surprising   care/careful

Exceptions: argue/argument, true/truly, change/changeable, judge/judgment, acknowledge/acknowledgment

Exception: Keep the silent -*e* if it is needed to clarify the pronunciation or if the word would be confused with another word without the -*e*.

hoe/hoeing (to avoid mispronunciation)
dye/dyeing (to avoid confusion with *dying*)

▪ **Final -*y*:** When adding -*ing* to a word ending in -*y,* retain the -*y*.

enjoy/enjoying   cry/crying

Change the *y* to *i* or *ie* when the final *y* follows a consonant but not when it follows a vowel.

happy/happier   defray/defrayed

- **Final consonants:** When adding a suffix to a word that ends in a consonant preceded by a vowel, double the final consonant if the root word has only one syllable or an accent on the last syllable.

    grip/gripping   refer/referred
    stun/stunning   transmit/transmitted

Exceptions: bus/busing, focus/focused

3. Forming plurals

- **-s or -es:** Add a final -s to make most nouns plural. Add a final -es to form a plural when the singular form of a noun ends in -s, -x, -ch, or -sh.

    cobra/cobras   kiss/kisses
    scientist/scientists box/boxes

Exception: The plural of a few nouns ending in -is is formed by changing -is to -es: analysis/analyses, basis/bases

- **Other plurals:** If a noun ends in -y preceded by a consonant, change the -y to -i and add -es to form the plural; if the final -y is preceded by a vowel, keep the -y and add -s to make the plural.

    beauty/beauties   boy/boys

Exception: Always keep the final -y when forming the plural of a person's name: Joe and Mary Kirby/the Kirbys

When a noun ends in a consonant and an -o in the singular, form the plural by adding -es. If the -o is preceded by a vowel, add an -s.

    hero/heroes   folio/folios

Exception: solo/solos

■ **Irregular plurals:** Most plurals follow standard rules, but some have irregular forms (*child / children, tooth / teeth*), and some words with foreign roots create plurals in the pattern of the original language, as do these words derived from Latin and Greek.

alumnus/alumni   datum/data
criterion/criteria   medium/media
stimulus/stimuli   phenomenon/phenomena

Note: Some writers now treat data as though it were singular, but the preferred practice is still to recognize that data is plural and takes a plural verb.

➤   The *data are* clear on this point: the pass/fail course has become outdated by events.

■ **Compound nouns:** Compound nouns with hyphens generally form plurals by adding *-s* or *-es* to the most important word.

mother-in-law/mothers-in-law
court-martial/courts-martial

Note: Standard British spelling differs from American spelling for some words—among them, *color / colour, canceled / cancelled, theater / theatre, realize / realise,* and *judgment / judgement.*

Glossary
of Grammatical Terms

This glossary defines key terms used in this handbook to discuss editing for style, for grammar conventions, and for punctuation and mechanics. References in parentheses following most of the terms indicate the chapters or chapter sections in which those terms are discussed.

absolute phrase (44f) A phrase made up of a noun or pronoun and a participle that modifies an entire sentence: *Their heads hanging, the boys walked off the field.*

abstract noun See *noun.*

active voice (28c; 33b) The form of a transitive verb in which the subject of the sentence is doing the acting. See *voice.*

adjective (42b, c) A word that modifies a noun or pronoun with information specifying, for example, which one, what kind, or how many: *a delicious orange.*

adjective clause or **relative clause** (44e) A dependent clause that begins with a relative pronoun or adverb (such as *who, whom, whose, which, that,* or *where*) and modifies a noun or pronoun (see *adjective*): *The house that I grew up in eventually sold for a million dollars.*

adjective phrase (44e) A phrase that begins with a preposition or verbal and modifies a noun or pronoun: *The game, by far the longest of the season, lasted twenty-one innings.*

adverb (42a, c) A word that modifies a verb, an adjective, or another adverb with information specifying, for example, when, where, how, how often, how much, to what degree, or why: *She was terribly unhappy.*

adverb clause (44k) A dependent clause, usually introduced by a subordinating word (such as *after, because,* or *when*), that modifies a verb, an adjective, or another adverb (see *adverb*): <u>*After he lost the tennis match,*</u> *Rodrigo went straight to the gym.*

agreement (39; 41a) The appropriate pairing in number, person, and gender of one word with another. See *pronoun agreement* and *subject-verb agreement.*

antecedent (39g; 41) The noun that a pronoun replaces. In the sentence <u>*Katya,*</u> *<u>who</u> was at the concert, saw <u>her</u> picture in the paper,* the antecedent of the pronouns *who* and *her* is *Katya.* See *pronoun reference.*

appositive (37c; 41c; 44e.3) A noun or noun phrase that appears next to a noun or pronoun and renames it: *My friend Max, <u>the best dancer on campus,</u> is a chemistry major.*

articles (43a) The words *a, an,* and *the. A* and *an* are **indefinite articles;** *the* is a **definite article.**

auxiliary verb (43b) See *helping verb.*

block quotation (48a) A long direct quotation that is not enclosed by quotation marks but is set off from the text.

case (41c) The form of a noun or pronoun, determined by the grammatical role it plays in a sentence. See *pronoun case.*

clause (37, 44c) A group of related words containing a subject and a predicate. An **independent (main) clause** can stand on its own as a sentence: *We can have a picnic.* A **dependent (subordinate) clause** cannot stand on its own as a sentence: *We can have a picnic <u>if it doesn't rain.</u>*

cliché (35d) An overworked expression or figure of speech.

collective noun (39c; 41a.3) See *noun.*

comma splice (38) An error in which two independent clauses are joined by a comma without a coordinating conjunction.

common noun See *noun.*

comparison (42c) The form of an adjective or adverb that indicates its degree or amount. The positive degree is the simple form and involves no comparison: *large, difficult* (adjectives); *far, confidently* (adverbs). The comparative degree compares two things: *larger, more difficult; farther, more / less confidently.* The superlative degree compares three or more things, indicating which is the greatest or the least: *largest, most difficult; farthest, most / least confidently.*

complement See *subject complement* and *object complement.*

complete predicate See *predicate.*

complete subject See *subject.*

complete verb (37; 40h) A main verb and any helping verbs needed to indicate tense, person, and number.

complex sentence See *sentence.*

compound predicate (37c) Two or more predicates connected by a conjunction.

compound sentence See *sentence.*

compound-complex sentence See *sentence.*

compound structures (41c.1) Words or phrases joined by *and, or,* or *nor.*

compound subject (39b) See *subject.*

concise (25) Of writing, employing as few words as needed to be clear and engaging.

concrete noun See *noun.*

concrete word (35b) A **concrete** word names things that can be perceived with the senses, such as *chocolate* or *jacket.*

conjunction (31; 39b) A word that joins words, phrases, or clauses and indicates their relation to each other. **Coordinating conjunctions** (such as *and, but, or, nor, for, so,* or *yet*) join words or ideas of equal weight or function: *The night grew colder, <u>but</u> the boys <u>and</u> girls kept trick or treating.* **Correlative**

conjunctions (such as *both . . . and, neither . . . nor, not only . . . but also*) link sentence elements of equal value, always in pairs: *She knew that either her mother or her father would drive her to the airport.* **Subordinating conjunctions** (such as *after, although, as if, because, if,* or *when*) introduce dependent or subordinate clauses, linking sentence elements that are not of equal importance: *They waltzed while the band played on.*

conjunctive adverb (38b; 45b) A word or expression such as *for example, however,* or *therefore* that indicates the relation between two clauses. Unlike conjunctions, conjunctive adverbs are not grammatically strong enough on their own to hold the two clauses together, requiring the clauses to be separated by a period or semicolon: *The night grew colder; however, the boys and girls kept trick or treating.*

connotation (35a) The secondary, or implicit, meaning of a word that derives from the feelings and images it evokes.

contraction (47c) A shortened word formed when two words are combined and letters are replaced with an apostrophe: *doesn't* for *does not.*

coordinate adjectives (44d) Two or more adjectives that act individually to modify a noun or pronoun: *It was a dark and stormy night.* Coordinate adjectives are separated by a comma: *It was a dark, stormy night.*

coordinating conjunction or **coordinator** See *conjunction.*

coordination (31a) In a sentence, the joining of elements of equal weight. See also *subordination.*

correlative conjunction See *conjunction.*

count noun (43a) See *noun.*

cumulative adjectives (44d) Adjectives that act as a set and should not be separated by a comma. The first adjective modifies the following adjective or adjectives as well as the noun or pronoun: *world-famous American sculptor.*

cumulative sentence (32c) A sentence that begins with a subject and verb and then accumulates information in a series of descriptive modifiers: *The reporters ran after the film star, calling out questions and shoving each other aside.*

dangling modifier (30e) A modifier that confusingly implies an actor different from the sentence's subject: _Being so valuable, thousands of people flooded into California during the Gold Rush._

definite article See _articles._

demonstrative pronoun A pronoun such as _this, that, these,_ and _those_ that points out nouns and pronouns that come later: _This is the house that Jack built._

denotation (35a) The primary, or dictionary, definition of a word.

dependent or **subordinate clause** See _clause._

dialect A variant of a language that is used by a particular social, geographical, or ethnic group.

diction (35) Word choice.

direct address (44g) A construction that includes a word or phrase that names the person or group being spoken to: _Are you coming, Vinny?_

direct object See _object._

direct question (49b) A sentence that asks a question and concludes with a question mark. Contrast with _indirect question._

direct quotation (48a) The reproduction of the exact words someone else has spoken or written. In academic writing, direct quotations are enclosed in quotation marks or, if long, set off in a separate block of text.

doublespeak (34d) The deceitful use of language to obscure facts and mislead readers.

euphemism (34d) An innocuous word or phrase that substitutes for a harsh, blunt, or offensive alternative: _pass away_ for _die._

excessive coordination The use of coordination to string together too many ideas at once.

excessive subordination (31c) The use of subordination to string together too many subordinate expressions at once.

exclamatory sentence (32d; 49c) A sentence that expresses strong emotion and ends with an exclamation point.

expletive construction (25c) The use of *there, here,* or *it* in the subject position of a sentence, followed by a form of *be*: <u>Here are</u> *the directions.* The subject follows the verb.

faulty coordination (31a) The use of coordination to join sentence elements that aren't logically equivalent, or elements joined with an inappropriate coordinating word.

faulty parallelism (29) An error that results when items in a series, paired ideas, or items in a list do not have the same grammatical form.

faulty predication (27b) An illogical, ungrammatical combination of subject and predicate.

figure of speech or **figurative language** (35e) An imaginative expression, usually a comparison, that amplifies the literal meaning of other words. See also *metaphor* and *simile.*

fused sentence (38) See *run-on sentence.*

gender (41a) The classification of nouns and pronouns as masculine (*he, father*), feminine (*she, mother*), or neuter (*it, painter*).

generic noun (41a.2) A noun used to represent anyone and everyone in a group: *the average <u>voter</u>; the modern <u>university</u>.*

gerund (39h; 41c.7) The present participle (*–ing*) form of a verb used as a noun: *Most college courses require <u>writing</u>.* See *verbal.*

gerund phrase (39h) A word group consisting of a gerund followed by objects, complements, or modifiers: <u>*Walking to the mailbox*</u> *was my grandmother's only exercise.*

helping or **auxiliary verb** (40h; 43b) Verbs that combine with main verbs to indicate a variety of meanings, including tense, mood, voice, and manner. Helping verbs include forms of *be, have,* and *do* and the modal verbs *can, could, may, might, shall, should,* and *will.* See *modal verb.*

idiom (35c) An expression whose meaning is established by custom and cannot be determined from the dictionary definition of the words that compose it:

Boston Red Sox fans were in seventh heaven *when their team finally won the World Series in 2004.*

imperative mood (28c; 40i) Of verbs, the mood that expresses commands, directions, and entreaties: *Please don't leave.* See *mood.*

indefinite article See *articles.*

indefinite pronoun (39d; 41a.1) A pronoun such as *someone, anybody, nothing,* and *few* that does not refer to a specific person or item.

independent or **main clause** See *clause.*

indicative mood (28c; 40i) Of verbs, the most common mood, used to make statements (*We are going to the beach*) or ask questions (*Do you want to come along?*). See *mood.*

indirect object See *object.*

indirect question (49b) A sentence that reports a question and ends with a period: *My mother often wonders* if I'll ever settle down. Contrast with *direct question.*

indirect quotation (48a) A sentence that reports, as opposed to repeating verbatim, what someone else has said or written. Indirect quotations are not enclosed in quotation marks.

infinitive (30d; 41c) A verbal consisting of the base form of a verb preceded by *to: to run, to eat.* See *verbal.*

infinitive phrase An infinitive, plus any subject, objects, or modifiers, that functions as an adverb, adjective, or noun: *When I was a child, I longed* to be a famous soprano.

intensive pronoun A pronoun ending with the suffix *–self* or *–selves* that adds emphasis to the noun or pronoun it follows. It is grammatically optional: *I* myself *couldn't care less.*

interjection A forceful expression, usually written with an exclamation point: *Hey! Beat it!*

interrogative pronoun A pronoun (*who, whose, whom, which, what, whatever*) used to ask questions.

interrogative sentence A sentence that poses a direct question.

intransitive verb (40b) A verb that describes an action or a state of being and does not take a direct object: *The tree fell*.

inversion (32d) In sentences, a reversal of standard word order, as when the verb comes before the subject: *Up jumped the cheerleaders*.

irregular verb (40a) A verb that forms the past tense and past participle other than by adding *–ed* or *–d*.

jargon (34c) One group's specialized, technical language used in an inappropriate context; that is, used with people outside the group or when it does not suit a writer's purpose.

limiting modifier (30b) A word such as *only, even, almost, really,* and *just* that qualifies the meaning of another word or word group.

linking verb (39f; 40h; 41c.2) A verb that joins a subject to its subject complement. Forms of *be* are the most common linking verbs: *They are happy*. Others include *look, appear, feel, become, smell, sound,* and *taste: The cloth feels soft*.

main verb The part of a verb phrase that carries the principal meaning.

mechanics (50–54) Conventions regarding the use of capital letters, italics, abbreviations, numbers, and hyphens.

metaphor (35e) An implied comparison between two unlike things: *Your harsh words stung my pride*. See *figure of speech*. Compare to *simile*.

misplaced modifier (30a–c) A modifier placed confusingly far from the expression it modifies, that ambiguously modifies more than one expression, or that awkwardly disrupts the relationships among the grammatical elements of a sentence.

mixed construction (27) A sentence with parts that do not fit together logically or grammatically.

mixed metaphor (35e) A confusing combination of two or more incompatible or incongruous metaphoric comparisons: *His fortune <u>burned a hole</u> in his pocket and <u>trickled away</u>.*

modal verb (43b.4) A helping verb that signifies the manner, or mode, of an action: *You <u>should</u> get ready for your guests.*

modifier (30; 42) A word or group of words functioning as an adjective or adverb to describe or limit another word or group of words.

mood (40i) The form of a verb that reveals the speaker's or writer's attitude toward the action of a sentence. The **indicative mood** is used to state or question facts, acts, and opinions: *The wedding <u>is</u> this weekend. <u>Did</u> you <u>get</u> your suit pressed?* The **imperative mood** is used for commands, directions, and entreaties: *<u>Take</u> your dirty dishes to the kitchen.* The **subjunctive mood** is used to express a wish or a demand or to make a statement contrary to fact: *If I <u>were</u> rich, I would travel the world by boat.*

noncount noun (43a) See *noun.*

nonrestrictive element (44e) A nonessential element that adds information to a sentence but is not required for understanding its basic meaning.

noun A word that names a person, place, thing, or idea: *David, Yosemite, baseball, democracy.* **Common nouns** name a general class and are not capitalized: *teenager, dorm, street.* **Proper nouns** name specific people, places, or things and are capitalized: *Shakespeare, London, Globe Theater.* **Count nouns** name specific items that can be counted: *muscle, movie, bridge.* **Noncount nouns** name nonspecific things that cannot be counted: *advice, air, time.* **Concrete nouns** name things that can be perceived by the senses: *wind, song, man.* **Abstract nouns** name qualities and concepts that do not have physical properties: *love, courage, hope.* **Collective nouns** are singular in form but name groups of people or things: *crew, family, audience.*

noun clause A dependent clause that functions as a noun: *They told me <u>where to meet them</u>.*

noun phrase A noun plus all of its modifiers.

number (39) The form of a verb, noun, or pronoun that indicates whether it is singular or plural.

object A noun or pronoun that receives or is influenced by the action reported by a transitive verb, a preposition, or a verbal. A **direct object** receives the action of a transitive verb or verbal and usually follows it in a sentence: *Tom and I watched the sunrise together.* An **indirect object** names for or to whom something is done: *Tom promised me a pancake breakfast afterward.* The **object of a preposition** usually follows a preposition and completes its meaning: *We drove into town together.*

object complement A word or group of words that follows an object in a sentence and describes or renames it: *I call my cousin Mr. Big.*

object of a preposition See *object.*

objective case See *pronoun case.*

parallelism (29) The presentation of equal ideas in the same grammatical form: individual terms with individual terms, phrases with phrases, and clauses with clauses.

participial phrase (32a) A word group that consists of a participle and any objects or modifiers and functions as an adjective: *Jumping the fence, the dog ran down the street.*

participle (40a) The *–ing* (present participle) or *–ed* (past participle) form of a verb. (In regular verbs, the past tense and the past participle are the same.) Participles are used with helping verbs in verb phrases (*They are walking slowly*), as verbals (*Walking is good exercise*), and as adjectives (*The walking dead haunt his dreams*). See *verb phrase* and *verbal.*

parts of speech The eight primary categories to which all English words belong: verbs, nouns, pronouns, adjectives, adverbs, prepositions, conjunctions, and interjections.

passive voice (28c; 33b) The form of a transitive verb in which the subject of the sentence is acted upon. See *voice.*

perfect tense See *tense.*

periodic sentence (32c) A sentence in which the key word, phrase, or idea appears at the end: *Despite a massive investment, the assembling of a stellar cast, and months of marketing hype, the movie flopped.*

person (39) The form of a verb or pronoun that indicates whether the subject of a sentence is speaking or writing (*first person*), is spoken or written to (*second person*), or is spoken or written about (*third person*).

personal pronoun (41) A pronoun that stands for a specific person or thing. The personal pronouns are *I, me, you, he, his, she, her, it, we, us, they,* and *them.*

phrasal verb (35c) A verb that combines with a preposition to make its meaning complete and often has an idiomatic meaning that changes when the preposition changes: *look out, dig into.*

phrase (37b) A group of related words that lacks either a subject or a predicate or both and cannot stand alone as an independent sentence. Phrases function within sentences as nouns, verbs, and modifiers.

plural Referring to more than one. See *number.*

possessive case See *pronoun case.*

possessive noun A noun that indicates possession or ownership: *Jesse's, America's.*

possessive pronoun A pronoun that indicates ownership: *mine, ours.*

predicate (27b) In a sentence, the verb and its objects, complements, or modifiers. The predicate reports or declares (*predicates*) something about the subject. The verb itself, including any helping verbs, constitutes the **simple predicate.** The simple predicate together with its objects, complements, and modifiers constitutes the **complete predicate.**

preposition A word that precedes a noun, pronoun, or noun phrase (the *object of the preposition*) and allows the resulting *prepositional phrase* to modify another word or word group in the sentence.

prepositional phrase A preposition and its object: *We went to the movies after completing our exams.*

present tense See *tense.*

pretentious language (34b) Language that is overly formal or full of fancy phrases, making it inappropriate for academic writing.

progressive tense See *tense.*

pronoun (41) A word that takes the place of a noun.

pronoun agreement (41a) The appropriate pairing in number, person, and gender of a pronoun with its antecedent: *Judi loved her tiny apartment.*

pronoun case (41c) The form of a pronoun that reflects its function in a sentence. Most pronouns have three cases: **subjective** (*I, she*), **objective** (*me, her*), and **possessive** (*my, hers*).

pronoun reference (41b) The nature of the relationship—clear or ambiguous—between a pronoun and the word it replaces, its **antecedent.**

proper adjective (42b) An adjective formed from a proper noun, such as *Britain / British.*

proper noun (50a) See *noun.*

quotation (48a, d, e) A restatement, either directly (verbatim) or indirectly, of what someone has said or written. See *direct quotation* and *indirect quotation.*

reciprocal pronoun A pronoun such as *each other* or *one another* that refers to the separate parts of its plural antecedent: *They helped one another escape from the flooded city.*

redundancy (25a) Unnecessary repetition.

reflexive pronoun A pronoun ending in *–self* or *–selves* that refers back to the sentence subject: *They asked themselves if they were doing the right thing.* Reflexive pronouns, unlike intensive pronouns, are grammatically necessary. See *intensive pronoun.*

regionalism (34a) An expression common to the people in a particular region.

regular verb (40a) A verb that forms its past tense and past participle by adding *–d* or *–ed* to the base form.

relative clause See *adjective clause.*

relative pronoun A pronoun such as *who, whom, which,* or *that* used to relate a relative (adjective) clause to an antecedent noun or pronoun: *The woman who came in second is a friend of ours.*

restrictive element (44e) A word, phrase, or clause with essential information about the noun or pronoun it describes. Restrictive elements are not set off by commas: *The house that Jack built is sturdy.*

rhetorical question (32d) A question asked for effect, with no expectation of an answer.

run-on sentence or fused sentence (38) An error in which two independent clauses are joined together without punctuation or a connecting word.

sentence A subject and predicate not introduced by a subordinating word that fit together to make a statement, ask a question, give a command, or express an emotion. A **simple sentence** is composed of only one independent clause: *I am studying.* A **compound sentence** contains two or more coordinated independent clauses: *I would like to go to the movies, but I am studying.* A **complex sentence** contains one independent clause and one or more dependent clauses: *If you try to make me go to the movies, I'll be really annoyed.* A **compound-complex sentence** contains two or more coordinated independent clauses and at least one dependent clause: *I'm staying home to study because I'm failing the course, but I'd much rather go to a movie.*

sentence fragment (37) An incomplete sentence that is treated as if it were complete, with a capital letter at the beginning and a closing mark of punctuation.

sexist language (34e) Language that demeans or stereotypes women or men based on their sex.

simile (35e) A comparison, using *like* or *as,* of two unlike things: *His eyes were like saucers.* See *figure of speech.*

simple predicate See *predicate.*

simple sentence See *sentence.*

simple subject See *subject*.

simple tense See *tense*.

singular Referring to one. See *number*.

slang (34a) An informal and playful type of language used within a social group or discourse community and generally not appropriate for academic writing.

specific word (35b) A word that names a particular kind of thing or item, such as *pines* or *college senior*.

split infinitive (30d) One or more words interposed between the two words of an infinitive: *The team hoped to immediately rebound from its defeat.*

subject (37; 39b) The words that name the topic of a sentence, which the predicate makes a statement about. The **simple subject** is the pronoun or noun that identifies the topic of a sentence: *The dog was in the yard.* The **complete subject** includes the simple subject and its modifiers: *The big black dog was in the yard.* A **compound subject** contains two or more subjects connected by a conjunction: *The dog and cat faced each other across the fence.*

subject complement (39f; 41c.2; 42b) A word or word group that follows a linking verb and renames or specifies the sentence's subject. It can be a noun or an adjective.

subject-verb agreement (39) The appropriate pairing, in number and person, of a subject and a verb: *The student looks confused. The students look confused.*

subjective case See *pronoun case*.

subjunctive mood (28c; 40) Of verbs, the mood used to express a wish or a request or to state a condition contrary to fact: *I wish I were home.* See *mood*.

subordinating conjunction or **subordinator** See *conjunction*.

subordination (31b, c) In a sentence, the joining of a secondary (subordinate) element to the main element in a way that shows the logical relationship between the two: *Although we shopped for hours, we didn't find a dress for the party.*

synonyms (35a) Words with similar meanings, such as *scowl* and *frown*.

syntax The rules for forming grammatical sentences in a language.

tag question (44g) A question attached at the end of a sentence. *It's hot today, isn't it?*

tense (40e) The form of a verb that indicates its time of action, whether present, past, or future. There are three **simple tenses:** present (*I laugh*), past (*I laughed*), and future (*I will laugh*). The **perfect tenses** indicate actions that were or will be completed by the time of another action or time: *I have spoken* (present perfect), *I had spoken* (past perfect), *I will have spoken* (future perfect). The **progressive forms** of the simple and perfect tenses indicate ongoing action: *I am laughing* (present progressive), *I was laughing* (past progressive), *I will be laughing* (future progressive), *I have been laughing* (present perfect progressive), *I had been laughing* (past progressive), *I will have been laughing* (future progressive).

transitive verb (40b) A verb that takes a direct object. *He bought a new bike last week.*

verb (37) A word that reports an action, a condition, or a state of being. Verbs change form to indicate person, number, tense, voice, and mood.

verb phrase A main verb plus its helping verbs: *Louie is helping with the party preparations.*

verbal (37b) A word formed from a verb that functions as a noun, an adjective, or an adverb, not as a verb.

verbal phrase A verbal plus an object, a complement, or a modifier.

voice (33b) The form of a verb used to indicate whether the subject of a sentence does the acting or is acted upon. In the **active voice,** the subject acts: *The crowd sang "Take Me Out to the Ballgame."* In the **passive voice,** the subject is acted upon: *"Take Me Out to the Ballgame" was sung by the crowd.*

wordy phrase (25b) A phrase that provides little or no information: *The fact is, the planets revolve around the sun.*

Index

Index
for Multilingual Writers

Credits

Abbreviations and Symbols for Editing and Proofreading

abbr	Faulty abbreviation **51**	*p*	Punctuation error
ad	Misused adjective or adverb **42**		⌃ Comma **44a-j**
agr	Problem with subject-verb or pronoun agreement **39, 41a**	*no ,*	Unnecessary comma **44k**
appr	Inappropriate word or phrase **34**		; Semicolon **45**
art	Incorrect or missing article **26d, 43**		: Colon **46**
awk	Awkward		⌄ Apostrophe **47**
cap	Faulty capitalization **50**		" " Quotation marks **48**
case	Error in pronoun case **41c**		. ? ! Period, question mark, exclamation point **49a-c**
cliché	Overused expression **35d**		— ( ) [ ] Dash, parentheses, brackets,
com	Incomplete comparison **26c**		. . . / ellipses, slash **49d-h**
coord	Problem with coordination **31**	*para*	Problem with a paraphrase **11b, c**
cs	Comma splice **38**	*pass*	Ineffective use of passive voice **33b**
d	Diction problem **34, 35**	*pn agr*	Problem with pronoun agreement **41a**
dev	More development needed	*quote*	Problem with a quotation **12b, 48a, e**
dm	Dangling modifier **30e**	*ref*	Problem with pronoun reference **41b**
doc	Documentation problem	*rep*	Repetitious words or phrases **25a**
	APA **19, 20, 21, 22**	*run-on*	Run-on (or fused) sentence **38**
	Chicago **23**	*sexist*	Sexist language **34e, 41a**
	CSE **24**	*shift*	Shift in point of view, tense, mood, or voice **28**
	MLA **14, 15, 16, 17, 18**	*sl*	Slang **34a**
emph	Problem with emphasis **31**	*sp*	Misspelled word **55**
exact	Inexact word **35**	*sub*	Problem with subordination **31**
frag	Sentence fragment **37**	*sv agr*	Problem with subject-verb agreement **39**
fs	Fused (or run-on) sentence **38**	*t*	Verb tense error **40e**
hyph	Problem with hyphen **54**	*usage*	See Glossary of Usage **36**
inc	Incomplete construction **26**	*var*	Vary your sentence structure **32**
ital	Italics or underlining needed **53**	*vb*	Verb problem **40**
jarg	Jargon **34c**	*w*	Wordy **25**
lc	Lowercase letter needed **50**	*ww*	Wrong word **35f**
mix	Mixed construction **27**	*//*	Parallelism needed **29**
mm	Misplaced modifier **30a-d**	*#*	Add a space
mng	Meaning not clear	*^*	Insert
mood	Error in mood **40i**	*◯*	Close up space
ms	Error in manuscript form **6**	*x*	Obvious error
	APA **21**	*??*	Unclear
	Chicago **23d**		
	MLA **17**		
num	Error in number style **52**		
¶	Paragraph		

Contents